Apple Training Series

Mac OS X
Help Desk Essentials

Edited by Owen Linzmayer

D1451459

Apple
Certified

Apple Training Series: Mac OS X Help Desk Essentials
Edited by Owen Linzmayer
Copyright © 2005 by Apple Computer Inc.

Published by Peachpit Press. For information on Peachpit Press books, contact:

Peachpit Press
1249 Eighth Street
Berkeley, CA 94710
(510) 524-2178
(800) 283-9444
Fax: (510) 524-2221
http://www.peachpit.com
To report errors, please send a note to errata@peachpit.com
Peachpit Press is a division of Pearson Education

Editor: Owen Linzmayer
Project Editor: Bob Lindstrom
Apple Series Editor: Serena Herr
Production Coordinator: Laurie Stewart, Happenstance Type-O-Rama
Technical Editors: John Parenica, Dirk Johnson
Copy Editor: Darren Meiss
Compositor: Kate Kaminski, Happenstance Type-O-Rama
Indexer: Jack Lewis
Cover Design: Frances Baca Design and Tolleson Design
Cover Illustration: Tolleson Design; images © Getty Images, Inc.

ISBN 0-321-27848-8
9 8 7 6 5 4 3 2
Printed and bound in the United States of America

Acknowledgments Thanks to John Parenica, Dirk Johnson, and the rest of the Apple training team responsible for the development of the Mac OS X Help Desk Essentials course on which this book is based.

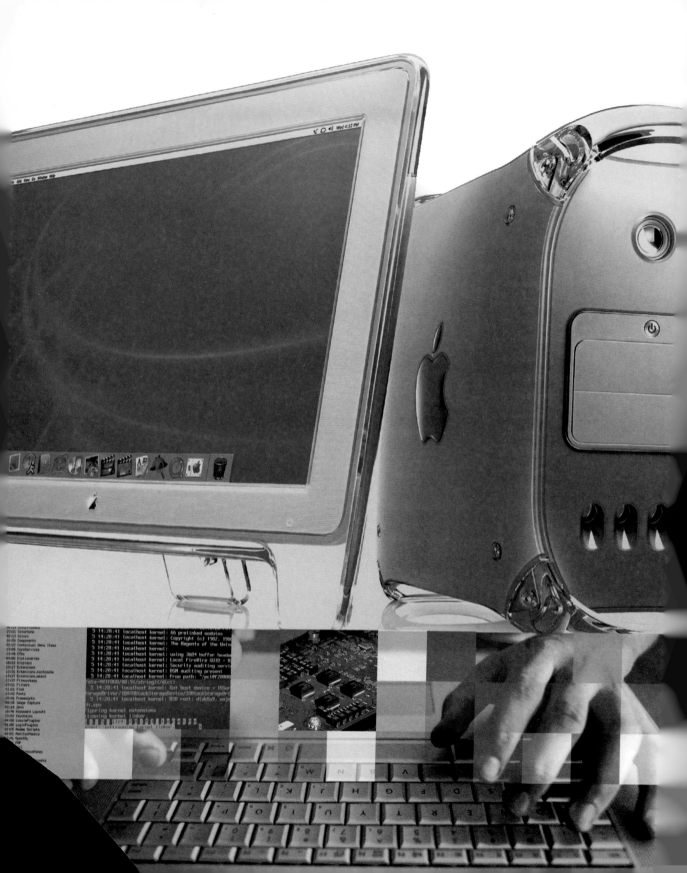

Contents at a Glance

Introduction 1

Lesson 1 Installation 7

Lesson 2 Users and Permissions 37

Lesson 3 File Systems 97

Lesson 4 Application Environments 143

Lesson 5 Command-Line Interface 179

Lesson 6 Networking Configuration and Troubleshooting 209

Lesson 7 Accessing Network Services 263

Lesson 8 File and Internet Sharing 301

Lesson 9 Peripherals 333

Lesson 10 Printing 369

Lesson 11 Startup Sequence 403

Lesson 12 Troubleshooting 427

Appendix A Apple General Troubleshooting Flowchart 465

Appendix B Networking Technologies 473

Appendix C Startup Sequence Processes 483

Glossary 491

Index 505

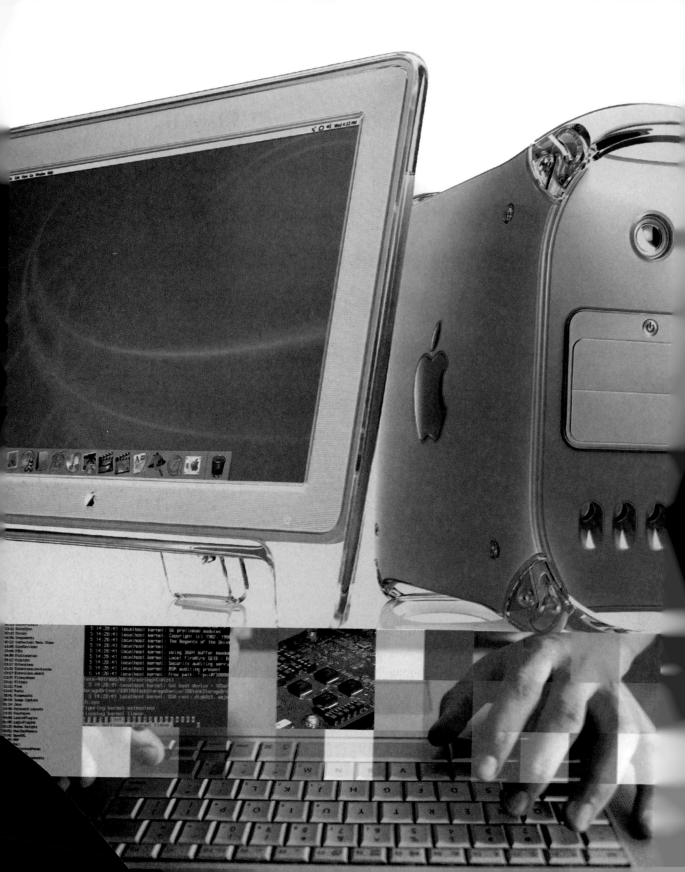

Table of Contents

Introduction 1

Lesson 1 Installation 7
Understanding Mac OS X 8
Installing Mac OS X 10
Completing the Installation 22
What You've Learned 32
Review Quiz 34

Lesson 2 Users and Permissions 37
Understanding User Types 38
Creating and Editing User Accounts 40
Securing Your Macintosh 62
What You've Learned 93
Review Quiz 95

Lesson 3 File Systems 97
File Locations in Mac OS X 98
Mac OS X Volume Formats 110
Working with Disk Utility 117
Managing Files and Folders 127
Troubleshooting the File System 138
What You've Learned 138
Review Quiz 140

Lesson 4   Application Environments 143
Macintosh Application Environments 144
Native Applications 144
Classic 146
Java 162
Using BSD/X11 165
Managing Applications 166
What You've Learned 174
Review Quiz 176

Lesson 5   Command-Line Interface 179
A Word of Caution 180
Command-Line Interfaces 180
File System Representations 188
Managing Processes from the Command Line 202
Monitoring System Usage 203
Managing Disks and Volumes 203
Using the Command Line with the
Graphical Environment 204
Advanced Commands 204
Command-Line Issues 205
What You've Learned 206
Review Quiz 207

Lesson 6   Networking Configuration and
Troubleshooting 209
Network Configuration Applications 210
Understanding Network Routing 212
Networking in Mac OS X 215
Creating and Choosing Locations 221
Managing Ports 222
Configuring Virtual Private Networks 243
Configuring 802.1X 245

Troubleshooting Network Issues 246
What You've Learned 258
Review Quiz 260

Lesson 7 Accessing Network Services 263
Discovering Services 264
Connecting to Servers 277
Authenticating Your Identity 286
What You've Learned 296
Review Quiz 298

Lesson 8 File and Internet Sharing 301
Sharing Services 302
Using AFP File Sharing 303
Using SMB File Sharing 312
Enabling FTP Access 314
Troubleshooting File Sharing 317
Understanding Personal Web Sharing 318
Enabling Personal Web Sharing 321
Modifying the Home Page Files 324
Sharing Your Internet Connection 327
Protecting Your Mac with the Firewall 328
What You've Learned 330
Review Quiz 331

Lesson 9 Peripherals 333
Understanding Buses 334
Understanding Device Classes 357
Understanding Device Drivers 360
Configuring Universal Access 363
Troubleshooting Peripherals 364
What You've Learned 365
Review Quiz 366

Lesson 10 Printing 369
Using CUPS 370
Managing Printers 371
Printing Documents 388
Using Other Print Options 393
Troubleshooting Printing 398
What You've Learned 399
Review Quiz 400

Lesson 11 Startup Sequence 403
BootROM 404
BootX 405
Kernel 407
mach_init and init 408
Startup Scripts and Startup Items 410
The loginwindow Process 413
User Environment Setup 414
Identifying Startup Processes 415
Troubleshooting the Startup Sequence 416
What You've Learned 422
Review Quiz 424

Lesson 12 Troubleshooting 427
Goals of Troubleshooting 428
Things to Do While Troubleshooting 429
Order of Elimination 430
Using the Troubleshooting Flowchart 433
Gathering Information 435
Verifying the Problem 441
Trying Quick Fixes 442
Running Diagnostics 447
Performing Split-Half Search 448
Researching 450
Escalating the Problem 456

Repairing/Replacing Components 456
Verifying the Repair 457
Informing the User 459
What You've Learned 460
Review Quiz 461

Appendix A Apple General Troubleshooting Flowchart 465
Mac OS X Quick Fixes 467
Mac OS X Diagnostic Tools 469
Mac OS X Split-Half Search Techniques 469
Mac OS X Research Resources 470
Mac OS X Repair/Replace 470

Appendix B Networking Technologies 473
802.1X 474
Apple Filing Protocol (AFP) 474
AirPort and AirPort Extreme 475
Bootstrap Protocol (BOOTP) 475
Dynamic Host Configuration Protocol (DHCP) 476
File Transfer Protocol (FTP) 476
HyperText Transfer Protocol (HTTP) 476
IP Addressing (IPv4 and IPv6) 477
Network Address Translation (NAT) 479
Point-to-Point Protocol (PPP) 479
Point-to-Point Protocol over Ethernet (PPPoE) 480
Rendezvous 480
Server Message Block (SMB) 481

Appendix C Startup Sequence Processes 483

Glossary 491

Index 505

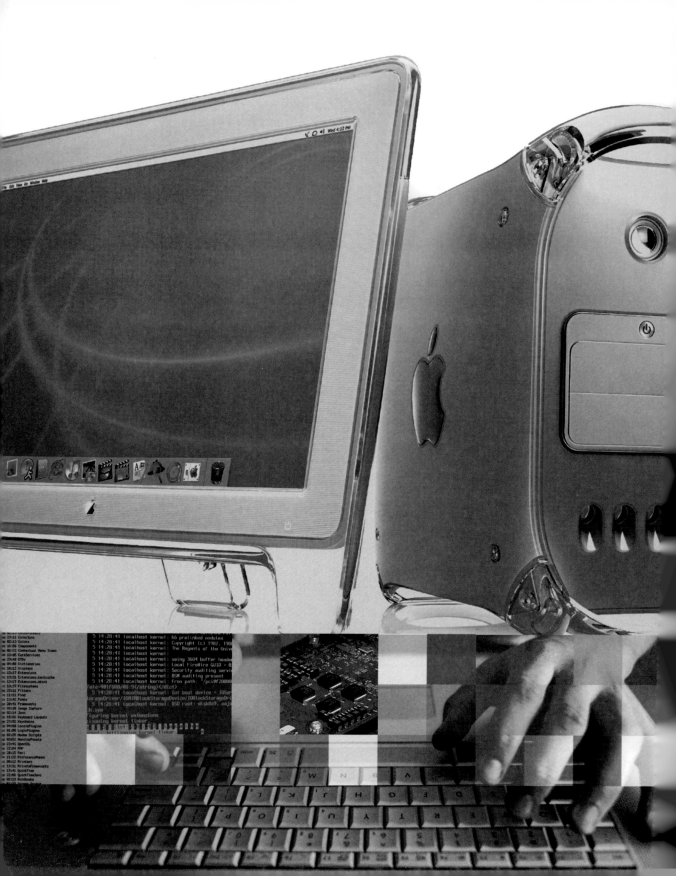

Getting Started

This book is based on Apple's official training course for Mac OS X Help Desk Essentials, an in-depth exploration of Mac OS X 10.3. It serves as a self-paced introduction to supporting and troubleshooting Macintosh computers running Mac OS X.

The primary goal is to prepare help desk personnel, technical coordinators, and system administrators to knowledgeably address customer concerns and questions. This includes the ability to return a Macintosh computer to normal operation, using the proper utilities, resources, and troubleshooting methodology.

Whether you are an experienced system administrator or just want to dig deeper into a Macintosh, you'll learn in-depth technical information and procedures used by Apple-certified technicians to install, configure, maintain, and diagnose Macintosh computers running Mac OS X 10.3.

This book assumes a basic level of familiarity with the Macintosh operating systems. Unless otherwise specified, all references to Mac OS X refer to Mac OS X 10.3.3.

Course Structure

This book is based upon material provided to students attending Mac OS X Help Desk Essentials, a three-day, hands-on course that provides an intense and in-depth exploration of troubleshooting Mac OS X. For purposes of consistency, we have maintained the basic structure of the course material, though you may complete it at your own pace.

Lessons 1 through 4 focus on setting up, configuring, and troubleshooting a standalone Mac OS X computer:

▶ Mac OS X installation
▶ Users and permissions
▶ File system
▶ Application environments

Lessons 5 through 8 deal with configuring Mac OS X to work in a networked environment. You will troubleshoot issues involving network services, such as file and Web servers, and configure Mac OS X to provide network services:

▶ Command-line interface
▶ Network configuration and troubleshooting
▶ Accessing network services
▶ File and Internet sharing

Lessons 9 and 10 introduce you to the support in Mac OS X for attaching hardware devices and printing:

▶ Peripherals
▶ Printing

Lesson 11 focuses on the technical details of how Mac OS X starts up, and Lesson 12 explains how to implement Apple's General Troubleshooting

Flowchart to correctly identify and fix machines that have unknown software issues:

▶ Startup sequence

▶ Troubleshooting

In an effort to be informative but not overwhelming, we have included several supplementary appendices. They may be valuable to you, though they are not considered essential or required for the course.

Lesson Structure

Each lesson in this book begins with an opening page that lists the goals for the lesson and an estimate of the time needed to complete the lesson.

The explanatory material is augmented with hands-on exercises essential to developing your skills. For the most part, all you need to complete the exercises is a Macintosh computer running Mac OS X 10.3. If you lack the equipment necessary to complete a given exercise, you are still encouraged to read the step-by-step instructions and examine the screen shots to understand the procedures demonstrated.

> **WARNING** ▶ The exercises are designed to be nondestructive if followed correctly. However, some of the exercises are disruptive—for example, they may turn off network services temporarily—and some of the exercises, if performed incorrectly, could result in data loss or damage to System files. As such, it's recommended that you run through these exercises on a Macintosh that is not critical to your productivity. Instructions are given for restoring your Macintosh to its functional state whenever necessary, but reasonable caution is recommended. Apple Computer, Inc. and Peachpit Press are not responsible for any data loss or any damage to any equipment that occurs as a direct or indirect result of following the procedures described in this book.

We refer to many Knowledge Base articles throughout this book, and close each lesson with a list of recommended articles related to the topic of the lesson. The Knowledge Base is a free online resource (http://kbase.info.apple.com) containing the very latest technical information on all of Apple's hardware and software products. You are strongly encouraged to read the suggested articles, as well as learn how to search the Knowledge Base for answers to your particular questions.

At the end of each lesson is a short review quiz that recaps the material you've learned. You can refer to various Apple resources, such as the Knowledge Base, as well as the lessons themselves, to help you answer these questions.

Certification

After reading this book, you may wish to take the Mac OS X Help Desk Essentials exam to earn the Apple Certified Help Desk Specialist certification. A $50 discount coupon for the exam is included on page 515. This is the first level of Apple's certification programs for Mac OS X professionals:

▶ Apple Certified Help Desk Specialist (ACHDS)—Ideal for help desk personnel, service technicians, technical coordinators, and others who support Mac OS X customers over the phone or who perform Mac OS X troubleshooting and support in schools and businesses. This certification does not include support of the Mac OS X Server platform. To receive this certification, you must pass the Mac OS X Help Desk Essentials certification exam. This book is intended to provide you with the knowledge and skills to pass that exam.

   NOTE ▶ Although all of the questions in the Mac OS X Help Desk Essentials exam are based upon material in this book, simply reading this book will not adequately prepare you for all the specific issues addressed by the exam. We recommend that before taking the exam, you spend time actually setting up, configuring, and troubleshooting Mac OS X.

▶ Apple Certified Technical Coordinator (ACTC)—This certification is ideal for Mac OS X technical coordinators and entry-level system administrators who provide technical support to Mac OS X users. In addition to user support, these professionals maintain the Mac OS X Server platform. This certification requires passing both the Mac OS X Help Desk Essentials and Mac OS X Server Essentials exams.

▶ Apple Certified System Administrator (ACSA)—This certification is designed for full-time professional system administrators and engineers managing medium-to-large networks utilizing Mac OS X Server in demanding and relatively complex multiplatform deployments. This certification requires passing both the System Administration of Mac OS X Clients and System Administration Using Mac OS X Server exams.

The Apple Certified Help Desk Specialist is also the first step towards the Apple hardware service technician certifications. These certifications are ideal for people interested in becoming Macintosh repair technicians, but also worthwhile for help desk personnel at schools and businesses, and for Macintosh consultants and others needing an in-depth understanding of how Apple systems operate:

▶ Apple Certified Desktop Technician (ACDT)—This certification requires passing the Mac OS X Help Desk Essentials and Apple Desktop Service exams.

▶ Apple Certified Portable Technician (ACPT)—This certification requires passing the Mac OS X Help Desk Essentials and Apple Portable Service exams.

About the Apple Training Series

Mac OS X Help Desk Essentials is part of the official training series for Apple products developed by experts in the field and certified by Apple. The lessons are designed to let you learn at your own pace. You can progress through the book from beginning to end, or dive right into the lessons that interest you most.

For those who prefer to learn in an instructor-led setting, Apple also offers training courses at Apple Authorized Training Centers worldwide. These courses are taught by Apple certified trainers, and they balance concepts and lectures with hands-on labs and exercises. Apple Authorized Training Centers have been carefully selected and have met Apple's highest standards in all areas, including facilities, instructors, course delivery, and infrastructure. The goal of the program is to offer Apple customers, from beginners to the most seasoned professionals, the highest quality training experience.

To find an Authorized Training Center near you, go to www.apple.com/training.

1

Time   This lesson takes approximately 1 hour, 30 minutes to complete.

Goals   Ensure that a specific computer meets the minimum requirements to run Mac OS X

Perform an erase, update, or archive installation of Mac OS X
on either a single- or multiple-partition hard drive

Use Setup Assistant to configure Mac OS X on a computer so
that the computer is capable of running Mac OS X applications

Use Software Update to locate and install any available software updates from Apple

Perform quick fixes to troubleshoot installation problems

Lesson **1**

Installation

All Macintosh computers ship from the factory with Mac OS X already installed so that the user need only plug it in and turn it on to begin taking advantage of the world's most advanced operating system running on the most elegant hardware. However, not every Macintosh in use today is running the latest version of Mac OS X. (As of this writing, that's 10.3, also known as "Panther.")

This lesson provides a brief technological overview of Mac OS X, followed by detailed instructions for installing, updating, and troubleshooting the installation. Although you do not need to actually perform an installation of Mac OS X as you read this lesson, doing so will give you a better understanding of the various options. If you do decide to install Mac OS X, it is suggested you do so on an extra computer or external hard drive so that you don't lose any productivity should you encounter difficulties working with a new, unfamiliar operating system.

Understanding Mac OS X

Since its release in March 2001, Mac OS X has been praised for its simplicity, elegance, and powerful Unix-based core. Mac OS X combines three graphics technologies—OpenGL, Quartz Extreme, and QuickTime—which are all based on open file formats to take Macintosh graphics capabilities beyond anything previously seen on a desktop operating system. The Aqua user interface provides a fluid look and feel to Mac OS X and showcases the graphics capabilities of the Quartz 2-D graphics engine.

The power of Unix in Mac OS X is provided by Darwin—the open-source foundation of Mac OS X. Modern operating system features such as preemptive multitasking, protected memory, and symmetric multiprocessing provide Mac OS X with greater stability and performance than previous versions of the Mac OS.

Finally, because most of today's major Internet technologies were developed on Unix, the Unix-like core of Mac OS X makes it a very Internet-savvy operating system. For example, Mac OS X uses the Berkeley Software Distribution (BSD) TCP/IP networking stack, which serves as the backbone of most TCP/IP implementations on the Internet today.

Integration Through Standards

One of the strengths of Mac OS X is that it uses a rich set of standards, which enables Mac OS X computers to integrate with other platforms. At every level of the operating system, standards play a key role.

At the hardware level, Mac OS X supports key hardware buses such as Universal Serial Bus (USB) and IEEE 1394 (also known as FireWire), which allow Mac OS X computers to use devices that also work on other platforms. Mac OS X can read and write files on a wide variety of formats such as 32-bit File Allocation Table (FAT32), Unix File System (UFS), and ISO-9660, providing access to storage devices formatted by other operating systems. For networking, Mac OS X relies on TCP/IP, allowing the computer to communicate with systems around the world. For graphics and documents, Mac OS X uses Portable Document Format (PDF), which allows documents to be shared with non–Macintosh systems.

Layers of Mac OS X

From an architectural standpoint, Mac OS X consists of four distinct layers. Here they are from bottom to top:

▶ Core OS—The foundation of Mac OS X. This layer is responsible for handling all I/O (input/output) and for managing memory and processor usage. It is commonly referred to as Darwin.

▶ Core Services—System components that implement the operating system services used by applications, such as QuickTime for playing movies, Quartz for 2-D drawing, directory services, and so forth.

▶ Developer Frameworks—Application environments that allow you to run various applications on Mac OS X. Running applications in these environments is covered in Lesson 4.

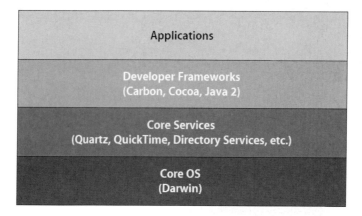

▶ Applications—The various programs you run, using the appropriate environment provided by the applicable Developer Frameworks layer just below. The applications layer is where users interact with the Macintosh. In addition to running traditional Mac OS–specific applications, Mac OS X includes support for running Java and Unix-style applications, including X11 applications, all of which are discussed in Lesson 4.

Installing Mac OS X

All new Macintosh computers come with Mac OS X preinstalled and most also come with Mac OS X provided on CD or DVD, in case the operating system needs to be reinstalled. This book assumes you are using Apple's Mac OS X retail package that contains several CDs with a simple Installer to guide you through the installation. If you are using the model-specific discs that came with your Macintosh, you may notice minor differences in the screens and examples used here. Although you can certainly dive right in and install Mac OS X without any forethought, you'll be better served in the long run if you take some time to prepare beforehand by verifying requirements and updating system components as necessary.

Verifying Requirements

The first step to take before attempting to install Mac OS X is to verify that the intended computer meets the minimum system requirements. If you don't know your computer's specifications, you can use System Profiler (/Applications/Utilities).

Mac OS X 10.3 requires the following:

▶ Power Mac G3, G4, or G5

▶ Built-in USB

▶ At least 128 MB of RAM

▶ A built-in display or a display connected to an Apple-supplied video card supported by your computer

▶ At least 2 GB of available disk space, or 3.5 GB if you install the developer tools

NOTE ► Mac OS X 10.3 cannot be installed on beige Power Mac G3 computers and PowerBook G3 computers without built-in USB. Mac OS X 10.2 is the latest version of the operating system that supports those computers. If you are installing Mac OS X on a PowerBook or an iBook, the laptop needs to be plugged into an AC power source to avoid exhausting battery power before the installation is completed.

NOTE ► For more information about installation requirements, see the complete list of supported computers at http://www.apple.com/macosx/upgrade/requirements.html.

Updating Hardware and Software

If your computer's firmware is out-of-date, the Mac OS X Installer will alert you when you attempt to install the OS. You can use the System Profiler utility to find the current version number of the firmware. (It's listed as the Boot ROM Version in the Hardware Overview.) You can also get the version number by rebooting the computer and holding down Cmd-Option-O-F, which places the computer in Open Firmware mode. The firmware version will be listed at the top of the screen.

Before installing Mac OS X, you must update your computer's firmware if an update is available. For a list of the firmware versions required by Mac OS X, and links to the necessary updates, refer to the Knowledge Base article #86117, "Mac OS X: Chart of Available Firmware Updates."

NOTE ► Older firmware updates do not run in Mac OS X; they run only in Mac OS 9. Firmware updates must be done from a writable partition. Review the update instructions for system requirements.

Updating your computer's firmware does not ensure that all of your existing peripherals and software will be compatible with Mac OS X. Therefore you should also check with the manufacturers of any devices you use with your computer to find the latest software updates for those devices. Likewise, you should check with the publishers of any third-party software you use to determine if updates are necessary for compatibility with the version of Mac OS X you intend to install.

If you are upgrading from one version of Mac OS X to another, it is likely that items will simply continue working as they always have. However, if you are upgrading from Mac OS 9, all of your programs must be run in Classic mode (which runs Mac OS 9 within Mac OS X), and you may find that some refuse to work at all and must be replaced with native Mac OS X alternatives.

Choosing a Partition Method

Mac OS X and Mac OS 9 can inhabit the same volume without any problems. The following table discusses the pros and cons of keeping the two together on a single volume (or partition) versus on separate partitions.

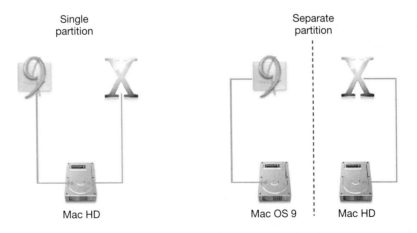

Partition Method Issues

Options	Pros	Cons
Single partition	Requires minimal preparation.	User could mistakenly delete Mac OS X files while working in Mac OS 9.*x*.
Separate partition	It's easy to upgrade, reinstall, or uninstall each operating system (Mac OS X and Mac OS 9.*x*); user is less likely to move or delete Mac OS X files.	More preparation is required, such as partitioning the disk. If you partition the disk, you will need to back up data.

One of the advantages of having two separate partitions is that if the operating system on the main partition becomes corrupted and unbootable, you can use the Startup Manager to boot the computer from the operating system on the second partition. If you press the Option key while the computer boots, the Startup Manager will scan each partition on any connected drive and display an icon representing the operating system last used on that partition (if one exists). Select an icon, and the computer will boot using the selected System folder.

> **NOTE ▶** Be aware that some Macintosh computers start up only in Mac OS X and cannot boot Mac OS 9. For more information, refer to Knowledge Base article #86209, "Macintosh: Some Computers Only Start Up in Mac OS X."

If you install Mac OS X and Mac OS 9 on the same partition, the hard disk must be formatted as Mac OS Extended. If you are installing Mac OS X on its own partition, Mac OS Extended is the recommended hard disk format, but you can also use UFS if, for example, you want to develop Unix-based applications within Mac OS X.

> **NOTE** ▶ Although applications running in the Classic environment can read and write files from a UFS partition, the Classic environment can only start from a Mac OS 9 System Folder located on a Mac OS Extended partition. Also, you will be unable to read files from a UFS partition if you boot Mac OS 9.

It is not necessary to have Mac OS 9 installed when upgrading to Mac OS X. Mac OS 9 can be installed before or after installing Mac OS X. If Mac OS 9 is installed, you will be able to run Classic applications. Furthermore, on some computers you will also be able to restart the computer in Mac OS 9 for trouble-shooting or compatibility needs.

Given the preceding information, determine if you would like to install Mac OS X on its own partition, or if installing it alongside Mac OS 9 is acceptable. If you need to partition the drive, you can use Disk Utility (/Applications/Utilities), but be aware that partitioning a drive is a time-consuming process that necessitates a full backup before starting if you want to retain your files.

Preparing for Installation

Before upgrading any operating system, you should back up all important data for protection in case an error occurs during installation.

If you need to run older Mac OS 9 applications, the Classic environment must be set up in Mac OS X with a valid Mac OS 9 System Folder. If you are using a Macintosh that will boot Mac OS 9, first install Mac OS 9 and then install any print drivers or fonts that you will use in the Classic environment in that System Folder. Use the Software Update control panel to make sure you have updated to the latest version (9.2.2 as of this writing). On newer computers that cannot boot Mac OS 9, you will need to copy over a licensed Mac OS 9

System Folder from another machine or from the Mac OS 9 Restore CD that shipped with the computer.

Before beginning the installation of Mac OS X, review the PDF document "Read Before You Install" on Mac OS X Install Disc 1.

If you are upgrading a computer from Mac OS 9 to Mac OS X, while still using Mac OS 9, collect your current network settings from the TCP/IP, Internet, Remote Access, and Modem control panels. You can run Apple System Profiler to generate a report with information that may prove useful during the upgrade process. Also, if you have a .Mac account, have the member name and password available.

Performing the Mac OS X Installation

You can start the Mac OS X installation process by either booting from the Mac OS X Install Disc 1 (with the disc in the drive, press and hold the C key during startup) or by launching the Install Mac OS X application in the Finder, which will restart the computer and boot the computer from the disc.

The Installer is largely self-explanatory. When in doubt, let the onscreen instructions guide you. After selecting your language, you continue through several screens that welcome you, explain the requirements, and then request your agreement to the software license terms. It's only when you get to select where and how Mac OS X is installed that you need to think carefully about your choices.

Selecting the Destination

In the Select Destination window, you select which volume will receive the operating system installation. Mac OS X can only be installed onto Mac OS Extended (HFS Plus) or UFS volumes. If you have multiple volumes from which to choose, keep in mind the information discussed previously in the "Choosing a Partition Method" section.

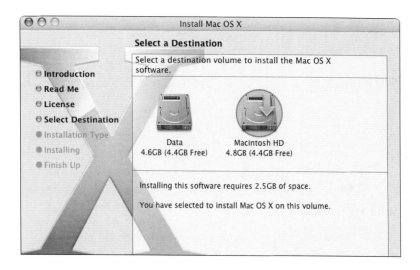

Choosing the Installation Type

If you wish to perform the default installation method, click Continue after selecting the destination. Otherwise, click Options to see the installation options. (The Options button appears only when a destination volume is selected.) The following table discusses the pros and cons of the three installation methods.

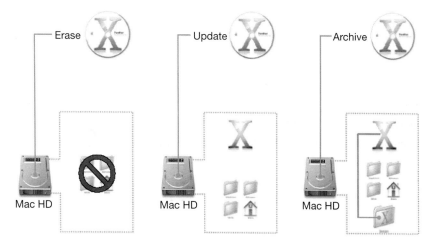

Installation Type

Options	Pros	Cons
Erase and Install	Provides a clean installation. Allows you to reset partitions. Can install on any partition.	All data on selected partition will be erased.
Update	Installer will update Mac OS X 10.0.x or later, maintaining preferences, fonts, applications, and files.	Requires that Max OS X 10.0.x or later is installed. Existing problems may not be fixed.
Archive and Install	Creates archive of current System directory and installs a new System directory optionally preserving user and network settings.	New System directory will not have any custom files from current System directory.

NOTE ▶ If you install Mac OS X on an iMac with a tray-loading CD-ROM drive, and the hard disk is an ATA hard disk with a capacity of 8 GB or larger, be sure to select a destination partition for Mac OS X that is completely within the first 8 GB of the disk, or the Mac OS X installer will not allow the installation to continue. This is due to a limitation in the firmware of this model. Refer to Knowledge Base article #106235, "Mac OS X: Disk Appears Dimmed (or 'Grayed Out') in the Installer" for information about installing Mac OS X on older Macintosh computers.

The Archive and Install option is similar to the Clean Install option in Mac OS 9—the existing System folder is archived into a Previous System folder, and a fresh install of the operating system will occur.

If you choose the Erase and Install option, you must specify whether to reformat the destination volume as either Mac OS Extended or UFS.

▶ Mac OS Extended, which is considered the "native" Macintosh volume format, has been used by Macintosh computers since Mac OS 8.1, and provides support for forked files. (Forked files are explained in Lesson 4.) If the drive will be accessed by a computer running Mac OS 9 or earlier, or by applications running in the Classic environment, you will need to use Mac OS Extended as the volume format and ensure that you install the Mac OS 9 drivers. The Mac OS X 10.3 version of the Mac OS Extended format includes journaling support to help protect the file system against power outages or other cases where the system is restarted or shut down prematurely.

▶ UFS is the volume format frequently used by other Unix-based operating systems. You might consider using the UFS volume format in the following instances:

  ▶ If you are installing Mac OS X on an external drive that will be later connected to another computer running Unix

  ▶ If you will be compiling and running Unix applications that rely upon UFS features such as case-sensitivity

  NOTE ▶ Keep in mind that Mac OS Extended is the recommended volume format for Mac OS X. If you do have a need for UFS, consider creating two partitions: a Mac OS Extended partition for Mac OS X and Mac OS applications, and a UFS partition for Unix applications.

For more information, refer to Knowledge Base article #25316: "Mac OS X 10.2 or Earlier: Choosing UFS or Mac OS Extended (HFS Plus) Formatting."

Customizing the Packages

By default, after selecting the destination and choosing the installation type, the installation proceeds with the Easy Install configuration, which installs the following packages:

▶ Essential System Software—The base system software.

▶ BSD Subsystem—Additional BSD command-line utilities. Install this package to use Developer Tools, FTP, Rendezvous, Internet sharing, Network Utility, or the Secure Shell (ssh) software.

▶ Additional Applications—Applications such as iCal, iPhoto, iSync, and iTunes.

▶ Printer Drivers—Drivers for some Canon, Epson, Hewlett-Packard, and Lexmark printers.

▶ Additional Asian Fonts—Additional fonts that expand the choices when writing in Chinese, Japanese, or Korean.

▶ Language Translations—Base Mac OS X support in languages in addition to your primary language.

These additional packages are not installed by default:

▶ Additional Speech Voices—Additional speech voices that enhance the speech technology in Mac OS X.

▶ Fonts for Additional Languages—Additional fonts with support for Armenian, Arabic, Cherokee, Cyrillic, Devanagari, Gujarati, Hebrew, Inuktitut, Punjabi, and Thai.

▶ X11—Software to enable X11 applications to run on Mac OS X.

If you click the Customize button, the Installer shows you a list of packages to be installed. Some packages, such as the BSD Subsystem and Printer Drivers, are optional, but are selected for installation by default. If a checkbox contains a minus sign (–), the package is made up of smaller packages, and not all of the subpackages will be installed. Click the disclosure triangle next to the package to list the subpackages.

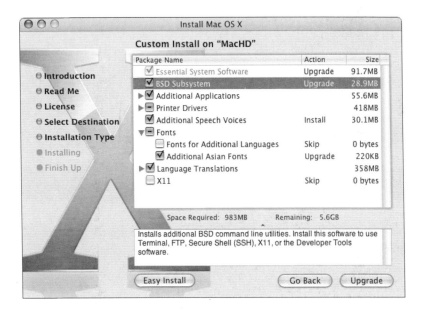

Customizing the list of packages to be installed could affect the number of discs needed to install Mac OS X. The default installation using the retail version of Mac OS X 10.3 uses the first two installation CDs. If you select additional packages, such as X11 or Fonts for Additional Languages, the third CD will be required to complete the installation. If you don't have the second or third CD available, you can quit the Installer when it asks for them. Later, you can manually install any needed packages from those CDs.

Once installation has begun, the Installer shows the percentage completed. The time required to complete the installation depends upon the options chosen and the speed of your Macintosh computer and its optical drive. If the screen goes blank during the installation process, press any key. *Do not* interrupt the process, lest the computer be left inoperable with only a partially installed operating system. This is why it's important to ensure laptops are plugged into working AC outlets during installation.

Completing the Installation

When the Mac OS X Installer is finished with Disc 1, the computer automatically restarts and installs any required software from the Mac OS X Install Disc 2 and 3. When the Mac OS X Installer has run its course, the bulk of the installation process is complete, but you still need to complete a few recommended steps to ensure an optimal user experience with the new operating system.

Configuring with Setup Assistant

When the installer is completely through installing the software, Setup Assistant opens to gather information necessary to register Mac OS X and create a new user account. If you are updating Mac OS X to version 10.3 and did not erase the destination volume, Setup Assistant will not run automatically because the user accounts and configurations are kept from the original installation.

For purposes of following the exercises in this book, it's best if you make the selections explained on these pages. However, if you are comfortable with the process and know what you are doing, feel free to configure Mac OS X differently.

1   In Welcome, select United States and click Continue.

2   In Personalize Your Settings, select U.S. and click Continue.

3   In Your Apple ID, select "Don't create an Apple ID for me" and click Continue.

If you already have an Apple ID or create a new one, the system will be configured to use your Apple ID for tasks such as buying songs from the iTunes Music Store.

4   In registration, press Cmd-Q and click Skip when prompted to skip the remaining registration and setup process.

There's no need to register Mac OS X for purposes of following the exercises in this book; but if you fill out this screen, your information is sent to Apple along with some basic system configuration details to be used for statistical purposes. You can read more about Apple's privacy policy at http://www.apple.com/legal/privacy.

5   In Create Your Account, enter the following information:

▶   Name: *Apple Admin*

▶   Short Name: *apple*

▶   Enter a password and hint of your own choosing.

▶   Select a picture.

If you are on a network that uses NetInfo directory services, you are prompted to use your account information from a server or to create a new local account. If your network does not use NetInfo, you are prompted to create a local account. The initial local account is an administrator account that allows you to change settings in System Preferences, install applications, and use certain utilities. For purposes of following along with the examples in this book, use Apple Admin as the name of your new administrator account.

NOTE ▶ Information about creating and managing additional user accounts is presented in Lesson 3.

When you create a local account, a short name is derived from the account name you entered. You can change the short name now if you like; however, once you create the account, the short name is permanent and you cannot change it. The short name is commonly used for command-line login, File Transfer Protocol (FTP) or ssh login, and email accounts. The short name is typically eight lowercase characters. However, with Mac OS X 10.3, the short name can be up to 255 bytes in length. (The number of characters can vary depending upon the language used, but using two bytes per character is a safe rule of thumb.) The short name cannot contain spaces or special characters ($< > $ "" $*$ {} [] () $\wedge$! \ # | & \$? ~). You can use either the user name or the short name to log in to Mac OS X.

6   Click Continue.

7   Select your time zone, and click Continue.

8   If prompted, set the time and date, and click Continue.

9   Click Done and the Finder appears. Welcome to Mac OS X!

You can quit the Setup Assistant after you have created the first user account, but you will need to complete the Mac OS X configuration, including network settings, using other utilities.

Configuring System Preferences

After you have used Setup Assistant to complete the initial configuration of Mac OS X, you can further configure the operating system using System Preferences. System Preferences is located in the main Applications folder, but it can also be opened by choosing it from the Apple menu or by clicking its icon in the Dock.

System Preferences displays a collection of icons, each representing a collection of settings that can be configured. By default, the icons are grouped into four categories: Personal, Hardware, Internet & Network, and System. If you prefer, you can change System Preferences to display the icons in alphabetical order by choosing View > Show All Alphabetically. The View menu also provides a complete list of the panes, allowing you to go directly from one System Preferences pane to another. Be aware that the System Preferences window may look different than this screenshot if the user has customized the toolbar at the top or added third-party preference items.

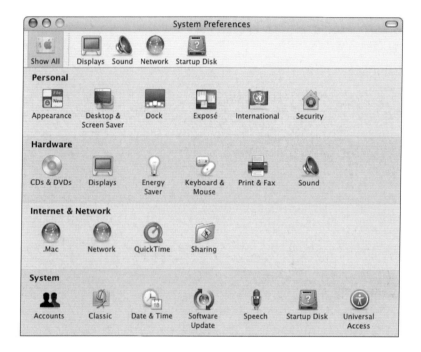

Finding System Information
You can choose Apple > About This Mac to find basic system information such as the operating system version, amount of memory installed, and the processor type and speed. Click the version number to display the Apple engineering build number; click it again to display the computer's serial number.

NOTE ► Earlier Macintosh computers, such as Power Mac G3 (Blue and White), are unable to display the computer's serial number.

Click the More Info button to launch System Profiler, which provides detailed system information.

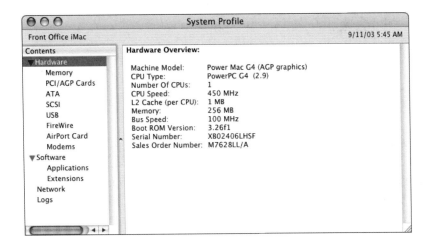

Updating System Software

After you install Mac OS X, Software Update will run automatically, provided you have a working Internet connection. (If it does not, choose Apple > Software Update.) This process checks Apple's software download site for the latest software updates for Mac OS X and lists available updates. When you select an update from the list, Software Update displays information about the update. Usually the information includes a URL you can click to see additional details.

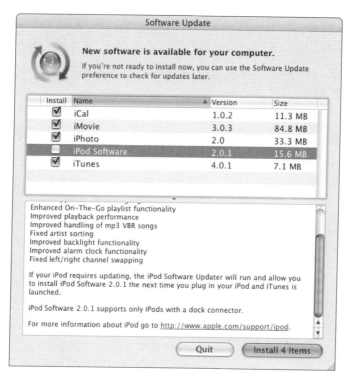

Software Update provides some options for how you want handle an update. If you don't want to install a particular update (if, for instance, you don't have an iPod and don't need iPod updates), you can select it and then choose Update > Ignore Update. In the future, Software Update will not include that specific update when it checks for available updates. However, when a later version of the update is posted, it will be added back to the updates to install. If you need to update multiple computers running Mac OS X, you may want to download the update by choosing Update > Download Checked Items. Then, instead of installing, the update package will be downloaded to /Library/Packages where it can be opened and installed manually.

> **NOTE** ▶ Sometimes an update will be available only after a prior update has been installed. To ensure that you have a fully up-to-date system, after you complete an update of your system, you should have Software Update recheck to see if any newer updates are available.

To verify whether a software update was installed successfully, look for its receipt in the folder /Library/Receipts. The Installed Updates pane also lists the updates that have been installed. Clicking "Open as a Log File" displays the installer log file, which lists installed updates and any errors encountered.

Checking Console Logs

The Console application lets you see technical messages from the Mac OS X system software and Mac OS X applications. Processes that do not have a graphical interface will output messages to Console as well as to the system log. Most of the information sent to Console is captured in the system log. Opening the Console application while you are troubleshooting will give you a better sense of what is happening on Mac OS X, because the Console application displays information and errors from processes you may not know are running.

Lines displayed in Console are usually made up of a date stamp, the name of the process, and the message. For instance:

2003-10-01 08:25:11.582 Classic Startup[513] CFLog (20): Classic is Starting: You have the preference set to warn before starting Classic. Click Start Classic to continue starting.

This message is simply informational. It shows that at 8:25 am on October 1, 2003, Classic was starting up.

Using Console to View Installation Log

During installation, any errors and informational messages are stored in a log file. After installing, or when you are experiencing problems that you think may be related to installation, check the installation log to see if any errors occurred.

1   Open Console (/Applications/Utilities).

2   If the list of available log files is not listed on the left side of the Console window, choose View > Show Log List.

3   Click on the disclosure triangle next to /var/log to see the list of log files in that folder.

4   Select install.log. This is the log file created during installation.

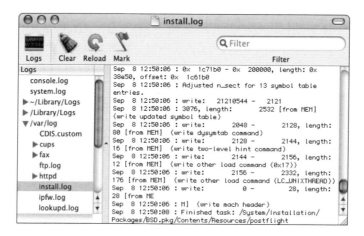

Look for any errors that may have occurred during installation.

5   Quit Console.

Troubleshooting Mac OS X Installation

If you encounter problems during the installation of Mac OS X or any software updates, there are several troubleshooting steps you can take to eliminate the problem and complete the installation:

► Turn off the Screen Saver and Energy Saver in System Preferences so that they do not activate while you are downloading or installing. If you are installing Mac OS X on a portable computer, make sure that it is plugged in to AC power while you are downloading and installing.

► Check the installation log by choosing File > Show Log or by viewing /var/log/install.log. Error messages listed here can help you troubleshoot the problem.

► Try restarting the computer and installing the update again. Since some installation issues are not reproducible, you may succeed the second time.

► Check to make sure that the latest version of the firmware is installed. An outdated version of the firmware can cause a range of problems, including no video display or erratic behavior.

► There could be problems with the disk drive onto which you are installing the update. Start up from the Mac OS X Install Disc 1 and use the Disk Utility application to verify the volume you are trying to install onto. After verification or any necessary repair, try the installation again.

► If the issue persists, disconnect any other drives you may have connected to your computer and retry your installation. Other devices could potentially affect your installation. Disconnect or remove anything that did not come with your computer. If removing all non-Apple memory leaves you with insufficient memory to install Mac OS X, then remove everything but the memory. If your issue persists, you may have an issue with your non-Apple memory.

▶ "Erase" installs often succeed where installations without erasing fail. You should make sure you have a working backup of your important data before erasing the volume. Due to the extreme nature of this solution, you may wish to try all other options first.

▶ If you need to install an older version of the operating system, first delete the files in /Library/Receipts, or better yet, move the files to a backup folder.

For more tips, see the Knowledge Base article #106692, "Mac OS X: Trouble-shooting Installation and Software Updates."

What You've Learned

▶ Mac OS X uses standards throughout the operating system. These standards enable Macintosh computers to integrate into networks and share data and peripherals with other computers.

▶ Mac OS X can install on any Macintosh computer with a G3 processor or later that also has built-in USB, 128 MB of memory, and 2 GB of available disk space.

▶ Before you install Mac OS X, you need to make key decisions about how you want to configure the system, including if you want to partition your drive or not. If you are upgrading from Mac OS 9, you should also note your network configuration information so that you can use it when you configure Mac OS X.

▶ After using Setup Assistant to do the initial configuration, you can use System Preferences to perform additional system configuration.

▶ Apple provides updates to the Mac OS X through the Software Update preferences. To ensure that your system is up-to-date, you should check for updates on a regular basis.

▶ Use Knowledge Base to research known installation issues.

References

The following Knowledge Base articles (located at http://kbase.info.apple.com) will provide you with further information regarding installing Mac OS X.

Apple Software Restore

▶ 42929, "Using Restore Discs with Mac OS X 10.2 or Later"

▶ 106451, "Using Apple Software Restore to Install or Reinstall Parts Without Erasing"

Firmware Issues

▶ 42642, "To Continue Booting, Type 'mac-boot' and Press Return Message"

▶ 58492, "Differences Between the Mac OS ROM and BootROM"

▶ 60351, "Determining BootROM or Firmware Version"

▶ 86117, "Mac OS X: Chart of Available Firmware Updates"

Installation Issues

▶ 75187, "Mac OS X: Software Installations Require Administrator Password"

▶ 106178, "Startup Manager: How to Select a Startup Volume"

▶ 106235, "Mac OS X: Disk Appears Dimmed (or 'Grayed Out') in the Installer"

▶ 106442, "Mac OS X 10.0, 10.1: Installer Does Not Display Hard Disk"

▶ 106464, "Your Mac Won't Start Up in Mac OS X"

▶ 106692, "Mac OS X: Troubleshooting Installation and Software Updates"

▶ 106693, "Mac OS X: Troubleshooting Installation from CD-ROM"

▶ 106694, "Mac OS X: Troubleshooting the Mac OS X Installer"

▶ 106695, "Mac OS X: Troubleshooting Automatic Software Update"

Miscellaneous

▶   2238, "Macintosh: How to Reset PRAM and NVRAM"

▶   86209, "Macintosh: Some Computers Only Start Up in Mac OS X"

▶   86246, "Using the Software Install and Restore DVD with PowerBook G4 (12-inch)"

UFS and Mac OS Extended

▶   25316, "Mac OS X 10.2 or Earlier: Choosing UFS or Mac OS Extended (HFS Plus) Formatting"

Review Quiz

Use the following questions to review what you have learned:

1.   What are the different configuration choices when installing Mac OS X?

2.   What are five things you should do before you upgrade Mac OS 9.*x* to Mac OS X?

3.   What is the purpose of the local account?

4.   What are the quick fixes to consider when troubleshooting an installation problem?

Answers

1.   Mac OS X can be installed on a single partition along with Mac OS 9.*x*. You can also install Mac OS X on one partition or volume while Mac OS 9.*x* is installed on another. Mac OS X can also be installed by itself, without Mac OS 9.*x*. You can also choose to update a previous version of Mac OS X install to Mac OS X 10.3.

2.   Before installing Mac OS X, you should make a backup of the data on your hard disk, upgrade to Mac OS 9.*x* (if you plan on using Classic applications), read the Read Before You Install document, collect network configuration information from Mac OS 9.*x*, and decide on an installation method.

3.   The initial local account is automatically an administrator account with which you can change settings in System Preferences, install applications, and use certain utilities.

4.   Check the installation log; confirm that firmware is up to date; restart/ reinstall; check for disk problems; disconnect non-essential hardware; and turn off Energy Saver and Screen Saver preferences.

2

Time   This lesson takes approximately 2 hours to complete.

Goals   Describe the types of user accounts and the differences between them

Use Accounts preferences to create, manage, and delete local user accounts

Reset user account passwords with Accounts preferences, the Mac OS X Install Disc 1, or the master password feature

Manage access to applications and data files by storing them in specific folders created by Mac OS X or by setting file and folder permissions

Troubleshoot user and permissions issues

Lesson 2
Users and Permissions

Mac OS X is a true multiuser operating system, which means that the computer can be used by more than one user, and every resource, file, and program is associated with a user on the system.

In Mac OS 9, the Multiple Users control panel allowed you to configure the system for more than one user. This feature was added to the operating system to give each user a unique workspace. Microsoft Windows implements multiple user accounts with functionality similar to Mac OS 9. Unix, on the other hand, was designed to be a multiuser environment because most computers in existence at the time Unix was developed were large computers that had to be shared by many people.

This lesson introduces you to the three types of user accounts; how to create and manage user accounts; options for increasing account security; managing user access to files and folders; and troubleshooting user account and file permission issues.

Understanding User Types

There are tens of millions of Macintosh users in the world today, performing a wide variety of tasks from accounting to layout to writing. However, as far as Mac OS X is concerned, there are only three types of users: normal, administrator, and System Administrator.

Your user type doesn't dictate the tasks you can perform with the Macintosh, but it does determine the level of privileges you enjoy for changing how the Mac operates.

You can configure three types of users in Mac OS X:

▶   Normal users can use a basic set of applications and tools and are limited to making configuration changes that affect only the user's own account, such as what applications and files are opened when the user logs in and what picture is displayed as the user's background pattern. A normal user cannot make changes to any settings that are system-wide, such as the Network, Date & Time, Sharing, Energy Accounts, Saver, or Startup Disk panes of System Preferences. A normal user is also restricted from using Directory Setup and NetInfo Manager to change configurations.

   If a normal user attempts to make a system-wide modification, the user will need to provide the user name and password of an administrator user before the changes can be made.

▶   An administrator user, or admin user, has basic use of the tools to configure and customize Mac OS X. The initial local account configured in Setup Assistant is an administrator user.

   One of the most powerful attributes of an administrator is that this user type can change settings on any of the panes in System Preferences. An administrator can make changes using certain utilities, such as NetInfo Manager. An administrator can also install applications and resources that can be used by all users on the system.

Startup Disk is restricted to keep anyone but an administrator from starting up in Mac OS 9.x. When in Mac OS 9.x, none of the file security in Mac OS X is in place, leaving the operating system and other users' files open to modification.

► A System Administrator (also called superuser or root) has read and write access to all settings and files on the system, including hidden system files that a regular administrator account cannot modify.

By default, System Administrator is disabled. The user exists, but you can't log in using that account. Mac OS X was configured this way to help avert unintentional deletion of important files and folders. System Administrator can be enabled using either NetInfo Manager or the command line. When viewing items owned by System Administrator in the Finder, the Info window will usually show the owner as "system."

NOTE ► There can be multiple normal and administrator users on any Mac OS X system, but only one System Administrator. Also, System Administrator is not a standard user account and does not have a home directory.

Each user has certain attributes: long name, short name, password, and a unique numeric user identification (UID). Although UID numbers aren't displayed in the user interface, Mac OS X uses the UID to internally identify users and these numbers can be viewed in NetInfo Manager. Each user account also has its own home folder in /Users and owns any files that are created when someone is logged in as that user.

Local vs. Network User Accounts

When you create a user account (administrator or normal), Mac OS X stores the user account information in a special database, called a directory, on the same computer. These user accounts are local user accounts. A user with a local user account can only log in to the computer that stores the account. Local user accounts are commonly used in home and small office environments.

In many networked environments, however, you might be given a network user account. These are user accounts that are stored in a network directory, a type of database hosted on a remote computer, such as a computer running Mac OS X Server or an Active Directory server running on a Windows Server machine, that provides resource information. Since the user account is stored on a remote computer, the user can log in to any computer that is configured to retrieve user account information from the remote computer. Network user accounts are commonly used in schools and larger enterprises.

> **NOTE ▶** This lesson covers creating and managing local user accounts only. Network accounts are also discussed in Lesson 7, but creation and management of network accounts is beyond the scope of this book.

Creating and Editing User Accounts

Both administrator and normal users use the Accounts pane of System Preferences to manage user accounts. Although normal users can change their own account information, such as the account password, only administrator users can add or delete user accounts. Throughout this lesson, we assume that you are initially logged in as an administrator using an account named Apple Admin. If you prefer to continue using your existing account, that's fine, as long as it's an administrator account. Whenever the Apple Admin account is discussed in the book, substitute your administrator account instead.

Accounts preferences is divided into five panes. However, only four are available at any time:

> **NOTE ▶** Startup Items is only available when you are configuring your own account, and Limitations is only available when you're editing other accounts.

▶ Password—You enter the user's full name and short name. You also enter the user's password and an optional password hint.

NOTE ▶ You can create a normal user without a password, but doing so is discouraged for security reasons.

When a user account is created in Mac OS X, a home folder is created for that user in /Users. The home folder has the same name as the user's short name. You can quickly access your home folder by clicking the home icon in the Sidebar at the left of the Finder window. The short user name can be as long as 255 Roman characters. However, if a short user name is longer than 32 characters, Classic applications (as well as some Mac OS X applications) may give errors while saving files to your home folder. In such a case, you can save the files in a folder that has a name less than 32 characters, and then move them later, using the Finder.

▶ Picture—You select a login picture. This picture is also used as your Address Book picture and as the default picture in iChat.

► Security—Used to enable the FileVault feature and administrative account capabilities for the account. FileVault is covered later in this lesson.

► Limitations—When logged in as an administrator user, the Limitations pane will allow you to limit what a normal user can do on the computer. You can allow or deny the user access to remove items from the Dock, open all System Preferences, change a password, or burn CDs or DVDs. You can configure the user to have access only to the applications and utilities of your choice.

You can also click Simple Finder to configure the user to use the Simple Finder. The Simple Finder displays only the folders that the user has access to in the Dock. Using the Simple Finder, the user does not have permission to save anything to the Desktop. If you give a user access to a specific file, such as a Word document, but you do not give the user access to the Word application, that user will still be able to open Word by double-clicking on the file.

NOTE ▶ The accounts list identifies normal accounts as either Standard, Managed, or Simplified, depending upon the Limitations settings.

▶ Startup Items—If you are modifying your own account, you can specify which items to open automatically when you log in. This pane is available to administrator users only.

To apply your changes, switch to another pane, add a new user, or quit System Preferences.

Setting Login Options

The Login Options pane in Accounts preferences is used to set options that affect how users log in as well as what they can do once they are logged in. Begin by selecting a user in the list at the left, then click Login Options at the bottom left.

You can configure the login window to display a list of user accounts with a login picture for each one or a prompt for the user name and password. The latter is the best choice for computers with several user accounts, and it also provides an extra measure of security because users must know a valid name and password to log in. If you are connecting to a network account from the login window, "Other User" is automatically displayed in the login window.

If you are an administrator user, you can configure the computer to log in as a particular user every time it starts up or restarts. Select the "Automatically log in as" checkbox and choose a user from the corresponding pop-up menu. You will be prompted for a password (if any) for that account.

The next time the computer boots, Mac OS X will automatically log into that account. This option is best for computers with only one user account.

You can also hide the Sleep, Restart, and Shut Down buttons in the Login Options pane. This security feature can keep a user from restarting in an insecure mode, short of using the reset or power buttons on the computer itself.

In addition, you can enable fast user switching (discussed later in this lesson) in the Login Options pane. This feature lets multiple users share a computer without quitting applications and logging out. For the purposes of the following exercises, make sure fast user switching is enabled.

Creating Two Normal User Accounts

This exercise guides you through the process of creating two normal user accounts:

1   Open System preferences and click Accounts.

2 Click the Add User button (the plus sign beneath the accounts list), and enter the following information:

▶ Name: *Laura Smith*

▶ Short Name: *laura*

▶ Password: *laura*

▶ Verify: *laura*

NOTE ▶ Entering the user's name for the password is not recommended for real-world use; we suggest it here only for simplicity.

3   Click the Picture button and select a picture from the list on the right.

4   Verify that the Laura account is in the Other Accounts list on the left.

5   Repeat the previous steps to create a second user account for Warren Peece. Enter *warren* for both the Short Name and Password.

Creating an Administrator User

At this point you have at least one administrator user account (Apple Admin) and two normal user accounts (Laura Smith and Warren Peece). Typically a computer will have one administrator user account with several normal user accounts. However, you may find it useful to create additional administrator accounts. The following steps walk you through the creation of an additional administrator user account:

1   In Accounts preferences, click the Add User button, and enter the following information:

   ▶   Name: *MacOSX Admin*

   ▶   Short Name: *macosx*

   ▶   Password: *macosx*

   ▶   Verify: *macosx*

   NOTE ▶ If other users have access to your Macintosh, it's prudent to use a different password than the one suggested in this book.

2   Click the Picture button and select a picture.

3   Click the Security button.

4   Select the "Allow user to administer this computer" option.

   Verify that MacOSX Admin is in the Other Accounts list and that the account type is Admin.

Configuring a User's Limitations

The following steps walk you through the configuration of user limitations:

1 Log in as Apple Admin, if you aren't already.

2 Open Accounts preferences.

3 Select Laura Smith's account and click the Limitations button.

4   Click Simple Finder.

5   In the Applications list, verify that only Applications is allowed.

6   Click the Password button.

Notice that the type of account for Laura Smith in the Other Accounts list has changed to Simplified.

7   Quit System Preferences.

Testing the New User Limitations

In the following steps, you will experience Laura's newly designated limitations:

1   Choose Laura Smith from the user accounts menu at the far right in the menu bar. This invokes fast user switching, which is discussed in detail later in this lesson.

2   Log in as Laura.

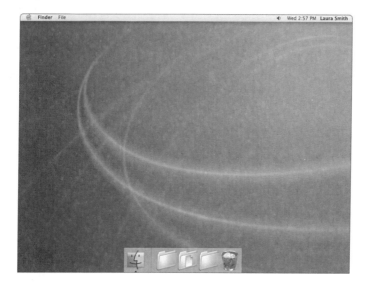

Note the Simple Finder environment.

3   Click My Applications in the Dock.

Note the limited number of applications Laura can access.

4   Choose Apple > Log Out Laura Smith.

5   Log in as Apple Admin.

6   Open System Preferences and click Accounts.

7   In Accounts preferences, select Laura and click Limitations.

8   Restore Laura's original capabilities by clicking No Limits.

9   Select any other account to save the changes for Laura Smith's account.

    Notice that the type of account for Laura Smith has reverted to Standard.

Deleting User Accounts

As an administrator user, you can use Accounts preferences to delete any user account. However, you cannot remove all the administrator users because there must be at least one.

To delete an account, select it, then click the Delete User (minus sign) button. The system will prompt you to put the contents of the user's home folder in a disk image (.dmg) file in the /Users/Deleted Users folder or to delete the home folder contents immediately.

If you click OK, the user's home folder will be moved into a disk image file in /Users/Deleted Users. If the files need to be transferred to another user account, an administrator user can move the disk image to that user's home folder. The user can then mount the disk image and retrieve the needed files. (Disk image files are covered in Lesson 3.)

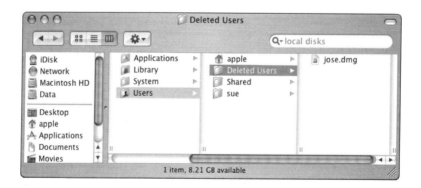

Deleting an Administrator User Account

The following steps walk you through deleting an administrator user account:

1   In Accounts preferences, select the MacOSX Admin user account.

2   Click the Delete User button (the minus sign).

A dialog appears, informing you that the contents of the user's folder will be put in the Deleted Users folder.

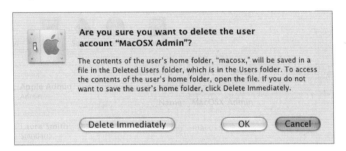

You have two options when deleting a user account: you can save the contents of the user's home directory in a disk image, or you can immediately delete the user's home directory.

Because you will want to access the user's documents after his account has been deleted, you need to archive the user's home folder as part of the account deletion.

3   Click OK.

4   Verify that MacOSX Admin is no longer listed in the Other Accounts list.

5   Quit System Preferences.

6   Open the /Users folder in the Finder.

Verify that the folder macosx has been deleted and that a macosx.dmg file has been placed in the Deleted Users folder.

Reviewing the Deleted User's Files

The contents of the macosx home directory have been stored in the macosx.dmg disk image. Disk image files will be covered later in Lesson 4, however, the following steps show you how to open the file and examine its contents:

1   Navigate to /Users/Deleted Users.

2   Double-click macosx.dmg.

   The macosx volume will be mounted on your desktop.

3   Double-click the macosx volume icon on your desktop.

You should be able to view the folders and files from the old MacOSX Admin home folder.

4 Unmount the macosx volume by dragging the icon to the Trash.

If you need to have another user take over the files from the MacOSX Admin account, you could copy the disk image to the new user's home directory, and that user could mount the disk image and copy out any needed files.

Switching Between Users

Mac OS X 10.3 introduced a new feature, fast user switching, which lets multiple users share a computer without quitting applications and logging out. When one user logs in to his or her own account, other accounts remain active in the background with applications running and documents still open.

Although the Unix-based security model in Mac OS X helps keep data and applications secure, enabling fast user switching can introduce some potential security risks. You should not enable fast user switching on a computer where you do not know and trust all of the users (in a computer lab or a kiosk, for example).

When you activate fast user switching in Login Options of Accounts preferences, a new menu appears on the right of the menu bar. You can use this menu to switch between accounts. If you switch to an active user account (an account that is logged in), you'll see the account in the same state in which it was last left, with any applications running. This feature enables you to keep each account's user environment distinct and intact without wasting time.

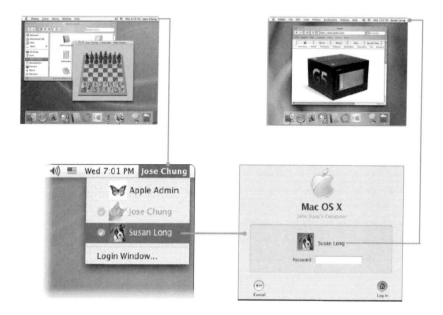

When using fast user switching, keep in mind that you might encounter resource conflicts. Many peripherals cannot be shared among multiple users on the same computer simultaneously. For example, if a user opens a scanner application and then switches out, a second user logging in may not be able to access the scanner. In some cases, applications that control peripherals will release control of the device when a user switches out. iChat, for example, will drop audio and video chats when a user switches out.

Some applications have issues when two or more people attempt to use the application at the same time. Mac OS X includes a list of versions of applications that are known to have issues when opened by more than one user. When a second user attempts to open the application, the system will warn the user that the application is already in use and cannot be opened. If you encounter an application that has problems with multiple switched users opening it, contact the application's developer—a more recent version may have fixed the problem.

You can also experience conflicts in accessing documents. A user with the right permissions can open the same document that a previous user was editing, and can make changes to it, even if the first user left the document open. This can result in conflicts. Therefore, you should coordinate work on shared documents with other users of the system to avoid problems.

Also, only one account at a time can use the Classic environment. If one account has a Classic application open, any other users on that Mac OS X computer will not be able to run Classic applications until the first user quits the running Classic application and stops the Classic environment.

> **NOTE ▶** If fast user switching is turned on, an administrator user cannot
> select or edit the account of any user that is currently logged in (the account
> name appears dimmed in Accounts preferences).

Experimenting with Fast User Switching

Fast user switching allows multiple user accounts to be active simultaneously on a computer and allows users to be able to quickly switch between them.

1   Click the Login Options button at the bottom of Accounts preferences.

2   Deselect the "Automatically log in as" option.

3   Select "Enable fast user switching."

4   In the Warning dialog, click OK.

Notice that a new user accounts menu appears at the right in the menu bar and displays the name of the logged-in user account.

5   Click the user accounts menu.

The menu expands to list each of the local user accounts. Notice that the menu item for Apple Admin is dimmed since it is the active account. It also has a checkmark next to it, indicating that the account is logged in.

6   Open Script Editor (/Applications/AppleScript).

7   In the untitled window that appears, enter the following simple script:

```
say "Hello there."

repeat

    display dialog "I am still here!" buttons "Cancel" giving up after 10

    say "I am still here!"

end repeat
```

This simple script displays a dialog and says "I am still here" every 10 seconds until the Cancel button is clicked.

8   Click Run. Provided the speaker volume is turned up loud enough, you should hear the computer immediately say "Hello there."

9   Choose Laura Smith from the user accounts menu.

The login window for Laura Smith appears.

10   Log in using Laura's password (laura).

The screen changes, and you are now logged in to the Laura account.

11   In Desktop & Screen Saver preferences, select a different background.

Notice that every once in a while you still hear the I'm Here script running, though it isn't visible. Even though the Apple Admin account is switched out, applications running in that account are still active.

12   Click Laura Smith in the menu bar.

Notice both Apple Admin and Laura Smith have checkmarks since both are logged in, but Laura Smith is dimmed since it's the active account.

13   Choose Apple Admin from the user accounts menu.

14   Enter the password for the Apple Admin account and log in.

15   In Script Editor, click Cancel to quit the I'm Here script.

16   Quit Script Editor, saving the I'm Here script if you wish.

17   Choose Apple > Log Out Apple Admin.

18   When asked to confirm logging out, click Log Out.

The screen clears, and the login window appears.

19   Log in as Laura Smith.

Laura's environment should be just as you left it, but you should no longer hear the I'm Here script.

Securing Your Macintosh

With its Unix core, Mac OS X has many robust built-in security features that restrict attempts to compromise the system, either intentionally or accidentally. However, as with any security system, there are ways to bypass or override the controls. In the end, to secure your machine, you must control physical access to the computer as well as user access to the files on the computer.

Creating Passwords

When you create a user account, or when a user changes his or her password, it is important to pick a password that will be easy to remember but difficult for other people to guess. People often resort to obvious passwords such as their own names or that of a loved one. Even combining common words is a poor choice since hackers employ automated cracking tools that generate millions of such combinations.

Much better is to combine alphanumeric characters and punctuation in a word that is seemingly random, but which actually has meaning if you know the secret. The mnemonics for the following good passwords are: gruesome threesome (gru "sum" three sum); look at me (replacing 0 with % and at with @); and early to bed, early to rise (replacing "to" with "2" and using the first letter of other words).

Bad	Good
John	gru+3sum
Johndoe	l%%k@me
browncow	e2be2r

A normal user can change his password. However, before doing so the user must enter the current password to authenticate himself or herself. If a user forgets his or her password, any administrator user on the computer can change the password using Accounts preferences. Any account password can be changed by booting the Mac OS X Install Disc 1 and choosing Installer > Reset Password.

If you want to protect the computer from a user booting an installation CD to change passwords, you can set an Open Firmware password, which you'll need to enter every time you turn on or restart the computer. Knowledge Base article #106482, "Setting Up Open Firmware Password Protection in Mac OS X 10.1 or Later," provides instructions for setting this up.

NOTE ▶ If you want to use FileVault to encrypt your home folder, you'll need to set the master password for the computer. This password is different from the password you set in the Accounts preferences. If you forget this password, it is difficult to recover. You'll learn more about the master password later in this lesson.

If you need to write down a password, it should be stored in a secure place to prevent unauthorized users from gaining access to the accounts. Mac OS X uses keychains for just this purpose (more on this topic later in this lesson).

Setting Security Options

Security preferences is a collection of options to help protect your system from unauthorized use. Most of the options are also in other System Preference panes, such as FileVault in Accounts preferences.

You can specify a password that will wake the system from sleep or screen saver. You can also disable automatic login to force users to authenticate, require users to enter a password to unlock a secure system preference, and specify how many minutes of inactivity after which to log out a user. These options also reside in Accounts preferences and Desktop & Screen Saver preferences.

Encrypting Home Directories with FileVault

Although Mac OS X provides some protection from other users gaining access to documents stored in an account's home directory, other users can still gain access to those files. For example, anyone with a Mac OS X installation disc or an administrator account on the computer can reset a password and log in to the account. Even without changing passwords, someone with System Administrator access can access any file on the system, including those in another home directory.

FileVault enables users to encrypt the contents of their home directories, allowing file access only when the user is logged in. When a user enables the FileVault feature, the user's entire home directory is transferred into an encrypted disk image (which is covered in more depth in Lesson 3). When the user logs in, the disk image is decrypted and mounted in the /Users directory, allowing the user to use his or her home directory. When the user logs out, the disk image is unmounted and re-encrypted, leaving only the disk image file in place of the user's home folder contents. Other users, including administrators, may get access to the disk image file, but because the disk image file is encrypted, they can't access the contents without the password. The time necessary to encrypt and decrypt the home directory depends upon the size of the directory and the speed of the computer.

NOTE ▶ When turning FileVault on or off for an account, there must be disk space available equal to or greater than the size of the user's home folder. If there is not enough disk space, the account can not be converted.

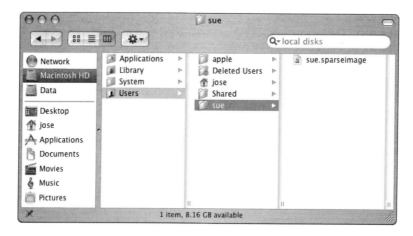

One of the drawbacks of encrypting data is that if the user forgets his or her password, access to the files in the home folder is lost. If an account has FileVault enabled, an administrator user cannot use Accounts preferences to change that account's password, nor can the administrator user turn off FileVault for the account; only the user can.

Because users invariably forget passwords, Mac OS X provides a master password feature to allow passwords on FileVault-protected accounts to be reset. The master password is used only as a back door for recovering FileVaults. If during login a user enters three incorrect passwords for their FileVault-encrypted accounts, the account's password hint is displayed along with a Reset Password button. After the user clicks Reset Password and enters the master password (obtained from the administrator), he or she can set a new account password.

To help prevent data from being completely lost when a user forgets the password, a master password must be set by an administrator user before any account can be encrypted by FileVault.

If you forget the master password, you can reset it, but you must know the passwords for any accounts with FileVault enabled:

1   As an administrator user, delete the master password keychain file (/Library/Keychains/FileVaultMaster.keychain). When the master password keychain is deleted, Mac OS X assumes that no master password is set yet.

2   In Accounts preferences or Security preferences, set a new master password.

3   Log in to each account that has FileVault turned on and use Accounts preferences to reset the password for that account.

NOTE ▶ Do not forget the master password! Although it is possible to reset the master password, it still requires all users with FileVault-protected accounts to know their passwords. If a user has forgotten his or her account password, and you have forgotten the master password, there is no way to recover the user's data.

Setting the Master Password

Before using FileVault, you should set the master password for the computer. If you don't and forget your login password, the data you encrypted using FileVault will be lost forever.

To set the master password:

1   Log in as Apple Admin.

2   Open System preferences and click Accounts.

3   Select Apple Admin in the left pane.

4   Click the Security button.

5   Click Set Master Password.

6   Authenticate as Apple Admin if requested.

7   Type *applemp* in the Master Password and Verify fields.

> **NOTE** ▶ If other users have access to your computer, it would be prudent not to use the passwords suggested in this book.

8   Click OK.

> **NOTE** ▶ The master password is set for the computer. You can change it later if you want by clicking the Change button in the Security pane.

9   Quit System Preferences.

10 Choose Apple > Log Out Apple Admin.

Encrypting a Home Folder

To encrypt Warren's home folder using FileVault:

1   Log in as Warren Peece (short name and password are both *warren*).

2   Open System preferences and click Accounts.

Because Warren is not allowed to administer the computer, he can only make changes to his account. Other accounts defined in the computer appear dimmed in the left pane.

3   Click the Security button.

4   Click the lock icon in the bottom left of the window, then authenticate as Apple Admin.

5   Click Turn On FileVault.

6 Type Warren's password (*warren*) in the Password field and click OK.

A warning message appears asking you if you are sure you want to turn on FileVault.

7 Take a moment to read the warning message and then click Turn On FileVault.

The system logs out Warren and displays a message indicating that the system is encrypting Warren's home folder and displays a progress bar. The system creates a sparse disk image, copies the home folder into the image, and deletes the old home folder. When the system is finished encrypting Warren's home folder, the login window appears.

Verifying the Home Folder Encryption

Once a home folder is encrypted, the contents of the home folder are inaccessible unless the owner of the home folder logs in. Do the following to verify that the system encrypted Warren's home folder:

1 Log in as Apple Admin.

2 Go to /Users/warren.

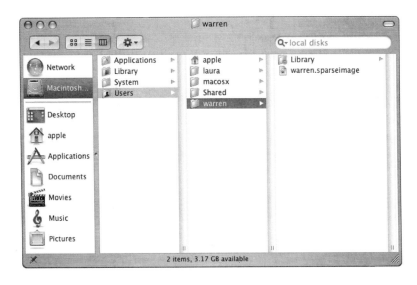

You should see a file named warren.sparseimage. This is the disk image file where Warren's home folder is stored. If you double-click the disk image file, the system prompts you to enter a password. If you enter Warren's password, the disk image mounts.

3   Click Apple Admin in the menu bar and choose Warren Peece from the user accounts menu.

4   Log in using Warren's password.

5   Go to /Users/warren.

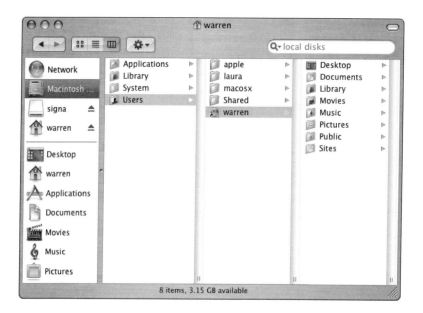

Notice that Warren can access the contents of his home directory.

6   Choose Apple > Log Out Warren Peece.

Resetting a User's Password

If Warren forgets his password, the contents of his home folder are inaccessible, unless his password is reset using the master password.

1   In the login window, select Warren Peece.

2   In the Password field, type *ABC*.

3   Click Log In.

    Since ABC isn't Warren's password, the window will shake.

4   In the Password field, type *123*.

5   Click Log In.

    Again, access will be denied.

6   In the Password field, type *xyz*.

7   Click Log In.

    Since logging failed three times, the login window will change to display the Reset Password button.

8   Click Reset Password.

9   In the Master Password field, type *applemp*.

10 Click Continue.

    An alert message appears explaining that the user's old keychain will be saved and a new one created.

11 Click OK.

12 In the New Password and Verify fields, type *peece*.

This will be Warren's new password.

13 Click Log in.

The computer will then log Warren in.

14 Choose Apple > Log Out Warren Peece.

Resetting the Master Password
If you forgot your master password, do the following to reset it:

1 Log in as Apple Admin.

2 Open Terminal (/Applications/Utilities).

Terminal is used to enter Unix commands. It is discussed in Lesson 5.

3 Type the following and press Return:

sudo rm /Library/Keychains/FileVault*

This command removes the files where the master password is stored.

4 When prompted for a password, enter Apple Admin's password.

You will not see any characters as you type but, if the password entered is correct, the Terminal prompt appears.

5 Choose Apple > Restart, then click Restart.

6 Log in as Apple Admin. For the Master Password, type *apple*.

At this point, Warren can still log into his account. However, if he forgot his password, he would not be able to use the master password to reset it. Warren needs to reset his password so that it is saved with the new master password.

7 Choose Warren from the user accounts menu and log in as Warren.

Remember that the password has been changed to *peece*.

8 Use Accounts preferences to change Warren's password to *warren*.

Warren's password is now saved with the new master password. If Warren should forget his password, he can use master password to reset his password.

Using a Normal Account to Change Passwords

Non-admin users can change their own passwords.

1 Log in as Laura.

2 Open Accounts preferences.

Notice that Laura's account is selected and all of the other accounts are dimmed.

Since Laura does not have administrator authority, she cannot modify any accounts other than her own.

3   Click in the Password field and press the spacebar.

4   A dialog appears asking for Laura's current password. This is to prevent other people from changing Laura's password when she steps away from the computer while she is still logged in.

5   In the Current Password field, enter Laura's password: *laura*.

6   Click OK.

7   In the Password and Verify fields, enter her new password: *smith*.

    Changes are saved when you attempt to leave the Password pane.

8   Click the Picture button.

    A dialog appears, stating that the keychain password will be changed.

9   Click OK.

    Laura has now changed her password.

10 Verify that you've changed Laura's password by logging out and then back in with the new password (*smith*).

Using an Administrator Account to Change Passwords

An administrator can change any of the passwords on a system.

1   Log out and then back in as Apple Admin.

2   Open Accounts preferences.

Because Apple Admin is an administrator, you can modify all of the accounts.

3   Select Laura's account.

4   In both the Password and Verify fields, enter *laura*.

Notice that you were not prompted for Laura's current password. An administrator does not need to know the user's current password in order to change it.

5   Click the Picture button.

A dialog appears, informing you that the keychain password has not been changed. Only the user for the account can change the keychain password.

6   Click OK.

Laura's password has been reset back to "laura."

Using the Mac OS X Install Disc 1 to Change Passwords

There will be times when you have a system where no passwords are known, including those for any administrator accounts. In these cases, you need to use the Mac OS X Install Disc 1 to change passwords.

1   Insert the main Mac OS X Install Disc 1.

2   Choose Apple > Restart, click Restart, then hold down the C key.

Holding down the C key during startup tells the computer to boot from the CD.

After a short while, the Installer appears. Do not proceed with the installation. Doing so causes the Reset Password option to disappear.

3   Choose Installer > Reset Password.

The Reset Password window appears.

4   In the upper portion of the window, select the icon that represents the hard drive with Mac OS X installed.

When you click the icon, Reset Password retrieves all of the user accounts.

5   Beneath "Select a user of this volume to reset their password," choose Apple Admin from the pop-up menu of user accounts.

6   In both of the Password fields, type *admin*.

7   Click Save.

8   When the Password Saved dialog appears, click OK.

9   Quit Reset Password (Cmd-Q).

10 Quit Installer (Cmd-Q).

11 When asked if you are sure you want to quit, click Quit.

    The system will restart from the hard drive.

12 Test the changing of the password by logging into the Apple Admin account with the new password set in step 6 (*admin*).

13 Eject the CD.

Using Keychains

Beyond the user account password, a user has to keep track of passwords for many other resources, such as Web sites, servers, and applications. When you connect to a server or Web site or open a keychain-aware application, the password used can be stored in the keychain. The next time you access those resources, the password is read from your keychain automatically. You can create more than one keychain for each user, based on types of resources or on particular locations.

The user's default keychain is automatically created at the same time the account is created. That keychain is named "login" and is stored in ~/Library/Keychains. A system-wide keychain named "System" is also created by default and is shared by all users on the system. Since the keychain is not "tied" to the system, it can be copied to other computers. For example, when a user upgrades to a new computer, he or she can copy the keychain from the old computer to the new one.

You can use Keychain Access (/Applications/Utilities) to create additional keychains for each user, based on types of resources or on particular locations. Users can also use Keychain Access to manage their keychains, including what passwords are stored in a keychain and what password is used to unlock the keychain.

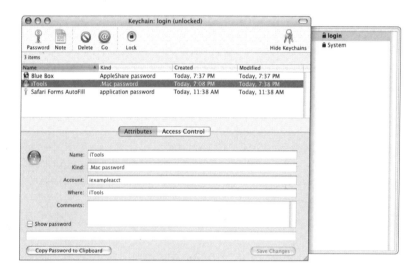

You can change the password to unlock a keychain at any time, however, if you want your default keychain to be unlocked automatically when you log in, make sure your keychain password is the same as your Mac OS X login password. If an administrator changes an account password, the keychain password for that account does not get changed as well. As a result, the user can log in with the new password, but the keychain will not automatically open.

Troubleshooting User Account Issues

Here are some basic user account troubleshooting topics and solutions:

▶ If you are unable to log into a computer because the administrator account passwords are lost, boot from a Mac OS X installation disc and use the Reset Passwords command. If you can log in using an administrator account, you can reset a user's password in Accounts preferences.

NOTE ▶ If the account is protected by FileVault, the only way to reset the password is to first enter the master password. If you forget your master password in addition to your account's password, there is no way to recover the data that was encrypted by FileVault.

▶ Whenever you have a problem with your computer, one troubleshooting technique is to log in with a different user account and see if the problem is reproducible. If the problem does not occur with the other user account, you can focus on the things that are user-specific, such as permissions and preferences.

▶ If you change the password of your Mac OS X user account, the system does not change the old password stored in the keychain to the new one. To fix this problem, you'll have to do the following:

1. Log in using the new password.

2. Open Keychain Access (/Applications/Utilities).

3. Choose Edit > Change Password for Keychain "login." (If the operating system had been upgraded from an earlier version of Mac OS X, the keychain will be named using the user's short name instead of "login.")

4. Enter the old password in Current Password.

5. Enter the new password of your user account in the "Password or phrase" and Verify fields.

6. Click OK.

▶ When using fast user switching to switch to another account, you might not be able to access certain resources. For example, if a previous user was using an iSight camera to do video chatting and didn't quit iChat, you will not be able to access the iSight camera because it's being used by another application. In this case, you'll have to disconnect the iSight camera from the computer and then reconnect it.

▶ In other cases, it might not be possible to resolve resource contention without disrupting another user's activity. For example, another user might be using QuickTime Broadcaster to broadcast audio captured by a microphone connected to the computer. In this case, resolving the resource contention will interrupt the other user's activity and may cause unforeseen problems. So, the best way to deal with resource contention when using fast user switching is for users of the system to agree in advance how to resolve contention issues.

▶ If you can't make changes to certain System Preferences such as Network, Sharing, and Energy Saver, or you cannot install applications in the Applications folder, it's because you are a normal user and not an administrator. As a normal user, you are limited to making configuration changes that affect only your account, such as what applications and files are opened when you log in and what picture is displayed as the background pattern. You cannot make changes to system-wide settings.

Setting File and Folder Permissions

In multiuser operating systems like Mac OS X, permissions allow you to determine how other users access the files and folders you create. To support permissions, each file and folder in the file system is associated with an owner and a group. As the owner of a file or folder, a normal user can use the Get Info (Cmd-I) command in the Finder to set separate permissions for the Owner, Group (see following section), and Others. The permissions you assign determine the access permitted to each of these three classes of users.

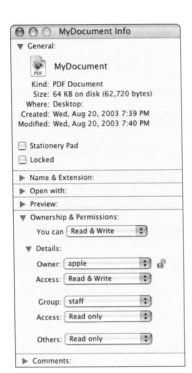
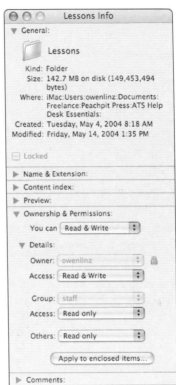

Files have three assignable access levels: Read & Write, Read only, and No Access. If you have Read & Write access to a file, you can open the file and change its contents. If you have Read only access to a file, you can open the file but cannot change its contents. No Access means that you cannot open the file.

Folders, by contrast, have four assignable access levels. The access levels you can set for a folder are Read & Write, Read only, Write only (Drop Box), and No Access. If you have Read & Write access to a folder, you can change the contents of the folder by adding, removing, or renaming files within the folder. If you have Read only access to a folder, you can open the folder and see what it contains, but you cannot add, remove, or rename files in the folder. Write only (Drop Box) access implies that you can add files to the folder but cannot see the folder's contents. No Access means that you will not be able to add files to the folder nor can you see the contents of the folder.

To view and set the permissions on a file or folder, select it in the Finder and choose File > Get Info (Cmd-I). Click the Ownership & Permissions disclosure triangle to reveal the current access levels for the Owner, Group, and Others. To change the permissions, choose the access levels you require using the appropriate pop-up. Owners get the access level that appears in the Owner access pop-up. Non-owners who belong to the indicated group get the access level appearing in the Group access pop-up. Users who are not the owner, and who do not belong to the group, get the access level that appears in the Others pop-up. (As a result, you can assign permissions such that others have a higher access level than the owner!) Once you set permissions for a folder, you can set the same permissions on all of the items within the folder by clicking the "Apply to enclosed items" button.

Although not represented in the Info window, there is also an Execute permission. The Execute permission tells Mac OS X to run a set of instructions within a file. The Execute permission also makes a directory functional. Unless you have Execute permission on a folder, you cannot list the contents of that folder, even if you have Read permission.

> **NOTE ▶** Permissions can be misassigned when creating files using Mac OS 9 or by some programs running under Mac OS X. To fix permissions problems on bootable Mac OS X volumes, open Disk Utility (/Applications/ Utilities), click the First Aid button, and click Repair Disk Permissions. Knowledge Base article #106712, "Troubleshooting Permissions Issues in Mac OS X," describes how to use the repair-permissions functionality included in Mac OS X 10.2 and later.

NOTE ▶ Sometimes you may find that a particular application doesn't seem to respect the file permissions. It may allow you to modify a file, even though the file was marked Read only. Some applications don't modify files directly. Instead, they duplicate the file and modify the copy. When you use the Save command, the application then deletes the original file and renames the duplicate to match the original file.

Groups

Mac OS X relies on the concept of groups to give permissions to sets of users that perform similar functions. Mac OS X does not provide an application to easily create and manage groups. Instead, it uses some preset groups to give users certain permissions and functionality. If you need to create and manage groups, Mac OS X Server may be a more suitable product.

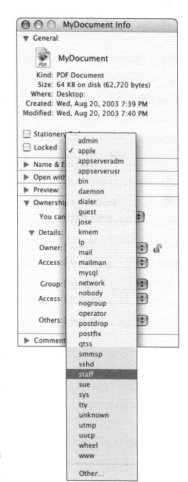

When you create a new normal user account, Mac OS X behind the scenes creates a new "group" with that user as the only member. The group's name is the same as the short user name. When you create a new administrator user account, it also gets a new exclusive group named after it, and all administrators automatically become members of the "admin" group. The root user, or System Administrator, is special. Not only is this account a member of the admin group, it is also the sole member of many different groups used only by the Unix underpinnings of Mac OS X.

Most users need only concern themselves with groups when setting permissions for files and folders as explained in the previous section.

Folder and Document Permissions in Context

Folder and document permissions interact in potentially surprising ways. For example, you may have Read & Write access to a file but still not be able to open the file because the file resides in a folder to which you have no access. The combinations presented here are even less intuitive.

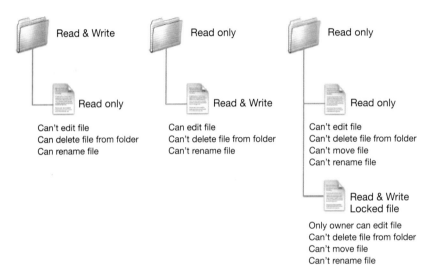

Consider the leftmost example pictured above. If you assign the indicated permissions to a folder and a file within it, can you safely assume that no harm can come to your file? At first glance, the document appears safe, and it is certainly true that the contents of the file cannot be changed. However, the document can be deleted or renamed since the folder permissions are Read & Write. Consequently, a user could delete the file and replace it with a file of the same name but with different contents.

Now, take a look at the second set of permissions. What, if any, modifications can you make to the document? You can change the contents of the file using applications that rewrite document data in place. However, applications that attempt to make backup copies or create a new file when saving documents will not be able to edit the file since the Read-only folder permissions prevent you from adding files to or removing files from the folder. Similarly, you will not be able to rename the file.

In addition to permissions, files have a locked attribute that you can set in the Get Info window. Locked files cannot be edited, deleted, or moved.

Changing the Permissions on Three Folders

In this exercise, you will change the permissions on folders.

1   Log in as Apple Admin.

2   Go to Apple Admin's home folder.

3   Open the Public folder.

4   In the Public folder, create three folders (Cmd-Shift-N) with the following names:

   ▶   RO

   ▶   RW

   ▶   WO

5   Select the RO folder and open the Info window by choosing File > Get Info (Cmd-I).

6   Click the disclosure triangle for Ownership & Permissions and then for Details.

7   Change the Access permissions for Others to Read only.

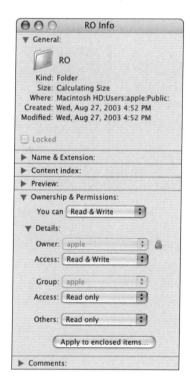

The lock next to the Owner must be unlocked in order for the user to change Owner and Group permissions.

8   Select the RW folder and open the Info window.

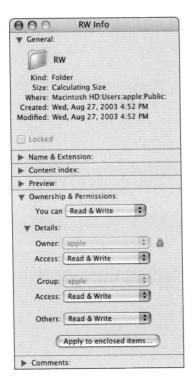

9   Change the Access permissions for Others to Read & Write.

10 Select the WO folder and open the Info window.

11 Change the Access permissions for Others to "Write only (Drop Box)."

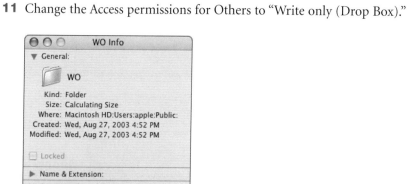

Changing the Permissions on Three Files

You will now create three text files and change their access permissions.

1 Open TextEdit (/Applications).

2 Choose Format > Make Plain Text.

3 Create the following three blank documents and save them in Apple Admin's Documents folder:

▶ NoAccess.txt

▶ ReadOnly.txt

▶ ReadWrite.txt

4 Quit TextEdit.

5 Open the Apple Admin's Documents folder.

6 Select the NoAccess.txt file and change the permissions for Others to No Access in the Info window.

7 Select the ReadOnly.txt file and change the permissions for Others to Read only in the Info window.

8 Select the ReadWrite.txt file and change the permissions for Others to Read & Write in the Info window.

9 Open a new Finder window and navigate to Apple Admin's Public folder.

10 Put the NoAccess.txt file in the RW folder.

11 Put the ReadOnly.txt file in the WO folder.

12 Put the ReadWrite.txt file in the RO folder.

Testing the Folder and File Permissions
This exercise demonstrates the effect of different permissions on files and folders.

1 Switch to Laura Smith's account and log in.

2 Open a Finder window and navigate to the RO folder in Apple Admin's Public folder.

3 Open the ReadWrite.txt file with TextEdit.

4 Add some text to the document and try saving.

Note that you cannot save the ReadWrite.txt file to the RO folder, and a normal user cannot delete the file. Only administrator users can delete this file.

NOTE ▶ This behavior is counterintuitive. The reason it behaves unexpectedly is because TextEdit (and most other applications) create temporary files when you try to modify and save a file. Since the folder is read-only, you can not add a temporary file. Thus, any attempt to save the file fails. However, if you were to use an application that does not create a temporary file, modifying your file would be allowed.

5   Use the Save As command to save the ReadWrite.txt file to the RW folder. (Do not change the name of the file.)

6   Open the RW folder and open the ReadWrite.txt file with TextEdit.

7   Add some more text to the document and try saving.

In this case, you can save the ReadWrite.txt file to the RW folder because both the file and folder allow Read & Write access.

8   In TextEdit, try to open the NoAccess.txt file in the RW folder.

You'll see that you cannot open the NoAccess.txt file with TextEdit because the permissions on the file are set to No Access. You can, however, delete the NoAccess.txt file from the Finder because the permissions on the folder are set to Read & Write, which allows changes to how files are stored in the directory.

9   In the Finder, try to open the WO folder.

When you try to open the WO folder, access to the folder is denied but you can move the ReadWrite.txt file from the RW folder into the WO folder.

10 In TextEdit, try opening the WO folder.

You should not be able to see the files in the WO folder.

11 Quit TextEdit.

12 Log out Laura Smith.

13 Log out Apple Admin.

Accessing Home Folders

Except for the Public and Sites folders, the folders in a user's home folder are private to that user, and no one, including administrator users, can access them without changing their permissions. By default, folders in a home folder have the No Access permission for Group and Others, and Read & Write access for the Owner.

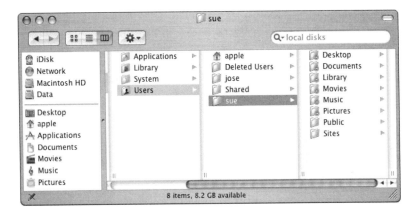

If a user would like to share files with other users, or keep some files in a location where they are accessible by others, he or she can do so by using the Public folder. The Public folder has Read & Write permissions for the Owner, and Read only for the Group and Others. The Drop Box folder within the Public folder has Read & Write for the Owner, and Write only for the Group and Others.

> **NOTE** ▶ When you create a new folder, by default it is Read only for Others, so other people can read its content if they can navigate to it. For this reason, it is best to keep your sensitive files and subfolders in your Documents folder. Otherwise, other users will have access to the files.

Testing Access to Files

The following steps walk you through creating two files and storing them in two separate locations, then testing whether you can access those files:

1   Log in as Laura.

2   In the Finder, navigate to the /Applications folder.

3   Using TextEdit, create a file, name it *Secret*, and save it in Laura's Documents folder.

4   Using TextEdit, create another file, name it *Shared*, and save it in Laura's Public folder.

5   Choose Apple Admin from the user accounts menu and log in.

6   Open a Finder window.

7   Go to the /Users folder.

8   Go to Laura's home folder.

You should not be able to access *Secret* in Laura's Documents folder, but you can access Laura's Public folder and the Shared document you created.

9   Quit TextEdit.

Troubleshooting Permission Issues

Here are some basic troubleshooting techniques for permission issues:

▶   Sometimes erratic system behavior such as inability to mount disk images, add files to the Applications folder as an administrator user, or spool print jobs is caused by incorrect file permissions. The First Aid pane in Disk Utility has a button that will scan and restore the permissions of Mac OS X system files and Apple-installed software to their default configurations on a bootable volume. Additional features of Disk Utility are covered in

Lesson 3. Knowledge Base article #106712, "Troubleshooting permissions issues in Mac OS X," contains additional advanced techniques to use when dealing with files with incorrect permissions.

▶ If you have problems accessing files and folders due to incorrect permissions, you can use your administrator account to fix the permission problems. Log in as an administrator and use the Get Info command to set correct permissions for Owner, Group, and Others in the Info window.

▶ If you need to restore a deleted user, the easiest method is to create a new user account and copy the deleted user .dmg file into the drop box in the new user account. After the user logs in with the new user account, the user can mount the .dmg file and copy the files from the disk image to the user's new home folder. This bypasses having to manually reassign ownership of the files from the old user account to the new one. Also, to retrieve files that belonged to a deleted user, log in as an administrator, which allows you to open the deleted user .dmg file and access the files inside.

What You've Learned

▶ There are three types of users—normal, administrator, and System Administrator—and each of these different users has different permissions.

▶ Creating and managing users is done in Accounts preferences.

▶ Security preferences provides options to increase user account security.

▶ How users are able to log in, including enabling the fast user switching option, is managed in the Login Options pane of Accounts preferences. Other available options include whether or not a list of users is displayed in the login window, and which account, if any, the computer should automatically log into.

▶ Permissions are used to grant different access levels to your files and folders. You can share them as Read only, or you can give users Read & Write permissions, or you can simply deny other users any access to your files and folders.

▶ How to troubleshoot user and permission problems.

References

The following Knowledge Base articles (located at http://kbase.info.apple.com) will provide you with further information regarding users and permissions in Mac OS X.

Files

▶ 106237, "Mac OS X: Unable to Move, Unlock, Modify, or Copy an Item"

Permissions

▶ 106712, "Troubleshooting Permissions Issues in Mac OS X"

▶ 107039, "Mac OS X 10.2: How to Change Ownership & Permissions Using the Finder"

Open Firmware Password

▶ 106482, "Setting Up Open Firmware Password Protection in Mac OS X 10.1 or Later"

Trash

▶ 106272, "You Can't Empty the Trash or Move a File to the Trash in Mac OS X"

User Access

▶ 107180, "Mac OS X 10.2: How to Manage User Access to Applications, System Preferences, and Disc Burning via 'Capabilities'"

Review Quiz

Use the following questions to review what you have learned:

1. What are the three types of user accounts in Mac OS X?

2. What are permissions, and why are they important?

3. What tool do you use to create, edit, or delete users?

4. What are limitations?

5. What tool do you use to repair permissions on a disk?

6. What is the master password?

7. What techniques are useful to consider when troubleshooting user and permissions issues?

Answers

1. Normal, administrator, and System Administrator.

2. Permissions provide security to keep one user from modifying or viewing another user's files. They are important because Mac OS X was designed to be used by more than one person.

3. Accounts preferences is used to create, edit, or delete users.

4. Limitations allow you to configure a user's access to applications, utilities, and the Finder.

5. Disk Utility.

6. If a user is unable to log in after three successive attempts, the user can enter the master password, which allows him or her to reset the account password. The master password must be set before an account can be encrypted with the FileVault feature.

7. Reset password; log in as different user; repair permissions with Disk Utility; restore deleted user account.

3

Time   This lesson takes approximately 1 hour, 30 minutes to complete.

Goals   Store files on the computer so that they are accessible to all
                computer users or only individual users

                Identify resources that only the system can access and those
                that the user can access

                Describe how to use Finder features, such as CD burning,
                matching file types with applications, and Secure Empty Trash

                Use Disk Utility for disk- and file system–related tasks

                Use System Profiler to identify storage devices and their
                properties

                Describe the different software RAID configurations supported
                by Mac OS X and configure two hard drives to use RAID 0 or 1

                Manage existing disk images

                Define a forked file and a file system bundle and access the
                contents of a bundle

Lesson **3**

File Systems

This lesson discusses several features of the file systems on your Mac OS X computer.

The first topic is the layout of the file system. You will learn how to interpret path names, where important directories are located, and how the system finds resources.

The second topic is volume formats. You will learn the features of different formats and how to configure and obtain information about volumes. You will also learn about file forks and their effect upon system behavior.

The main tool for managing disks on Mac OS X is Disk Utility. You will learn how to use Disk Utility to obtain information about a disk, and to repair, erase, partition, and restore a disk.

Mac OS X provides several features for transferring files and for creating archives and backups. These include disk images, the Finder's archive feature, and CD- and DVD-burning capability.

This lesson also introduces a few basic command-line utilities.

File Locations in Mac OS X

The World Wide Web was created on a NeXT Computer running a Unix-based operating system, so it's not surprising that Web addresses look a lot like Unix path names for files. A URL (Uniform Resource Locator), such as www.apple. com/macosx, is fundamentally a path to a file or other resource on a remote computer.

The convention of describing the location of a Web page on the Internet by a path is the same basic mechanism that Mac OS X uses to describe the location of a file or folder in the file system. For example, the location of the folder where users should install system-wide fonts is /Library/Fonts.

The first slash (/) represents the root of the file system or your boot volume. All other mounted volumes (such as Zip drives, FireWire disks, or network volumes) are mounted in a hidden folder called /Volumes. The boot volume contains many folders, and each folder contains many folders and files. You can think of a file system as a tree, with the hard disk at the bottom (root) of the tree, and folders containing subfolders and files as branches of that tree.

Understanding Absolute and Relative Paths

To describe the location of a particular item, you can use either an absolute path or a relative path. An absolute path begins with a forward slash (/) and indicates the path to the file starting at the root of the file system. A relative path indicates the path relative to where you are now. For instance, if you are logged in as usertwo and want to refer to the projects folder inside the Documents folder for userone, you would need to include the file path starting at root:

/Users/userone/Documents/project

If, however, you were already in the home folder for userone, you could refer to the same folder with just Documents/project.

You can also use some shortcuts to refer to relative paths. For instance, home directories can also be referred to by the tilde (~) character. It can be used to specify paths starting at your home directory. So typing

~mary

refers to Mary's home folder. If you want to refer to the Library folder in your home folder, type the shortcut

~/Library

If you want to refer to the current working folder, you can use a single period (dot):

./project

To refer to the parent folder of the working folder, you can use two periods (dot-dot), as in

../project

Path names can be up to 1024 bytes long, starting from root.

Viewing Hidden Folders

Some folders do not ordinarily appear in the Finder. These folders are used by the system and are not useful to ordinary users. To see these folders in the Finder, you must choose Go > Go to Folder, enter the path, then click Go.

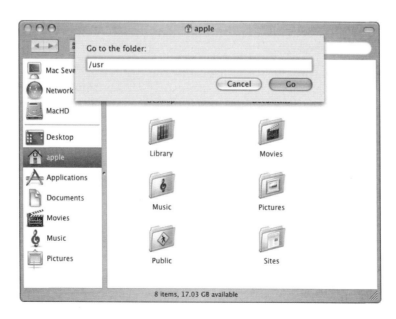

Hidden top-level directories include private, cores, etc, tmp, var, Volumes, bin, dev, sbin, and usr. Permissions for these hidden directories are set to allow only the root user to write to them. An administrator can read the files but cannot make changes.

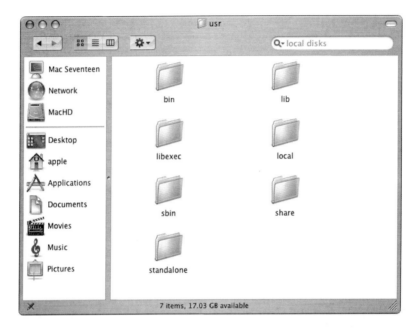

In addition, any folder or file with a name beginning with a period (.) will not appear in a Finder listing. You can go to a folder with a name beginning with a period if you navigate to it with Go to Folder. One folder that does not appear in the Finder is your Trash folder. The Trash icon is located in the Dock.

Understanding Special Folders

As you can see in the preceding discussion of hidden folders, Mac OS X automatically creates a number of different folders on each volume that it uses to organize the thousands of files necessary for a modern operating system. In addition to the hidden folders, a handful of special folders are visible to all users. Understanding where these folders are located and what they are used for can prove invaluable in troubleshooting Mac OS X systems.

Top-Level and Home Folders

Mac OS X permissions distinguish between system files and files that can be configured and modified by users and administrators. This gives greater protection to important system files.

The main top-level folders in Mac OS X are Applications, Library, System, and Users. If you have installed the developer tools, you will also have a top-level folder called Developer. If you have installed Classic on the same volume, you will also have the top-level folders Applications (Mac OS 9), Desktop (Mac OS 9), and System Folder.

When you create a user account (see Lesson 2), Mac OS X creates a home directory for you within Users. This location is where you store personal documents. Other users do not have write permissions for your home folder. The following subfolders appear under each user's home directory:

▶ Desktop—Any items on the Mac OS X desktop

▶ Desktop (Mac OS 9)—Classic subfolder containing any items on the Mac OS 9 desktop, if Classic is installed

▶ Documents—Default folder for the user's documents

▶ Library—User-specific application support, fonts, preference files, and so on

▶ Movies—Folder for movie files

▶ Music—Folder for music files such as MP3s

▶ Pictures—Picture files to be used by applications such as iPhoto

- ▶ Public—Shared folder for Mac OS X Personal File Sharing
- ▶ Sites—Folder for Mac OS X Personal Web Sharing

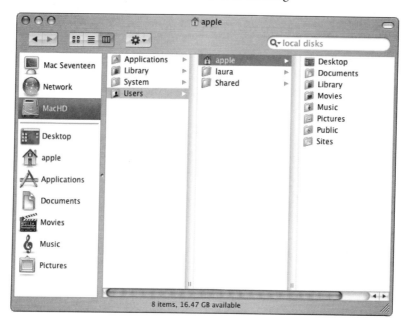

With the exception of the ~/Library folder, you needn't keep any of the other home folders if you don't want them. Also, there is nothing that prevents you from placing MP3 music files in the ~/Documents folder, or storing MPEG movies in the ~/Pictures folder. Keep in mind that some applications expect to find documents in specific places, so deleting these folders or placing your documents in other folders may cause problems.

Trash

As mentioned already in the "Viewing Hidden Folders" section, the Trash is actually a folder on the root volume. Items placed in the Trash remain accessible so that you can retrieve an unintentionally discarded document if you realize your mistake in time.

The Finder now provides a feature called Secure Empty Trash. Ordinarily, after you empty the Trash some data from deleted files remains on the disk until new files overwrite it. Someone could restore those deleted files by using special data-recovery software, such as UnErase (part of Norton Utilities from Symantec.)

The Secure Empty Trash feature overwrites deleted files with meaningless data so that data-recovery software cannot restore them. To delete files securely, choose Finder > Secure Empty Trash. Deletion may take some time, depending on the contents of the Trash directory.

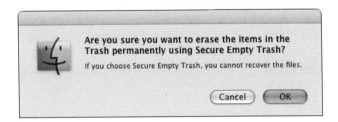

Shared Folder

Mac OS X provides a common folder for all users with accounts on the computer (called local users) at /Users/Shared. You can save files to the Shared folder from applications, or you can copy files into the folder. You cannot delete or rename a file in the Shared folder unless you are the owner of the file.

System and Library Folders

On Mac OS X, all important operating system files reside in a folder called /System. To better secure the integrity of the core system against malicious or accidental removal of files, /System is not accessible to even administrative users. Only the root user has permission to access these files.

System-wide resources that are not installed by the operating system are added to the /Library folder. This folder is accessible to administrative users. Administrators should add resources to /Libraries, not to /System.

The /Network directory is typically mounted from a server. It contains resources that are provided over the network.

Since Mac OS X is a multiuser system, each user has separate resources, such as personal fonts. These resources are stored in each user's home folder—specifically in the ~/Library folder. For example, the Mail application stores all of a user's mail in the ~/Library/Mail folder. This ensures that user-specific information is stored in each user's home folder, protecting that information from other users, and making it easy to back up and restore all of the documents and preferences for each user.

Search Paths

Mac OS X puts resources such as fonts, frameworks, and preference data in various places. Therefore, the system needs to search through multiple locations to find resources. The order of this search is known as the search path. The concept of search paths recurs in several contexts in Mac OS X administration.

The order in which Mac OS X searches for resources is

1. User (~/Library)
2. Local (/Library)
3. Network (/Network/Library)
4. System (/System/Library)

A good example of how search paths work involves fonts, which can reside in several possible locations. If you have multiple fonts of the same name installed, Mac OS X will load the first one it finds in the search path. This order also applies to preferences and other resources in the Library folders. For more information about fonts, refer to Knowledge Base article #106417, "Mac OS X: Font Locations and Their Purposes."

Fonts

All users can install fonts in the Fonts folder in the Library folder of their home folder (~/Library/Fonts). The fonts in a user's Fonts folder are not available to other users on the system. As administrator, you might want to make

certain fonts available only to a specific user by installing them in that user's
Fonts folder.

Fonts in /Library/Fonts, /Network/Fonts, and /System/Library/Fonts are available to all users on the computer. Only an administrative user can install fonts
in /Library/Fonts or /Network/Fonts.

Mac OS X installs its own special fonts in /System/Library/Fonts. Do not
attempt to remove the fonts in /System/Library/Fonts.

Classic applications use the fonts in /System Folder/Fonts. Fonts in this folder
are also available to Mac OS X applications and are used when booting into
Mac OS 9.

The Font Book application allows you to install fonts in ~/Library/Fonts,
/Library/Fonts, or /System Folder/Fonts. You do this by selecting "for me only,"
"for all users of this computer," or "for Classic Mac OS," respectively. If you are

logged in as a normal user and you select "for all users of this computer," Font Book prompts you for an administrator password.

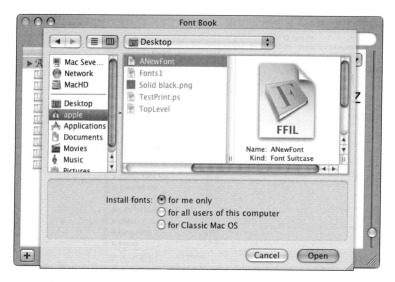

If you install fonts manually (by dragging and dropping font files in the Finder) while an application that uses fonts is open, you must quit and restart the application before the application can use the newly installed fonts. When you use Font Book to add a font, you don't need to do this.

The following font types are supported:

▶   TrueType

▶   PostScript Type 1

▶   OpenType

▶   Bitmap

Removing a Font
You can use the Font Book utility to move a font to the Trash.

1   Log in as Apple Admin, if necessary.

2   Quit all applications to ensure that no fonts are in use.

3   Open Applications > Font Book.

4   In the Collection column, click All Fonts.

5   In the Font column, click Arial.

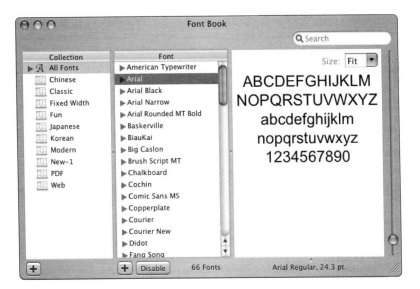

6   Choose File > Remove Font.

7   In the dialog that appears, click Remove.

8   The Arial font is now in the Trash. You will retrieve it from the Trash in
       the next exercise.

Adding a Font to Be Used by One User Only

You can use Font Book to install a font in your own Fonts directory.

1   Verify that you are still logged in as Apple Admin. Then, open the Trash.

2   Locate the Arial font that Font Book moved into the Trash and drag it to
       your desktop.

3 Choose File > Add Fonts.

4 In the dialog that appears, navigate to your desktop.

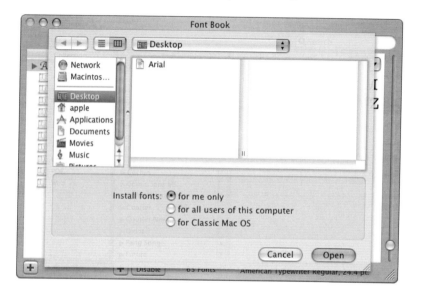

5 Select Arial.

6 Select the "for me only" radio button.

7 Click Open.

Arial appears in the Font column.

8 Quit Font Book (Cmd-Q).

9 Open a new Finder window and change to column view.

10 Navigate to /Users/apple/Library/Fonts and confirm that Arial is installed there.

11 Navigate to /Library/Fonts and confirm that Arial is not installed there.

12 Open TextEdit and, if necessary, choose Format > Make Rich Text.

13 Type several lines of text in a blank document.

14 Highlight a few lines of text.

15 Choose Format > Font > Show Fonts.

16 When TextEdit's Font pane appears, click Arial.

17 Confirm that the lines you highlighted now appear in the Arial font and that the rest of the document is in the default font, Helvetica.

18 Save the document as *Testdoc* on your desktop.

19 Close TextEdit.

20 Using Finder, drag Testdoc into the folder /Users/Shared.

Confirming That the Font Is Unavailable to Other Users

If you log in as a different user, you don't have access to the fonts in user Apple Admin's Fonts directory.

1   Log in as Laura Smith.

2   In Finder, navigate to /Users/Shared and open Testdoc.

3   Choose Format > Font > Show Fonts.

4   Confirm that the Arial font is not in TextEdit's Font pane, and that the lines that were previously in Arial are now in the default font, Helvetica.

5   Open Font Book and add Arial, installing it "for all users of this computer." This restores the font to its original location.

Mac OS X Volume Formats

The preceding sections in this lesson discuss how Mac OS X organizes files and folders as far as the user is concerned. The following sections discuss how those files are managed on volumes at a more technical level. Users that casually interact with documents through the Finder and Open and Save dialog boxes need not concern themselves with this information, but it can prove useful if you are trying to troubleshoot problems.

When you install Mac OS X, you can choose to optionally erase and format a hard disk or volume using the Mac OS Extended (HFS Plus) or UFS (Unix File System) format. Furthermore, Disk Utility allows you to format volumes in several other formats. Apple recommends that you always use the Mac OS Extended format unless you have a specific reason to use another format. Some of the characteristics of the volume formats supported by Mac OS X are as follows:

▶   Mac OS Extended (HFS Plus)—This is the format most familiar to Apple customers; it is used by both Mac OS X and Mac OS 9. The Mac OS Extended file system is case-preserving, but case-insensitive, which means if you name a file File1, the Mac OS Extended file system will retain the upper-case letter F whenever you view the file. You cannot, however, put files called file1 and File1 in the same directory because Mac OS X doesn't distinguish between the two names.

Mac OS X Server 10.2.2 introduced a new Mac OS Extended file-system feature known as journaling. Journaling is the default in Mac OS X 10.3. It helps protect the file system against power outages or unforeseen failures in server components, reducing the need for repairs. For more information, refer to Knowledge Base article #107249, "Mac OS X 10.2: About File System Journaling."

▶ Mac OS Standard (HFS, or hierarchical file system)—This is an older file system that Mac OS X can access, but you can't install Mac OS X on an HFS volume. Furthermore, HFS is somewhat inefficient in its use of available storage space; HFS Plus allows more information to be stored on the same volume and is therefore preferred.

▶ Unix File System (UFS)—This format is compatible with other Unix-like operating systems. It is case-sensitive, so you can create files called file1 and File1 in the same directory. UFS volumes are not visible to the Classic environment or Mac OS 9, nor is AirPort functional if Mac OS X is installed on a UFS volume. However, UFS may be preferable when developing Unix-based applications within Mac OS X.

▶ MS-DOS file system—This is the format used by Microsoft Windows. This will make files on the Windows formatted drive usable by both a Windows operating system as well as Mac OS X.

For more information about volume formats, refer to Knowledge Base article #25316, "Mac OS X 10.2 or Earlier: Choosing UFS or Mac OS Extended (HFS Plus) Formatting."

Viewing Volume Information with System Profiler

System Profiler provides information about your computer. The information is grouped into topics, which are listed in the Contents column on the left. The Hardware topic in System Profiler further groups devices by the bus or interface they are connected to. Some devices are used for data storage and might contain one or more file system volumes. If you select a storage device that contains file system volumes, System Profiler shows information about the volumes.

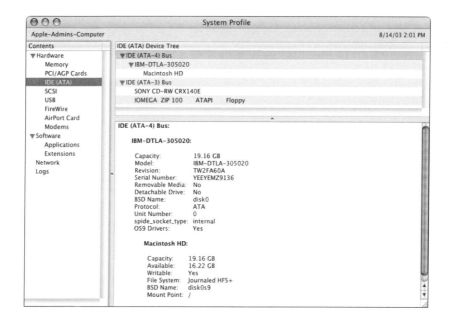

File Forks

On a Mac OS Standard or Extended file system volume, each file has two parts known as forks—a data fork and a resource fork. The data fork is similar to the traditional idea of a file on many operating systems—it contains a chunk of data, such as the actual executable code in an application. The resource fork is a way to put structured information into a file such as alert sounds, button icons, and dialogs for applications. Resource forks allowed earlier versions of the Macintosh operating system to provide a more intuitive, pleasing user experience. As far as the user is concerned, there is only one file to manipulate in the Finder, but programmers can edit the resources using a utility such as ResEdit.

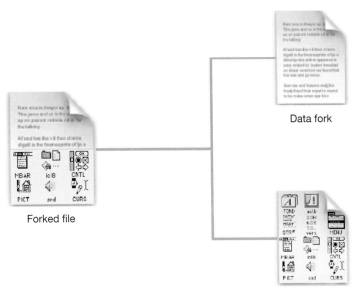

Data fork

Forked file

Resource fork

Resource forks were incredibly useful when Macintosh computers were used primarily in homogenous local networks, but in today's highly networked and Internet-connected world they have one big drawback. When you move files to non–Mac OS systems, other systems do not know how to deal with the resource fork, typically discarding it and stripping the file of important information. As such, Mac OS files that are moved between platforms can lose important information. Traditionally, to preserve both forks, Mac OS files needed to be put into an intermediary format such as BinHex before being transferred. To maintain backwards compatibility, Mac OS X still supports resource forks, and has added another more portable mechanism.

Unix file system volumes do not use a catalog to keep track of what applications were used to create different files on the volume. The file manager service in Mac OS X creates a shadow file for every file on the disk. This shadow, called an AppleDouble file, contains everything that would be in the resource fork on the Mac OS X Extended volume: the resource fork data and all of the file attributes of the file it shadows.

Mac OS X Bundles

Mac OS X has a mechanism to aid compatibility with the rest of the networked world but at the same time provide a way to store resources and structured information in what appears to users to be a single file. The solution is called a bundle.

Just as the Mac OS 9 Finder presented a forked file as a single item in the user interface, the Mac OS X Finder presents and treats a bundle as a single file, although in reality it is a specially marked folder that can contain files and other folders. An application package in Mac OS X is one example of a bundle.

The average user typically does not need to know about bundles, just as the typical Mac user may never have been aware of resource forks. However, a traditional Mac OS power user or administrator might use ResEdit in Mac OS 9 to edit the resource fork of a file.

Similarly, in Mac OS X, it is possible to view the contents of a bundle. You can see the contents of an application bundle by holding down the Control key while you click an application icon and selecting "Show Package Contents."

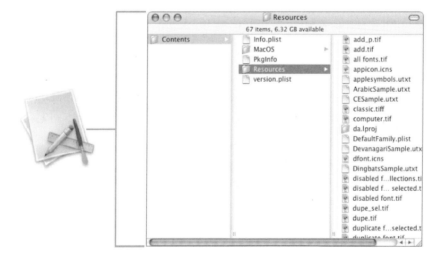

File Extensions and the Internet

On a Mac OS Standard or Extended file system volume, a catalog keeps track of what applications were used to create the different files on the volume. This information identifies which application to open when a user double-clicks a file. The applications keep track of the types of files they can read.

On the Internet, many files you download or receive are not from another Mac OS computer, so they do not have creator or type information. Instead, they use extensions. These multicharacter suffixes are preceded by a period in the filename. By default, the Finder in Mac OS X hides the file extensions of many common file types such as .rtf or .txt. In the Finder preferences, you can choose to hide all extensions, or you can use the Get Info (Cmd-I) command to hide the extension of an individual file. The Finder looks at file extensions as well as creator and type to determine how to open a file. If you double-click a file, the Finder first looks for a creator entry and, if it finds one, uses it to determine which application to use to open the file. If there is no creator, it looks at the extension and finds an application that can use files with that extension. If there is no creator or extension, it looks at the file type and finds an application that can use that file type. If there is no creator, extension, or file type, a dialog appears listing installed applications and asking you to choose an application to open the file.

Matching Files to Applications

As you learned in Lesson 2, you can get and set information about files, folders and disks using the Get Info command (Cmd-I). You can also set some additional options for documents, which control how they get used by applications.

Documents are associated with particular applications, so you can simply double-click a document to start the application for it. Most documents are identified by type or extension. A file extension consists of a dot (.) followed by several letters that identify the type of file.

Since extensions can be a bit cryptic for some users, you can have the Finder hide the extension of a file.

1   Select a document.

2   Choose File > Get Info (Cmd-I).

3   In the Info window, expand the Name & Extension section.

4   Select the "Hide extension" checkbox.

    When you choose to hide extensions, the Finder will display only the base name of the file. Even if the extension is hidden, you can still change it in the Info window.

You can change the application a file is associated with by using the Info window.

1   Select the document.

2   Choose File > Get Info (Cmd-I).

3   In the Info window, expand the "Open with" section.

4   From the "Open with" pop-up menu, choose an application.

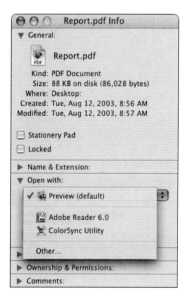

The next time the file is opened in the Finder, it will be opened with the newly chosen application.

5   If you want all files of the same type to be opened with the chosen application, click Change All.

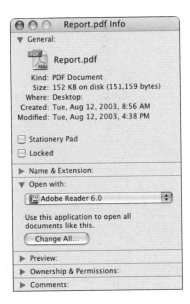

Working with Disk Utility

Disk Utility is a very useful tool for working with volumes. Beginning with Mac OS X 10.3, Disk Utility includes the functionality provided by Disk Copy in previous versions of Mac OS X. Disk Utility's user interface has changed to accommodate the feature set of both programs. This section discusses the various features of Disk Utility.

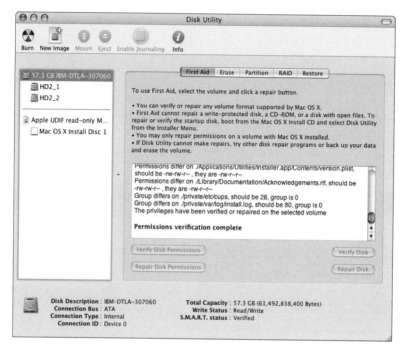

A copy of Disk Utility is included on the Mac OS X Install Disc 1. You can run it when starting up from the disc, which gives you a way to check and repair hard disks before you install Mac OS X. You can also use it on disks that already have Mac OS X installed on them, or you can use it to format disks. You have the following formats to choose from if you are booting your system from disc: Mac OS Extended (journaled or non-journaled), MS-DOS, and Unix File System; you can also leave it as free space.

Information

The Information pane in Disk Utility provides details about storage devices (such as internal drives and FireWire hard drives) connected to a system and the partitions they contain. To open the Information pane, click the Info button in the Disk Utility window. The left column of the window contains a list of all the connected drives.

After you select a drive from the list, you can click Info to display information about the drive such as its capacity and bus type.

Beneath each drive is an indented list of partitions on that drive. Starting with Mac OS X 10.3, CDs recorded with multiple sessions are now displayed correctly as separate partitions in the left column of the Disk Utility window. Unmounted partitions are dimmed, and information about them cannot be gathered. When you select a partition, Disk Utility displays details about the partition, including its capacity, free space, number of files, and volume format.

Although System Profiler provides information about storage devices, it provides only a subset of the information provided by Disk Utility. In addition, System Profiler does not provide any information about unmounted partitions. Disk Utility lists unmounted partitions and allows you to mount them.

Getting Information About a Storage Device

The Info window in Disk Utility allows you to see details about disk drives and their partitions.

1   Open Disk Utility.

2   Select the main hard drive icon in the list of devices on the left of the Disk Utility window.

3 Click the Info button.

The Info window lists details about the drive, including its capacity and the type of bus it uses.

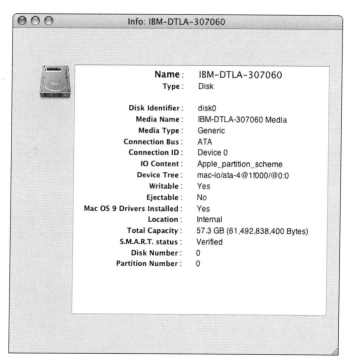

4 Close the Info window and go back to the main Disk Utility window.

Indented beneath the hard drive entry in the list of devices on the left are all of the partitions contained on the drive.

5 Select a partition and click the Info button.

The Info window changes to list details that are specific to the partition.

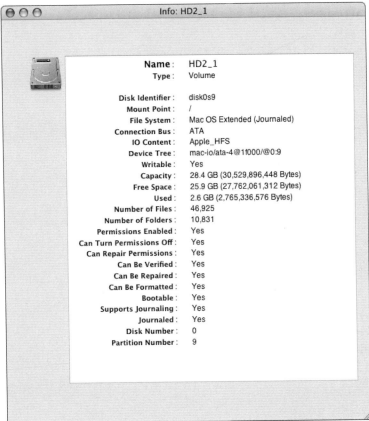

The volume format for this partition is Mac OS Extended (Journaled.) The capacity of the partition is 28.4 GB, and 25.9 GB of disk space are available.

First Aid

The First Aid pane of Disk Utility verifies and repairs the directory structure of your hard disk. You cannot use Disk Utility to repair the startup disk, so you must start the computer from the Mac OS X Install Disc 1 and run Disk Utility from there. Disk Utility can repair UFS, Mac OS Standard (HFS), Mac OS Extended (HFS Plus), and MS-DOS (FAT) formats.

Unusual behavior such as inability to mount disk images, add files to the Applications folder as an administrator user, or spool print jobs could be caused by incorrect file permissions. Clicking the Repair Disk Permissions button in Disk Utility restores the privileges of Mac OS X system files and Apple-installed software to their default configurations. Disk Utility checks and repairs the permissions on bootable volumes only.

Using Disk Utility from the Mac OS X Install Disc 1

With Disk Utility, you can format and configure storage devices connected to a Mac OS X computer. However, if you need to configure your main boot volume, you need to either boot from a secondary disk drive or boot from the Mac OS X Install Disc 1.

1   Insert the Mac OS X Install Disc 1.

2   Restart the system and hold down the C key to boot the system from the optical drive.

3   After the system begins booting, release the C key.

4   After the Installer starts, choose Installer > Open Disk Utility.

Using First Aid to Repair Disk Errors

With Disk Utility, you can scan and fix the most common disk drive errors.

1   Click the First Aid button in the Disk Utility window.

2   Select the partition on your main hard drive from the list of devices on the left.

3   Click Verify Disk.

Disk Utility scans your disk and reports any errors that it finds.

NOTE ▶ You can also use the First Aid pane to verify and repair disk permissions on bootable volumes.

4   If you find any errors, click the Repair Disk button.

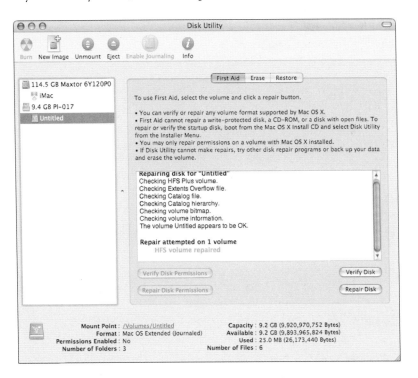

NOTE ▶ If you want to save time, don't click Verify Disk; simply click Repair Disk instead. If there's nothing to repair, Disk Utility essentially acts as if you had clicked Verify Disk.

5   Quit Disk Utility.

6   Quit Installer.

7   Click Quit to restart.

8   Remove the Mac OS X Install Disc 1 after your system restarts.

Erase

In the Erase pane of Disk Utility, you can erase the contents of a partition or drive (except the startup disk), and change its format. You can also use this utility to erase CD-RW and DVD-RW volumes.

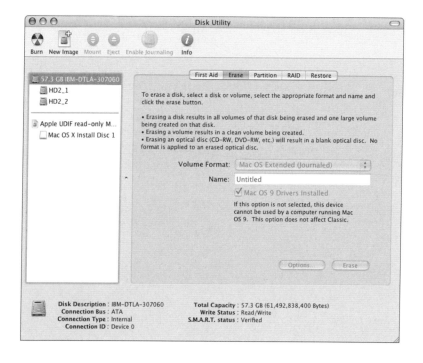

Partition

You can use the Partition pane of Disk Utility to partition hard drives. Again, you cannot make modifications to the startup disk.

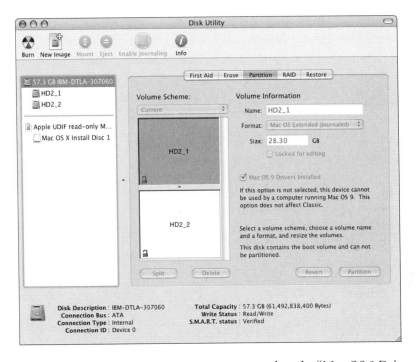

If you plan to boot Mac OS 9 on your computer, select the "Mac OS 9 Drivers Installed" checkbox when you partition your hard disk. This option causes Disk Utility to create a small partition and install Mac OS 9 drivers there. If this partition does not exist, you will not be able to boot the computer in Mac OS 9.

NOTE ▶ The Mac OS 9 Drivers Installed option is hardware dependent and is not displayed on systems that do not support Mac OS 9, such as the Power Mac G5.

RAID

Disk Utility provides a tool to configure a software RAID in Mac OS X. Redundant Array of Independent Disks (RAID) is used to configure multiple hard disks so that they appear as one volume in the operating system (sort of the opposite of partitioning, which makes one hard disk look like multiple volumes). You can configure the RAID scheme to use striping (RAID 0), which stores data across the disks, or mirroring (RAID 1), which stores the same data on all disks. With striping selected, a single volume will display the drive capacity as the total amount of all drives being used in the array.

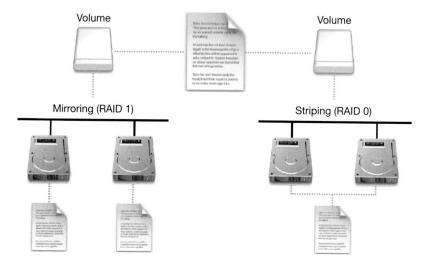

Although RAID 0 provides a speed advantage, there is no redundancy of the data and no easy way to recover complete files from the remaining good drive if one of the striped drives is lost.

Restore

Disk Utility uses Apple Software Restore (ASR) to restore a hard drive, using a customized disk image that you create. This allows you to very quickly restore your computer's original contents, including the Mac OS 9 system software, factory settings, and applications that came with your computer.

To use the restore feature, click the Restore button in the Disk Utility window and follow the onscreen instructions. Take extreme care that during the development of your image content or configuration setup you do not accidentally erase and overwrite data.

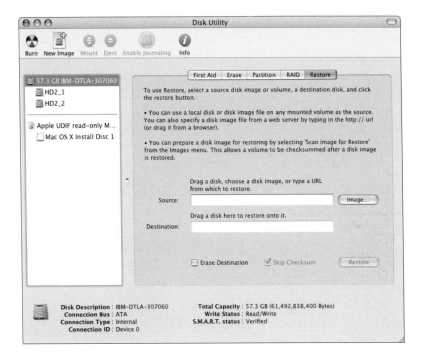

Managing Files and Folders

Users spend the bulk of their time managing files and folders in the Finder. Mac OS X builds upon the traditional features of the Finder with new capabilities such as creating archives and burning discs. Furthermore, programs such as Disk Utility and .Mac's Backup give users innovative new ways of storing and safekeeping files.

Using Disk Images

In addition to everything else we've discussed, Disk Utility can also be used to create disk images. A disk image is a file you can mount on your desktop as if it were a disk. It is a useful way to transfer files over the Internet or onto media such as CD-ROM or DVD-ROM discs because disk images are bit-for-bit copies of any number of original files (including their directory structure) copied into a single file. The integrity of the copied files and their original structure is maintained when the disk image is mounted on a system. There are two common types of disk image files produced by Apple software: Disk Utility and self-mounting.

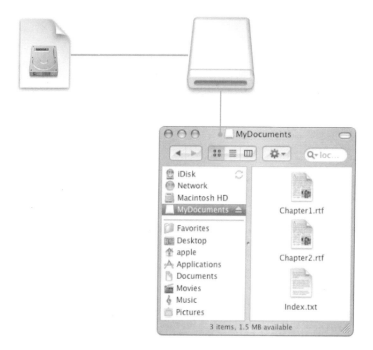

▶ Disk Utility images normally carry the extension .img or .dmg. A Disk Utility image icon looks like a picture of a hard disk printed on a piece of white paper with one corner folded down.

► Disk Utility can mount disk images, which means it can make them appear on the desktop or in the Finder as disks. When you download a file of this type, the Finder may open the disk image automatically, and the image may appear on the desktop as a plain white volume icon. If the disk image does not open automatically, double-click the disk image file. The disk icon will then appear on your desktop and in the Finder. It may appear as a plain white volume or with a custom icon. The disk image remains available until you drag the volume icon to the Trash or restart the computer.

► Mac OS X 10.2.3 introduced Internet-enabled disk images, which are identical to regular disk images except that when the disk image is opened, the contents of the disk image are copied to the hard drive and then the disk image is moved to the Trash. You can read more about Internet-enabled disk images at http://developer.apple.com/ue/files/iedi.html.

► Self-mounting images normally carry the extension .smi. This type of file can appear on the desktop without the use of Disk Utility. However, .smi files, originally created for Mac OS 9.*x* require that Disk Utility be present in the Mac OS X Utilities folder. The icon for a self-mounting image file looks like a blue floppy disk on top of a white diamond.

Creating a disk image file is a good way to archive or transfer a set of files and a directory structure in a single flat file. You can compress a file to reduce its size, and you can compress a whole directory and its contents into a single file. Compression is useful for speeding up file transfers and for archiving files when disk space is tight. You can also create disk images of bootable CDs and hard disks and encrypt your images for additional security.

The panes in Disk Utility allow you to select the destination folder, format, and encryption type, if any. You can create an image from the current drive selected in Disk Utility, a folder, or simply a blank image that you add to later. Image formats include read/write, read only, compressed, and DVD/CD master. Encryption types include none or AES-128 (128-bit Advanced Encryption Standard). When you click Save, Disk Utility creates a file on your computer with the extension .dmg.

NOTE ▶ If you create a blank image and want to resize it later you can only do so by using hdiutil, the command-line equivalent of the old Disk Copy .

Creating a Disk Image File with Disk Utility

In this exercise, you will use Disk Utility to create a disk image file on your computer.

1   Open Disk Utility (/Applications/Utilities).

2   Choose Images > New > Image from Folder.

An Open dialog appears.

3   Navigate to the /Library/Fonts folder.

4   Click Open.

The Convert Image dialog appears.

5   Specify Fonts in the Save As field.

6   Choose Where > Desktop (Cmd-D).

7   Choose Image Format > compressed.

8   Choose Encryption > none.

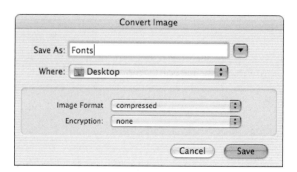

9 Click Save.

10 When prompted, enter your user name and password.

A Disk Utility progress dialog appears.

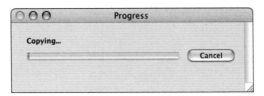

When Disk Utility has completed creating the image, the file Fonts.dmg appears on the desktop.

Mounting and Using a Disk Image File

The disk image file format is useful for software distribution. The image can be mounted and used like a drive.

1 Double-click the Fonts.dmg file on your desktop to mount it.

You will see a Fonts disk drive icon on your desktop.

2 Double-click the Fonts volume.

You will see all of the contents from the Fonts folder.

3 Drag and drop some files from the Fonts volume to the desktop.

4 Eject the Fonts volume.

5 Delete the Fonts.dmg disk image file and any other files you copied from the Fonts volume.

Creating Archives from Finder

Archiving files and folders creates a compressed file containing a copy of the items. Archived files take up less disk space than uncompressed files, so archiving is useful for making backup copies of your data and sending information over the Internet.

To archive files or folders, select an item or items in the Finder and choose File > Create Archive.

If you archive a single item, the archived file has the name of the original item with a .zip extension. If you archive multiple items at once, the archived file is called Archive.zip. Zip is a compression format commonly used on Windows systems and is similar to, but not compatible with, the StuffIt compression format more commonly used on the Mac.

When you double-click an archived file, the archive is replaced by uncompressed copies of the original items.

Expanding Compressed Files

In addition to the .sit or StuffIt compression format, Mac OS X also supports .tar, a Unix file archive format used by the tar command-line utility, and gzip, which is often used to compress tar archives.

To expand a .sit, .tar, or .gzip compressed file, all you have to do is double-click it. StuffIt Expander will open automatically and expand the compressed file. If you need even more compression options, consider purchasing StuffIt Deluxe (www.aladdinsys.com).

As you learned earlier in this lesson, some volume formats are case-sensitive and some are not. If an archive was created on a case-sensitive volume, it may contain files with the same name except for case. If you expand this archive in the Finder on a case-insensitive Mac OS Extended file system, the Finder will append a number to the name of the second file so that the names are different. If, however, you expand this archive from the command line using the tar utility, the second file will overwrite the first. If users report that files are missing when they extract a tar archive from the command line on a Mac OS Extended file system, recommend that they try expanding the archive in the Finder.

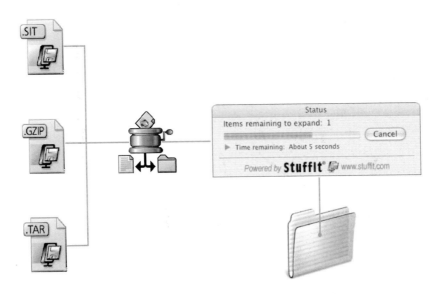

Using CDs or DVDs to Transfer Files

CDs and DVDs are convenient media for transporting and distributing files. Transferring files to CD or DVD is referred to as burning. In Mac OS X, the Finder and Disk Utility are commonly used for burning. To burn CDs, you must have a computer with a CD-R, CD-RW, Combo, or SuperDrive. To burn DVDs, you must have a SuperDrive. Discs labeled CD-R or DVD-R can be written only once. Discs labeled CD-RW or DVD-RW can be written and erased several times. You also need enough free space on your hard disk equal to the media you are burning.

> **NOTE** ▶ See Knowledge Base article #58804, "Mac OS 9: How to Burn a CD and Choose a Format," for more info on CD-ROMs.

Ignoring Volume Ownership

The permission to access removable media such as optical discs is determined by the ownership, just like any other Mac OS X volume. You can use the "Ignore ownership on this volume" checkbox in the Info window to gain access to a removable volume that is otherwise inaccessible due to ownership.

NOTE ▶ This feature was designed for convenience when using removable media. However, you can also use it to ignore ownership on disk partitions other than the boot volume, which means that file ownership alone is not sufficient to protect files on a nonroot partition. Users with more stringent security needs should use other techniques, such as encryption, to protect files.

1   In the Finder, select the volume and choose File > Get Info.

2   Click the disclosure triangle next to Ownership & Permissions.

3   Select the "Ignore ownership on this volume" checkbox.

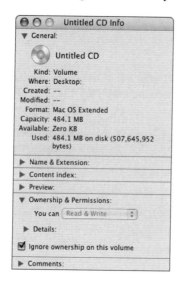

Using the Finder to Burn Discs

In CDs & DVDs preferences, you can specify that when you insert a blank piece
of optical media into a drive capable of burning, Mac OS X prompts you to
choose what to do. If you choose Open Finder, whenever you insert a blank disc
it is mounted in the Finder, then you can drag and drop files and directories
into it. Behind the scenes, Mac OS X creates a temporary file to store the
contents intended for the disc. The file grows on your hard disk equal to the
actual size of the items you are adding to the disc to be burned. Once you have
arranged the files and directories the way you want them, select the disc and
choose File > Burn Disc. A dialog appears. If you aren't ready to burn, click
Cancel and continue arranging the contents of the disc or click Eject to leave
the disc untouched. Otherwise, specify the burn speed and click Burn. Until
you do so, the disc remains blank. Once you click Burn, a dialog shows the
progress of the burn operation, and when it is complete, the newly burned disc
appears on the Finder desktop.

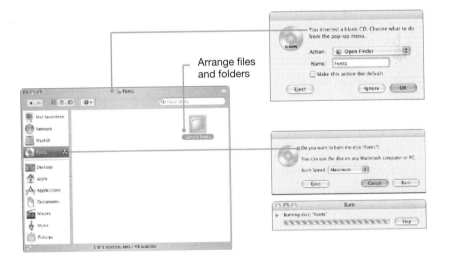

Arrange files
and folders

Using Disk Utility to Burn a Disk Image on a Disc

You can use Disk Utility to burn a disk image on a blank disc (CD-R, CD-RW, or DVD-R). When you click the Burn icon, you are prompted for the files to burn. You are then asked to insert a disc. When you burn a disk image using Disk Utility, the contents of the image are burned on the disc. If you burn multiple images on a CD, each will be its own session, appearing separately in the Finder when mounted. If you use the Finder to burn a disk image onto a CD, when you insert the CD, you see a disk image you can mount by double-clicking. If you use Disk Utility to burn a CD, when you insert the CD, you see the contents of the image instead of the disk image itself.

Backing Up

In general, users are strongly encouraged to back up their important personal data. Many common problems, such as viruses, theft, lost notebooks, file corruption, and user errors, can cause data loss. Even at sites where system administrators perform backups, users might need to do backups of their own. Typically, site backups exclude some personal data, such as mail folders. Also, computers might not be online at the time a site backup is performed.

Users who have a .Mac account can use the .Mac Backup feature. To back up to iDisk with .Mac Backup, users must be connected to the Internet and must have configured their account information in Internet preferences. A disadvantage to .Mac Backup is that its capacity is limited to 100 MB. An advantage to .Mac Backup is that you can easily schedule it to occur automatically. Scheduled backups require that the computer be connected to the Internet and turned on with the user logged in and Energy Saver preferences turned off.

As of Mac OS X 10.3, .Mac users can have a local copy of their iDisk available, even when they are offline. When the user has a network connection, the local iDisk automatically synchronizes with the remote iDisk. This feature ensures that the user's latest changes are accessible from any computer. However, this feature is not designed to be a backup solution.

Users can back up data onto CDs or DVDs using .Mac Backup, as well as the burn features of the Finder and Disk Utility described earlier in this lesson. The Finder's Archive feature is useful for compressing files and directories before backing them up. Command-line users can use the Mac OS X utility hdiutil. Users can also transfer files, folders, and archives to Zip drives and FireWire drives, including the iPod.

Several vendors provide backup solutions for Mac OS X. One of the most popular programs is Retrospect (www.dantz.com).

Troubleshooting the File System

When troubleshooting file system problems, try these suggestions:

▶ If you are having problems accessing files on a local hard drive, use Disk Utility's First Aid to check for and repair any problems.

▶ If a computer becomes unbootable, it might be that a corrupted or deleted system file might be the cause. To fix these problems, try the following:

1. Put the computer in target disk mode by pressing T while you reboot. In target disk mode, the computer acts as a FireWire drive and can be connected to another computer, allowing you to run diagnostics, examine the drive contents, and recover and back up the files on the drive, even though the drive is unbootable. See Lesson 9 for more information on target disk mode.

2. Reinstall the operating system to replace the missing files. When the operating system version on the installation disc is older than the one on the hard drive, you'll need to use the Archive and Install option, which will enable you to install the older operating system without having to erase the drive. You'll still need to apply updates to make the operating system version current.

What You've Learned

▶ Mac OS X is a flexible, mainstream operating system that provides support for Mac OS 9 volumes, modern Mac OS X volumes, and network volumes.

▶ Mac OS X integrates well with the Internet, and provides utilities with which you can troubleshoot and manage your storage devices.

▶ Mac OS X supports several volume formats. Mac OS Extended file system and UFS are the primary formats. The Mac OS Extended file format supports file forks and bundles.

▶ Mac OS X allows you to securely delete files in the Trash so that they cannot be recovered.

- ► Mac OS X uses paths to indicate the location of files and directories. The file system has a standard layout. Some directories are hidden until you navigate to them in the Finder by choosing Go > Go to Folder.

- ► Mac OS X has standard top-level folders and standard folders within each user's home folder. System files installed by the operating system are stored in /System.

- ► Mac OS X searches for resources in multiple locations in a specific order, known as a search path. Fonts are an example of a resource that uses a search path.

- ► Disk Utility allows you to configure, check, and repair hard disks.

- ► Disk image files are useful for encapsulating a directory and its contents.

- ► File compression and expansion allow you to conserve storage space and speed up transfer time.

References

The following Knowledge Base articles (located at http://kbase.info.apple.com) will provide you with further information regarding file systems in Mac OS X.

Backup

- ► 106941, "Mac OS X: How to Back Up and Restore Your Files"

Fonts

- ► 106417, "Mac OS X: Font Locations and Their Purposes"
- ► 106737, "Mac OS X: How to Add or Remove Classic Fonts"

Disk Utility/fsck

- ► 106214, "Using Disk Utility and fsck for File System Maintenance in Mac OS X"

HFS

▶   107249, "Mac OS X 10.2: About File System Journaling"

▶   25316, "Mac OS X 10.2 or Earlier: Choosing UFS or Mac OS Extended (HFS Plus) Formatting"

URLs

Visit the following Web site for more information:

▶   Internet-enabled disk images: http://developer.apple.com/ue/files/iedi.html

Review Quiz

Use the following questions to review what you have learned:

1.   You have a computer running Mac OS X with Classic installed. Sometimes, you boot it into Mac OS 9. What might be a drawback of using a UFS volume on this computer?

2.   List some top-level folders in Mac OS X.

3.   Someone has given you a file archive in .tar format. What do you do to expand it?

4.   What kind of hardware must your computer have in order to burn CDs?

5.   What two quick fixes are appropriate to consider when troubleshooting local file system issues?

Answers

1. UFS volumes are not visible to Mac OS 9.

2. /Applications, /Library, /System, and /Users.

3. Double-click the file icon. StuffIt Expander, which is included in Mac OS X, will expand .tar archives.

4. It must have a CD-R, CD-RW, Combo, or SuperDrive.

5. Repair with Disk Utility; use Target Disk mode to verify/install OS.

4

Time

This lesson takes approximately 1 hour to complete.

Goals

Install, run, and troubleshoot native Mac OS X applications

Configure the Classic environment to run Mac OS 9 applications on a Mac OS X computer

Use Classic preferences to identify what Mac OS 9 applications are running and help troubleshoot them as necessary

Install and run Java applets and JNLP applications

Use Activity Monitor to monitor applications' use of memory and processor

Creating Archives from Finder

Archiving files and folders creates a compressed file containing a copy of the items. Archived files take up less disk space than uncompressed files, so archiving is useful for making backup copies of your data and sending information over the Internet.

To archive files or folders, select an item or items in the Finder and choose File > Create Archive.

If you archive a single item, the archived file has the name of the original item with a .zip extension. If you archive multiple items at once, the archived file is called Archive.zip. Zip is a compression format commonly used on Windows systems and is similar to, but not compatible with, the StuffIt compression format more commonly used on the Mac.

When you double-click an archived file, the archive is replaced by uncompressed copies of the original items.

Expanding Compressed Files

In addition to the .sit or StuffIt compression format, Mac OS X also supports .tar, a Unix file archive format used by the tar command-line utility, and gzip, which is often used to compress tar archives.

To expand a .sit, .tar, or .gzip compressed file, all you have to do is double-click it. StuffIt Expander will open automatically and expand the compressed file. If you need even more compression options, consider purchasing StuffIt Deluxe (www.aladdinsys.com).

As you learned earlier in this lesson, some volume formats are case-sensitive and some are not. If an archive was created on a case-sensitive volume, it may contain files with the same name except for case. If you expand this archive in the Finder on a case-insensitive Mac OS Extended file system, the Finder will append a number to the name of the second file so that the names are different. If, however, you expand this archive from the command line using the tar utility, the second file will overwrite the first. If users report that files are missing when they extract a tar archive from the command line on a Mac OS Extended file system, recommend that they try expanding the archive in the Finder.

9 Click Save.

10 When prompted, enter your user name and password.

A Disk Utility progress dialog appears.

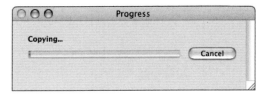

When Disk Utility has completed creating the image, the file Fonts.dmg appears on the desktop.

Mounting and Using a Disk Image File

The disk image file format is useful for software distribution. The image can be mounted and used like a drive.

1 Double-click the Fonts.dmg file on your desktop to mount it.

You will see a Fonts disk drive icon on your desktop.

2 Double-click the Fonts volume.

You will see all of the contents from the Fonts folder.

3 Drag and drop some files from the Fonts volume to the desktop.

4 Eject the Fonts volume.

5 Delete the Fonts.dmg disk image file and any other files you copied from the Fonts volume.

Lesson 4

Application Environments

An application environment consists of the libraries, library resources, application programming interfaces (APIs), and services that you need to run applications developed with those APIs. The application environments depend on the underlying layers of the system software: the core services (Quartz, OpenGL, QuickTime, and so on) and the core operating system (the kernel environment called Darwin).

In this lesson, you'll learn about the many application environments available to Mac OS X users. Those environments support programs created for present and past versions of Mac OS, as well as applications created for Java and Unix environments.

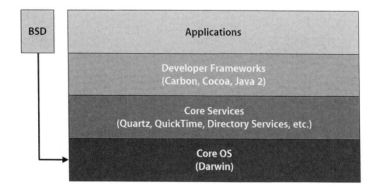

Macintosh Application Environments

The following types of applications can be run in Mac OS X:

- ▶ Carbon
- ▶ Cocoa
- ▶ Classic
- ▶ Java
- ▶ BSD

All the application environments are accessible through the Aqua graphical interface. This is true even for some BSD tools/applications, which provide a graphical user interface either through native applications such as Network Utility or through the X11 graphical system. However, to directly use pure BSD-only tools, you need to use a command-line interface utility such as Terminal.

Native Applications

Mac OS X provides two native application environments: Carbon and Cocoa.

Native applications are usually stored in /Applications or ~/Applications but function properly regardless of their location on disk. In addition, applications might install additional support files in the Applications Support folder in /Library and ~/Library. Classic applications, in contrast, are typically stored in /Applications (Mac OS 9) and might install support files in /System Folder.

Cocoa

Cocoa provides the environment for running applications that were developed specifically for Mac OS X in either Java or Objective-C using an advanced object-oriented development environment.

Carbon

Carbon applications can be written using a set of programming interfaces available on both Mac OS 9 and Mac OS X. The Carbon environment is important because it lets developers update existing Mac OS 9 applications quickly to run on both Mac OS 9 and Mac OS X.

When Mac OS X first shipped, the term "Carbon" was frequently used to describe an application that ran on both Mac OS 9 and Mac OS X. (Cocoa described applications that ran only on Mac OS X and took advantage of the operating system's new features like protected memory and true multitasking.) Originally that was true; almost all Carbon applications ran on both operating systems. However, with subsequent releases of Mac OS X, there have been more Carbon applications, such as Microsoft Office X, that are Mac OS X–only and take advantage of Mac OS X–specific features such as Quartz, the 2D graphics system.

When looking for applications to run on Mac OS X, you should not be concerned with whether the application uses Carbon or Cocoa; rather, look for an application that was "Built for Mac OS X." For a list of applications developed for Mac OS X, see www.apple.com/macosx/applications/.

Troubleshooting Mac OS X Applications

Troubleshooting a Mac OS X application that doesn't work correctly can be a potentially complex task. However, there are some simple steps you can take to fix application-level problems:

▶ If you can't open a document, the first step is to isolate the cause of the problem:

   ▶ Try opening a different document within the application.

   ▶ Try logging in as a different user. If the problem disappears, the problem could be improper preference or permissions settings or application support files in the other user account. If the problem still occurs, the application or its support files could be corrupted.

▶ If you are unable to open a Mac OS X application, a file used by the application might have been deleted or corrupted. Try the following to fix the problem:

   ▶ Try removing the application's files from the Application Support folders in /Library and ~/Library.

   ▶ Try deleting and reinstalling the application to restore the application files that have been corrupted or deleted.

▶ If a Mac OS X application is not running correctly, it might be due to a corrupted preference or cache file:

   ▶ Locate and rename the application's preference file in /Library/Preferences for system-wide preferences or in ~/Library/Preferences for user-specific preferences and then relaunch the application. A new preference file will be created. Don't delete the preference file, because if you find that the preference file was not the cause of the problem, you might want to restore the old preference file.

   ▶ If the issue does not appear to be related to preferences, a login item, or a kext (kernel extension) file, and it persists in Safe Mode (hold down Shift while starting up), there may be an issue with a cache file in your home folder. Delete the ~/Library/Caches folder.

Classic

The Classic environment supports legacy applications—those applications that ran in Mac OS 9 or earlier. With the Classic environment, you do not need to upgrade all of your applications immediately after upgrading to Mac OS X. To use the Classic environment, you must install Mac OS 9.2 in addition to Mac OS X. As discussed in Lesson 1, both operating systems can be installed on the same or different volumes.

The Classic Process

Unlike other applications, Classic applications do not run as standalone processes on Mac OS X (for more on processes, read "Monitoring System

Activity" later in this lesson). Instead, all Classic applications run within a single, shared process named TruBlueEnvironment. This single process contains the entire running version of Mac OS 9, along with any Classic applications and extensions.

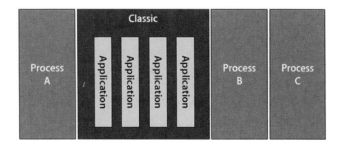

Because Classic applications share a common process and memory space, just as they do on a standard Mac OS 9 system, they are not protected from each other. If a Classic application crashes, it can overwrite and crash other applications running in the Classic environment. It cannot, however, crash native Mac OS X applications because they run in separate, memory-protected spaces.

Starting the Classic Environment

If Classic is not set to start automatically when you login, the Classic environment typically starts up like this:

1. You double-click a Classic application such as SimpleText.
2. The application icon appears in the Dock. Classic Startup (an application that starts the Classic environment) starts and a "9" icon appears in the Dock.
3. The TruBlueEnvironment process starts. This is the Classic environment that runs in the background.
4. After the environment process starts, Mac OS 9.2 loads.

5. The Classic startup window displaying a progress bar appears.

If an error occurs during startup, the system expands the window to show the error message. You also can manually expand the window by clicking the disclosure triangle. This is useful if you want to see the extensions loading for troubleshooting purposes.

6. The Classic application (in this case, SimpleText) starts up.

7. After Mac OS 9 loads, Classic Startup quits.

8. The "9" icon disappears from the Dock, and the Classic environment continues to run in the background.

Once Classic is running, it remains available for all Classic applications and need not be started again each time you open a different application.

Additions to Mac OS 9.2 Under Classic

When the Classic environment is started for the first time, you will be presented with a dialog requesting permission to update a set of files in the Mac OS 9.2 System Folder.

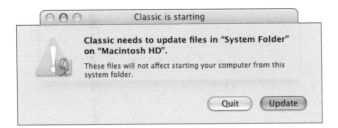

These files enable Mac OS 9.2 to run in the Classic environment. These files include updates to such items as Startup Disk and AppleScript, and new files such as Classic, Classic RAVE, Classic Support, and Classic Support UI. If you click Quit in the dialog, Classic can not start.

To view the files that Mac OS X uses to update Mac OS 9.2, do the following:

1   In the Finder, choose Go > Go to Folder.

2   In the "Go to the folder" field, type the following path:

    /System/Library/CoreServices/Classic Startup.app/Contents/Resources/ English.lproj/SystemFiles

3   Click Go.

If you encounter issues using Classic, you can use these files to verify and replace corrupted files in /System Folder by comparing file dates and sizes.

Control Panels in Classic

Many tried and true Mac OS 9 control panels and extensions function properly in Classic mode, and they may even be necessary to use certain applications or peripherals. However, there are some Mac OS 9 control panels that can not be used in the Classic environment because the features they configure are provided by Mac OS X in System Preferences. Attempting to use them causes a dialog to appear:

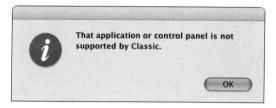

Knowledge Base article #107135, "Mac OS X 10.2: About Using Mac OS 9 Control Panels in the Classic Environment," provides details on the limitations of control panels under Classic. You can't use the following control panels in Classic. You should use their counterparts in System Preferences instead:

- ▶ AppleTalk
- ▶ Control Strip
- ▶ Date & Time
- ▶ Energy Saver
- ▶ File Exchange
- ▶ Infrared
- ▶ Location Manager
- ▶ Memory
- ▶ Modem
- ▶ Mouse
- ▶ Multiple Users
- ▶ Password Security
- ▶ PowerBook SCSI Disk Mode
- ▶ Remote Access
- ▶ Startup Disk
- ▶ TCP/IP
- ▶ Trackpad
- ▶ Web Sharing

It's a good idea to use Extensions Manager to create a startup set that excludes these items, and use it when launching Classic within Mac OS X.

Setting Classic System Preferences

All of the options for running Mac OS 9 applications within Mac OS X are controlled in Classic preferences.

Start/Stop

The Start/Stop pane in Classic preferences lists all Mac OS Standard and Extended volumes including those on mounted disk images. Those with System Folders usable by Classic are selectable; all others are dimmed. Each volume can contain more than one usable System Folder; Classic on Mac OS X 10.2 or later does not require a System Folder to be "blessed" in order to be usable, as was the case with Mac OS 9 and earlier.

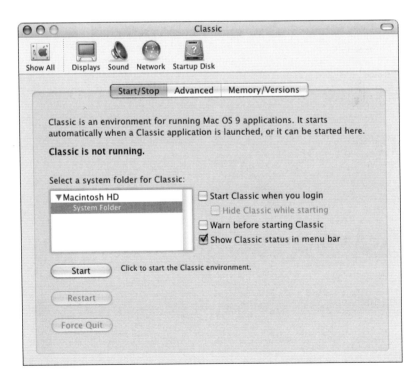

If "Start Classic when you login" is not selected, the Classic environment is opened automatically the first time you open a Classic application such as SimpleText. However, you can also start the Classic environment manually in Classic preferences. Since Classic consumes memory and processing cycles, it's a good idea not to start Classic unless you know it is needed.

In the Start/Stop pane, you can manually start, restart, force-quit, or stop Classic. You can also force-quit either an individual Classic application or the entire Classic environment by pressing Cmd-Option-Esc. However, using the Force Quit button in Classic preferences is a more reliable way to stop the Classic environment.

Remember that stopping Classic quits all running Classic applications. If you are having problems with one particular Classic application, you should first use the Force Quit command, which is covered in more detail in the "Force Quitting Applications" section later in this lesson. If the operating system is unable to quit the Classic application, it will automatically quit the Classic environment for you.

Selecting the checkbox labeled "Show Classic status in menu bar" in Classic preferences creates a menu extra that lets you determine whether Classic is running, start or restart Classic, and open Classic preferences.

Advanced

Click Advanced in Classic preferences to set startup options, configure sleep, or rebuild the Classic desktop. You can set the following options for starting Classic:

▶ The Turn Off Extensions option allows starting Mac OS 9.2 in Classic with all extensions disabled. This is useful for troubleshooting because it loads the bare bones Mac OS 9 components, avoiding all potential third-party extension conflicts.

▶ The Open Extensions Manager option brings up the Extensions Manager when Mac OS 9.2 starts in Classic. This is useful for resolving extension conflicts because you can selectively load items for testing.

▶ The Use Key Combination option lets you specify simulating key combinations when Classic starts up. For instance, some extensions can be disabled individually by pressing particular keys during startup. You can configure those keys in Use Key Combination.

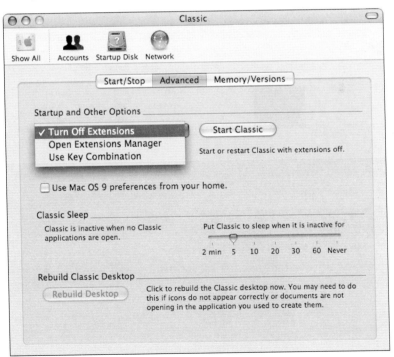

The settings in the Startup and Other Options section of the Advanced pane are not persistent. They apply only once when you click Restart Classic.

> **NOTE** ▶ If you have multiple user accounts on the Mac OS X system, you may find it useful to select "Use Mac OS 9 Preferences from your home." With this option on, the Mac OS 9 Preferences folder, along with other user-specific parts of the Mac OS 9 System Folder, is mapped into the user's home folder (~Library/Classic/). This enables different users to use the same Mac OS 9 System Folder, yet keep their own unique preferences for Classic applications. The first time you start Classic after selecting this option, Classic Startup will offer to make a copy of the user's preferences from the Mac OS 9 System Folder and put these into your home folder. It is strongly recommended that you allow this.

You can configure the Classic environment to sleep after a set amount of time with no Classic foreground applications running. Changes made to the inactive time take effect the next time the Classic environment runs. While Classic sleeps, it puts no load on the system. For this reason, if Classic is configured to start upon login it's a good idea to also configure it to sleep when inactive. The environment will wake from sleep with a little delay when you open a Classic application. No background Classic applications run while the Classic environment sleeps. If you need Classic background applications to remain running (for scanner button monitoring, for example), set the value to Never. Otherwise, the default value of 5 minutes is a good choice.

You can manually rebuild the desktop in Classic by clicking the Rebuild Desktop button. For more about this, see the Knowledge Base article #10182, "Mac OS: Rebuilding Desktop File and Icon Recovery." This process rebuilds only the desktop on the Classic startup volume. To rebuild the desktop on all volumes, start Classic from the Advanced pane with the Use Key Combination option set to Cmd-Option. This preference item is persistent, so unless you want to rebuild the desktop on every startup, click Clear Keys.

Memory/Versions

The Memory/Versions pane provides you with details about the state of the Classic environment including what applications are running within it, memory usage, and the version of Mac OS 9 being used. The information this pane provides is very similar to the information provided by choosing Apple > About This Mac in the Finder for Mac OS 9.

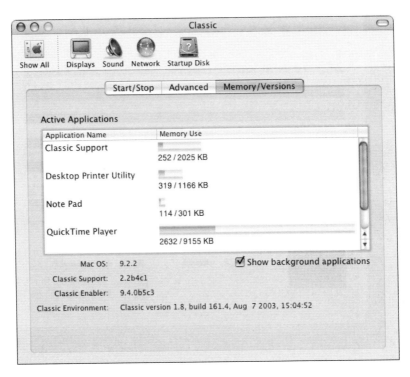

In the Active Applications portion of the Memory/Versions pane, all of the currently running Classic applications are listed along with how much memory the application is using and how much it was assigned. With versions of the Mac OS prior to Mac OS X, applications were allocated a fixed amount of memory that was assigned in the Info window in the Finder. Native Mac OS X applications are able to get additional memory as needed, but Classic applications cannot use more memory than they have been assigned. Symptoms of a Classic application running with insufficient memory allocations are out-of-memory errors, sluggish performance, and erratic behavior such as crashing. If you see any of these symptoms, check the memory usage in the Memory/Versions pane to see if the application has used all of its memory allocation. If it has, you can quit the application, assign it more memory, and restart it.

Some Classic applications and drivers use background processes to provide their functionality. Turning on the "Show background applications" option will add these processes to the list, helping you determine if you want to set Classic sleep time in the Advanced pane to Never.

Configuring Mac OS X to Run Classic Applications

Before you can run older Mac OS applications, you need to install a copy of Mac OS 9 and configure Classic to use that copy of Mac OS 9.

1   If Mac OS 9 is not installed on your Macintosh computer, install it now using the installation CD from a retail package of Mac OS 9, according to the onscreen instructions.

2   If you don't have a Mac OS 9 Install CD, but do have another computer on your network with a valid Mac OS 9 System Folder, copy the System Folder and Applications (Mac OS 9) folders from that computer to the root level of your Mac OS X boot hard drive.

3   Open Classic preferences.

4   If a dialog appears with the warning "No system folder selected," click OK.

5   Select System Folder from the boot volume in the "Select a system folder for Classic" list.

6   Select the "Show Classic status in menu bar" checkbox.

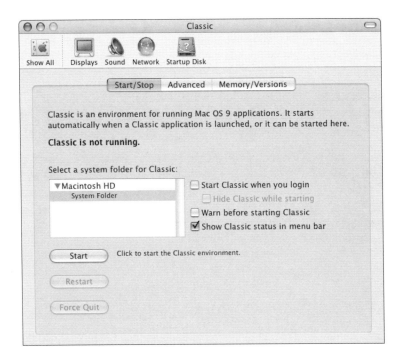

7 Test that Classic is able to correctly start by clicking the Start button.

Classic will begin to start up.

8 When the "Classic needs to update files" dialog appears, click Update.

9 When the Classic startup window closes, open SimpleText, which should be located in /Applications (Mac OS 9).

SimpleText should launch successfully.

Troubleshooting Classic

Classic preferences provides you with tools that help troubleshoot problems occurring in the Classic environment.

1   In Classic preferences, click Memory/Versions.

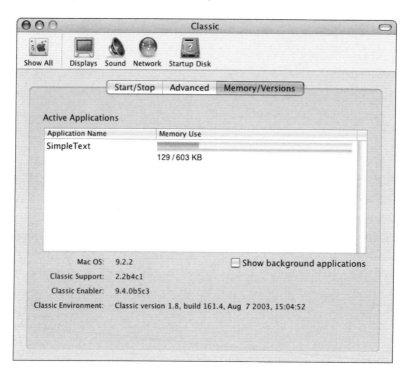

The Memory/Versions pane displays details about the Classic environment, including the version of Mac OS 9 running, what Classic applications are running, and the memory usage of each application. If you find that a Classic application is running erratically, you can check its memory usage.

It could be that the application has used up the memory allocated to it. If this occurs, try quitting the application and increasing the memory for the application via the Get Info window in the Finder.

2   Click Advanced.

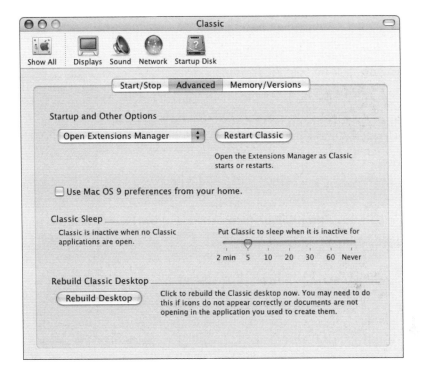

The Advanced pane allows you to do common Mac OS 9 troubleshooting tasks such as rebuilding the desktop and controlling the loading of extensions.

3   From the pop-up menu under Startup and Other Options, choose Open Extensions Manager.

4   Click Restart Classic.

5   If a dialog appears warning, "There are extensions in this set that are not installed on your computer," click Don't Save.

As the Classic environment restarts, it will display the Extensions Manager, allowing you to enable and/or disable extensions during the Mac OS 9 boot process.

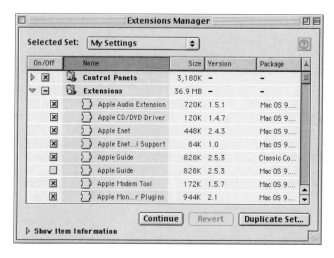

At this point, you can disable any extensions you think might be causing problems, just as you would with a standard Mac OS 9 system. For now, do not disable any of the extensions.

6   Click Continue to finish booting Mac OS 9.

Using the Classic Menu

The Classic menu provides you quick access to some Classic-related actions you may perform frequently, such as starting and stopping the Classic environment or opening Classic preferences. It also provides access to the items in the Mac OS 9 Apple menu without having to launch or switch to a Mac OS 9 application.

1 Click the Classic menu in the menu bar and choose Apple Menu Items > Chooser.

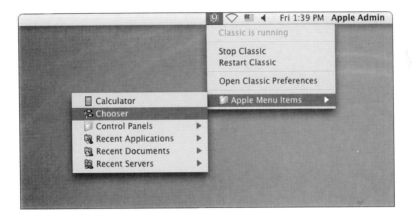

The Chooser opens, enabling you to select and set up a printer for use by a Classic application. Do not select a printer at this time.

2 Close the Chooser.

3 Choose Classic > Stop Classic.

This quits all running Classic applications and then stops the Classic environment. This is similar to choosing Special > Shut Down in Mac OS 9, and it is the graceful method for shutting down Classic. If you have unsaved documents open, you will be prompted to save them before quitting.

Troubleshooting Classic Applications

Try the following to troubleshoot problems running Classic and Classic applications:

▶ If Classic does not start up, check to make sure that a valid Mac OS 9 System Folder is listed and selected in Classic preferences.

▶ If Classic begins to start up but does not finish, it could be caused by a bad alias in the Servers folder in the Mac OS 9 System Folder. Try dragging the /System Folder/Servers folder to the Trash and restarting Classic.

▶ If you still encounter problems starting Classic, select Turn Off Extensions in the Advanced pane of Classic preferences and click Restart Classic. If Classic is able to fully start up, troubleshoot for an extension conflict just as you would with a regular Mac OS 9 system. (See the "Troubleshooting Classic" exercise earlier in this lesson.)

Java

Native Mac OS X and Classic applications are written to run on Macintosh computers exclusively. However, there are programming languages that can be used to create applications capable of running on a wide range of platforms. One such cross-platform language is Java, developed by Sun Microsystems (www.sun.com).

Mac OS X has a Java application environment that allows you to develop and run Java applications and applets, whether they were created on a Mac or some other platform.

Applet Launcher (/Applications/Utilities/Java) runs Java applets on your disk or on the Internet without opening a Web browser. To run an applet on the Internet, type the URL for the applet location in the text field and click Launch. You can also click Open to select an HTML file that uses the applet.

Java Web Start (/Applications/Utilities/Java) runs full-featured Java applications that are downloaded and launched by your Web browser. Web Start applications are launched by clicking a Web page link that downloads a small .jnlp (Java Network Launching Protocol) file and launches it. If the application is not present on the computer, the Java Web Start utility automatically downloads the necessary Java class files and starts the application. (The class files are stored in a Web Start cache in ~Library/Caches.) Once running, the application is independent of the browser, which allows you to quit the browser or surf to another page. If you launch the same application a second time, Web Start will allow you to convert the .jnlp file into a standalone application that you can double-click and run without having to use the Web Start utility. More information about Java Web Start can be found at http://developer.apple.com/java/javawebstart/.

Java support varies greatly from browser to browser. Currently, Safari and Internet Explorer are the most reliable browsers for running Java applications. Netscape, Mozilla, and OmniWeb all run Java but, currently, not as well as Safari and Internet Explorer. This is subject to change with future releases of those browsers.

Applet Launcher is useful when a user wants to run an applet without the overhead of running a browser, particularly when the applet is stored locally.

Using a Web Browser to Run an Applet

Frequently, Web sites include Java applets to provide functionality beyond displaying images and text. If you have a Java applet from the Web, here's one way you can run it:

1   Double-click a Java applet file (it may have an .html extension) to open it in Safari.

Safari interprets the HTML code in the file and runs the associated Java applet, as in this TicTacToe example.

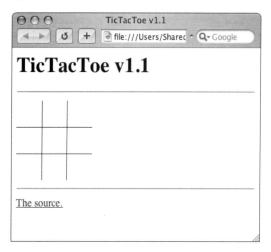

2 Quit the applet by closing the browser window or quitting Safari.

Using Applet Launcher to Run an Applet

You do not need a browser to run an applet. Mac OS X includes Applet Launcher, which enables you to run and control applets without using a full Web browser.

1 Open Applet Launcher (/Applications/Utilities/Java).

The Applet Launcher window appears.

2 Click Open.

3 Navigate to a Java applet.

NOTE ▶ Files that open with Applet Launcher end with ".html".

4 Select a Java applet file and click Open.

5 Stop the applet by choosing Applet > Stop.

6   Restart the applet by choosing Applet > Restart.

7   Open another applet.

You can have multiple applets open at the same time.

8   Choose Applet > Tag to view the HTML source that controls the applet.

9   Choose Applet > Info to display information about the applet, such as who created it and what it is supposed to do.

10 Quit Applet Launcher.

Using BSD/X11

Since Darwin, the core operating system of Mac OS X, uses BSD (Berkeley Software Distribution) 5.0 Unix, you can write and run Unix shell scripts to use any of the command-line interfaces in Mac OS X. (The primary one is Terminal.) You can also run Unix-style applications and tools that have been ported to Mac OS X. The BSD layer provides yet another platform for professional developers and scripters. You will learn how to use the command-line interface in Lesson 5.

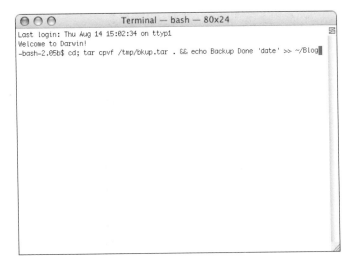

NOTE ▶ To learn more about BSD, visit www.bsd.org.

Initially, applications running on Unix-based operating systems were limited to the command line. Later, the X Window System, more commonly called X11, was created to allow developers to write graphical applications. X11 for Mac OS X (not installed by default) offers a complete X Window System implementation for running X11-based applications on Mac OS X. It includes the full X11R6.6 technology, including a window server, libraries, and basic utilities such as xterm, a terminal emulator. For more information about X11 for Mac OS X, refer to the Apple's X11 Web page at www.apple.com/macosx/x11/.

NOTE ▶ You can launch an X11 application by double-clicking its icon in the Finder.

Managing Applications

When things are working properly in Mac OS X, there's not much need to manage your applications. You simply install them, then use them as needed. However, Mac OS X includes some tools that are useful for troubleshooting application problems.

Getting Information with System Profiler

There are times when you will find it handy to have a list of applications installed on a system. System Profiler is a utility that creates reports about how a system is configured. System Profiler is located in /Applications/Utilities. You can also open System Profiler by choosing Apple > About This Mac and clicking More Info.

Finding Applications

To see a list of the applications installed on your system, open System Profiler and in the Contents pane on the left, click the Software disclosure triangle and then select Applications. System Profiler scans the /Applications folder, including any subdirectories it contains, to create a list of applications. It presents the

list of found applications on the right, listing each application's name, version
number, and date of last modification.

When you select an application in the list, System Profiler displays information
about the application in the lower pane. System Profiler does not search for
files outside of /Applications. If an application is not installed in /Applications
or in one of its subdirectories, the application will not be listed. As such, an
application can be stored in and run from an individual user's home directory,
but it won't appear in this list.

Finding Frameworks

A framework (.framework) is a bundle of shared library code that is automatically and dynamically loaded and linked to programs. For example, rather than
include the same printing code in all four applications of an office suite, the
programs could share a single framework for that task. Apple's frameworks are
stored in /System/Library/Frameworks.

Just as an application package makes it easier for a program to locate its own
resources, a framework makes it easy for a shared library to locate its resources.

It also simplifies installation or removal of libraries. Frameworks are comparable to .dll (Dynamic Link Library) files found in Windows.

Just as it does with applications, the System Profiler Frameworks pane provides a list of frameworks installed in the operating system, along with their version numbers. To see the Frameworks pane, choose View > Extended Report. In the Contents pane on the left, click the Software disclosure triangle, then select Frameworks.

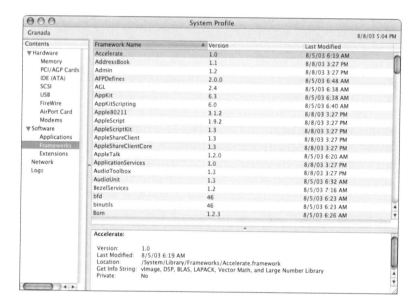

Monitoring System Activity

The Activity Monitor utility (/Applications/Utilities) allows you to view and monitor every application and process running on the computer.

A process is a running program or set of threads and an address space. A thread is a set of instructions that can be assigned independently to the CPU. Therefore, different threads of a single process can run on one processor at different times or at the same time on different processors. This is called symmetric multiprocessing. The job of a process is to manage memory and other resources related to the execution of its threads. Two types of processes

that run without an explicit user interface are system-level processes, called daemons (pronounced "demons"), and applications running in faceless mode.

As stated in Lesson 2, every program (and therefore every process) is owned by
a user. Activity Monitor tells you who owns each process, its status, how much
of the CPU is being used to run the process, and how much memory is used
by the process. You can identify the process by its ID number, which appears in
the Process ID column. Each process ID (PID) is unique.

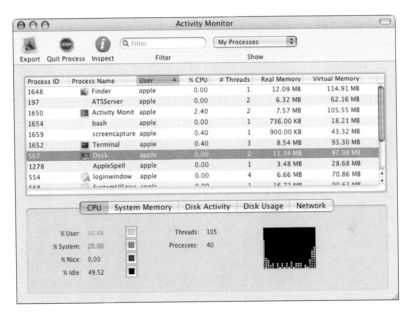

In Activity Monitor, you can sort processes by column heading. Click the column heading to select it and click it again to sort up or down. Although it might
seem easy to match a process to a running application, don't always make that
assumption. For instance, if Classic is running, its process is actually called
TruBlueEnvironment, and all of the applications running in Classic are merely
threads of that process. Also, Activity Monitor displays some Carbon applications as LaunchCFMApp, rather than listing their individual application names.

To see more information about a process, including memory usage, statistics, and
files open by a process, select the process in the Activity Monitor window and
click the Inspect icon in the toolbar.

To quit a process, select it in the Activity Monitor window and click the Quit Process icon in the toolbar or choose Process > Quit. This is just like typing *kill* in a command-line interface, except that the kill command doesn't display any prompt. You can also elect to use the more severe Force Quit, which is equivalent to the kill command, but with a more severe halting of the process (*kill -9* at the command line).

The lower pane of the Activity Monitor contains buttons that provide you with system-wide information covering CPU, system memory, disk activity, disk usage, and network statistics.

Using Activity Monitor to Force a Process to Quit

Occasionally, you may find it necessary to forcibly quit a process that is running in the background. You can do this using Activity Monitor.

1   Open Activity Monitor (/Applications/Utilities).

Activity Monitor displays a list of all processes currently running.

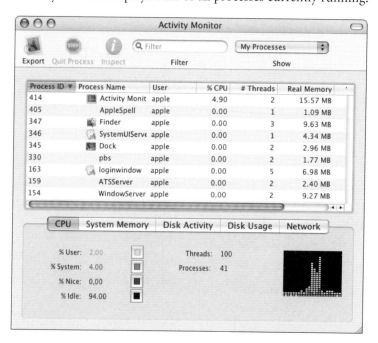

2 Select the Dock entry.

You can scroll through the list to locate it, or you can narrow the list down by typing the beginning of the name in the Filter field.

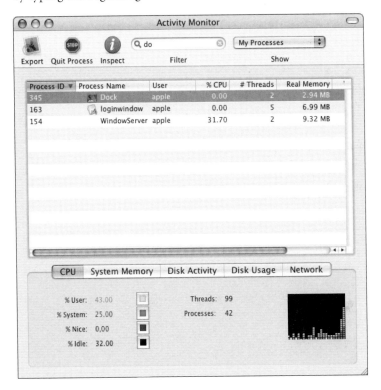

3 Click the Quit Process button.

4 In the Quit Process dialog, click Force Quit.

The Dock disappears and then reappears almost immediately because Mac OS X automatically reopens it.

5 Quit Activity Monitor.

Force Quitting Applications

As you've seen in the preceding exercise, you can use Activity Monitor to force-quit a misbehaving process or application. However, you can also use several other methods that don't require you to open that utility. You can forcibly quit any applications that are visible by using the Force Quit Applications window or the Dock. Press Cmd-Option-Esc or choose Apple > Force Quit to open the Force Quit Applications window. You can select any running application in this window and click Force Quit. You can also click and hold the application's icon in the Dock until a menu appears. One of the choices will be Quit, but if you hold down the Option key, it will change to Force Quit. Theoretically, choosing this option will have the same effect as clicking Force Quit in the Force Quit Applications window. However, in practice the latter method sometimes fails to get a program to actually quit whereas the former method almost always works. Another way to force an application to quit is to Ctrl-Option-click the application's icon in the Dock and choose Force Quit.

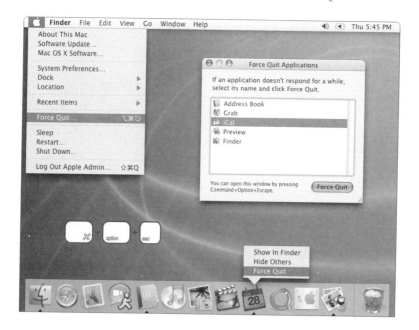

Due to protected memory, the Force Quit command has no effect on any other application. The only exception to this is Classic applications. Forcing a Classic application to quit might impact other Classic applications but does not affect applications running in Mac OS X. If the Force Quit command fails for an individual Classic application, the entire Classic environment will automatically be shut down.

> **NOTE ▸** You should always restart Classic if you force a Classic application to quit, because Classic then could be in an unusable state.

If you select the Finder in the Force Quit Applications window, the Force Quit button changes to a Restart button. You cannot quit the Finder, but you can restart it.

Forcing an Application to Quit

If an application becomes unresponsive, you can use the Force Quit Applications window to force the application to quit.

1   Open TextEdit.

2   Press Cmd-Option-Escape.

The Force Quit Applications window appears.

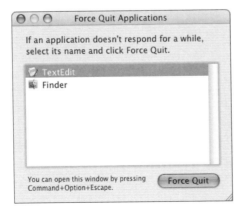

You can also open the Force Quit Applications window by choosing Apple > Force Quit.

3 Select TextEdit from the list.

4 Click Force Quit.

5 In the confirmation dialog that appears, click Force Quit.

The system will force TextEdit to quit, and it should no longer appear in the Force Quit Applications window.

6 Close the Force Quit Applications window.

What You've Learned

▶ A process is a running program. Each process on Mac OS X runs in its own protected memory space.

▶ Mac OS X includes five primary application environments:

  ▶ Carbon

  ▶ Cocoa

  ▶ Classic

  ▶ Java

  ▶ BSD/X11

▶ To use the Classic environment, Mac OS 9 must be installed. You select which Mac OS 9 System Folder to use, and you configure Classic options in Classic preferences.

▶ System Profiler provides a list of all applications located in /Applications and all of the installed frameworks.

▶ If an application does not respond to input from the keyboard or mouse, choose Apple > Force Quit or press Cmd-Option-Escape to display the Force Quit Applications window. Select the application to quit and click Force Quit. You can also use the Dock and Activity Monitor to force an application to quit.

References

The following Knowledge Base articles (located at http://kbase.info.apple.com) will provide you with further information regarding installing Mac OS X application environments.

Classic

▶ 10182, "Mac OS: Rebuilding Desktop File and Icon Recovery"

▶ 106601, "Mac OS X 10.1: 'The Classic Environment is Not Responding' Message"

▶ 106677, "Mac OS X: Troubleshooting the Classic Environment"

▶ 106678, "Mac OS X: Classic Will Not Start Up—Mac OS 9 Not Installed or Not Blessed"

▶ 106679, "Mac OS X: Classic Will Not Finish Starting Up—Extension Conflict or 'Bus Error'"

▶ 106719, "Mac OS X: How to Use Mac OS 9 Applications"

▶ 106874, "Mac OS: Web Browser Quits Unexpectedly or Stops Responding"

Final Cut Pro

▶ 61477, "Final Cut Pro 3: Troubleshooting Installation Issues"

iApps (iMovie, iPhoto, iTunes)

▶ 42567, "iPhoto: Unable to Import Photos From Kodak Photo CD"

▶ 61018, "iPod: Troubleshooting Songs That Skip iCal/iChat/iSync"

▶ 61771, "iPod: Does Not Appear in iTunes or on Desktop, Exclamation Point, or Sad iPod Icon Appears on Screen"

▶ 75336, "iPhoto: Troubleshooting Camera Connections"

▶ 106137, "iMovie: FireWire 2.7 May Resolve Dropped Frames"

iSync

▶ 35013, "iSync 1.0: Troubleshooting Issues Synchronizing Palm OS Device"

▶ 61755, "iSync 1.0: About Using the Log to Troubleshoot Issues"

▶ 107350, "Mac OS X 10.2.3 and Later: Some Window Buttons Lack Drop Shadow, Appear Countersunk"

Mail

▶ 61153, "Mac OS X Mail: How to Troubleshoot Undeliverable Email"

Troubleshooting

▶ 25398, "Mac OS X: How to Troubleshoot a Software Issue"

URLs

Visit the following Web sites for more information:

▶ Java Web Start: http://developer.apple.com/java/javawebstart/

▶ Mac OS X applications: www.apple.com/macosx/applications

▶ X11 for Mac OS X: www.apple.com/macosx/features/x11/

Review Quiz

Use the following questions to review what you have learned:

1. What are the key application environments? What are the differences among them?

2. What are three methods you can use to force-quit an application in Mac OS X?

3. How do you start the Classic environment in Mac OS X?

4. What tool do you use to configure the Classic startup options?

5. What quick fixes should you consider when troubleshooting Mac OS X application issues?

6. What quick fixes should you consider when troubleshooting Classic application issues?

Answers

1. Carbon, Cocoa, Java, Classic, and BSD

    ▶ Carbon—One of Mac OS X's two native application environments, Carbon provides a set of APIs that exist on both earlier versions of Mac OS (8.1 through 9) and Mac OS X. Many Carbon applications run on both Mac OS 9 and Mac OS X.

    ▶ Cocoa—The other "native" application environment, Cocoa is a framework developers can use to create applications that take advantage of Mac OS X–specific features.

    ▶ Java—Java is a cross-platform application environment that allows developers to create applications that run on multiple operating systems.

    ▶ Classic—The Classic application environment allows Mac OS X users to run applications built for Mac OS 9 and earlier.

    ▶ BSD—The Unix-style environment allows Mac OS X users to run command-line based tools and utilities.

2. You can use the Activity Monitor utility to quit the process, Ctrl-Option-click the application icon in the Dock and choose Force Quit from the pop-up menu, or use the Force Quit Applications window to force-quit an application. You can access the Force Quit Application window by pressing Cmd-Option-Escape or by choosing Apple > Force Quit.

3. The Classic environment is typically started when a Classic application is started. However, you can configure it to start at login or start it manually using Classic preferences or the Classic menu.

4. Classic preferences is used to configure the Classic startup options.

5. Try a different document; try a different user account; force-quit; reinstall the application; remove application support files (such as preferences files).

6. Verify that a valid System Folder is selected; restart Classic; remove server aliases; use Extensions Manager.

5

Time

This lesson takes approximately 1 hour to complete.

Goals

Identify reasons to use a command-line interface and ways to access the command-line interface

Describe the syntax of commands entered on the command line

Use the online manual to determine the syntax and sample usage for a command

Run commands to view hidden files and directories and to manipulate files and file attributes

Run commands to find files, manage processes, monitor usage, and manage disks and volumes

Exchange data between the Finder and the command line

Command-Line Interface

Mac OS X is designed to give users all the power of an industry-standard, Unix-based operating system without having to know anything about BSD (Berkeley Software Distribution) tools. From an administrator and technical coordinator's perspective, however, you may find it convenient to use a command-line interface to accomplish certain administrative or troubleshooting tasks. Using the command-line interface is optional, but for the purposes of obtaining Apple Help Desk Essentials certification, it is necessary to understand the basics of when, where, and how to use these tools.

Sometimes referred to in Unix environments as a shell, a command-line interface executes commands entered as text rather than from a menu selection or mouse click. The shell is the traditional interface to a Unix system, and many features of Mac OS X can only be accessed as commands on the command line.

Executing commands using a shell can be more efficient, or simply more convenient, than using the graphical user interface. For example, using the command line allows you to execute commands as some other user without first having to log out. Additionally, at the command line you can monitor and troubleshoot a remote machine accessible over the network.

A Word of Caution

The command-line interface is an incredibly powerful tool, and with that power comes the potential for doing accidental damage to your files. In the Mac OS X graphical user interface, if you make a mistake, you can usually choose Edit > Undo (Cmd-Z) to backtrack, and destructive actions usually are accompanied by dialogs requesting confirmation. There are no such safety nets with the command-line interface. If you enter the wrong command, you might delete documents or render the computer inoperable with no warning whatsoever, and you won't be able to undo the damage short of restoring from a backup or reinstalling.

The commands shown in the examples in this lesson are relatively harmless if entered as shown. But you should still be careful as you follow along with this lesson and don't experiment unless you know exactly what you are doing.

Command-Line Interfaces

In a graphical user interface, programs are controlled primarily by selecting and clicking menus and windows with buttons and text fields. As such, you can usually discover what a program is capable of doing just by examining the onscreen options. A command-line interface executes individual programs, called commands or tools, that you type. A command consists of the name of the command followed by any options (often called switches), that you choose to provide, and any arguments for the command. Note that command names are case-sensitive. To execute a typed command, you press the Return key.

The command prompt is the starting point for entering commands in a command-line interface. It can be daunting to stare at the command prompt if you're used to a graphical user interface because there are no helpful onscreen hints explaining what to do.

The information between the brackets indicates where you are—the name to the left of the colon (:) is the name of the computer. (If localhost is shown instead of the name of the computer, it is because a reverse DNS lookup could not be done on the computer's IP address.) The information to the right of the colon shows the working directory, or the folder, you are in. The tilde character (~) is shorthand for your home folder.

Immediately following the brackets are the name of the currently logged-in user and a separator character (% or #). If the character # is shown instead of the character %, it indicates that the current user is running commands as the System Administrator.

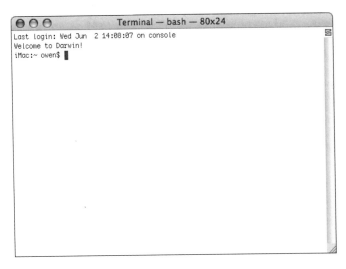

In this screen shot, the user named owen is logged in on a computer named iMac and is working within his home directory.

> **NOTE** ▶ The prompt is specific to each shell and is also user configurable. What we show here is the default prompt you get with bash (*Bourne Again Shell*), the default shell.

You can access the command line in Mac OS X in the following four ways:

▶ >console—If you enter >*console* as the user name with no password in the Mac OS X login window, the Mac OS X graphical user interface disappears, and you are prompted to log in from a command-line interface prompt. At this point, you are using Mac OS X solely from a command-line interface. If you type *exit* at the prompt, you return to the Mac OS X login window.

▶ Remote login using ssh (secure shell) or Telnet—You can log in to a remote Mac OS X computer from any computer by using ssh, provided that you use the user name and password of a user account on the remote Mac OS X computer. After you ssh into a remote Mac OS X computer, commands entered on your computer are executed on the remote computer as though you were using it locally. Note that Remote Login on Mac OS X is disabled by default. An administrative user can enable Remote Login in the Services pane of Sharing preferences.

▶ Single-user mode—By pressing Cmd-S after you hear the startup chime, you enter single-user mode. In single-user mode, you have access to the file system as the System Administrator without having to log in. You exit single-user mode by typing *exit*.

NOTE ▶ Single-user mode is a security risk because it gives the user System Administrator access to most of the files on the system. Setting an Open Firmware password on the computer will prevent a user from entering single-user mode. Knowledge Base article #106482, "Setting Up Open Firmware Password Protection in Mac OS X 10.1 or Later," provides instructions for setting this up.

▶ Terminal—For the remainder of this lesson, you will use Terminal (/Applications/Utilities) when you access the command line because it is the most convenient and secure method.

Entering Commands

Each command is entered on a single line after the shell prompt and in the following format:

command option(s) (arguments)

For instance, the ls command lists the contents of the named directories. Adding an option to this command gives you a little more information in the listing. Typing *ls -lA ~/Documents* lists the contents of your Documents folder along with their permissions for files and subdirectories.

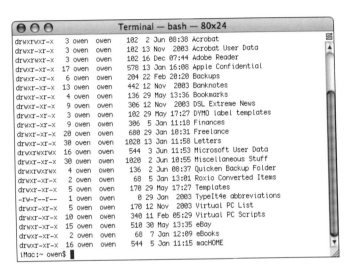

Many shell commands operate on or produce textual information. Shell commands that require input typically read their input from the default input device (the keyboard), and commands that generate output typically write to the default output device (the monitor).

Input/output redirection allows you to change the input device, the output device, or both for a given command. For example, you might want to redirect the output of an ls command to a file for inclusion in an email message. Such a command might look like this:

ls -lA ~/Documents > ~/Desktop/lstext.txt

The greater-than sign is used after the ls command (with its options and argument) to redirect output to a text file identified by path and filename. In this case, the list of items in the Documents folder would be saved to a text file named lstext in the current user's Desktop folder.

Accessing Online Help

All Unix-based systems provide online help using the man (for manual) command. This command formats and displays pages describing the command, configuration file, or other item. The man pages for a command contain

- ▶ The name
- ▶ A brief synopsis
- ▶ A description
- ▶ Examples of command syntax and usage (for most, but not all, commands)

The man command, followed by a command name, displays the manual pages for that command. For instance, on the command line, type

man ls

This command displays information about the ls command, including its many parameters.

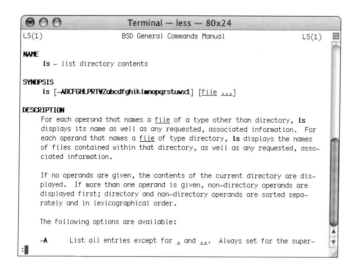

You can also search the man pages for specific words using:

apropos keyword

where *keyword* is the specific word you're searching for. This command displays a list of commands whose man pages include this keyword. Using apropos is a good way to discover new commands.

> **NOTE** ▶ A newly installed system may not have had time to create the database used by the apropos command. You can force the update of the database by entering the following command:
>
> *sudo /etc/weekly*

The man pages are organized in numbered sections. If there is more information than fits on the screen, press the spacebar to page down. Sometimes you have to specify the section number to find the page you want. For example, open is the name of a command, the name of a Perl language construct, and a Unix system call. To see the man page for the command, you need to use

man open

To find out what a section contains, type

man section *intro*

For instance:

- ▶ Section 1—General commands (tools and utilities)
- ▶ Section 2—System calls and error numbers
- ▶ Section 3—C libraries

Not all commands have man pages, and sometimes the man pages have errors.

Viewing man Pages Using Terminal

You can use a command-line interface to view the man pages for Unix commands.

1 Open Terminal (/Applications/Utilities).

2 At the command prompt, type

man ping

and press Return to obtain information on the Unix command ping that corresponds to the Ping pane in Network Utility.

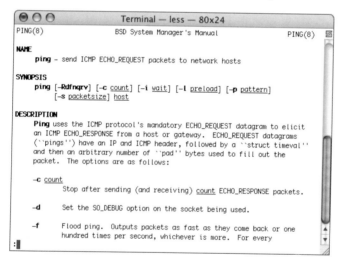

You can continue viewing the rest of the documentation by pressing the spacebar.

3 To quit viewing the documentation, press Q.

4 View the man pages for host and traceroute, which correspond to the Lookup and Traceroute commands used in Network Utility.

man host

man traceroute

5   If you don't remember the name of a command, but know something about it, you can search the keywords of the man pages with either *man -k (keyword)* or *apropos*.

man -k owner

6   Search through the results of *man -k owner* until you find the command that allows you to change ownership of a file or directory.

Using Edit Keys

Typing at the command line must be exact, and some file systems require you to enter case-sensitive filenames. Fortunately, most shells, including those included by default with Terminal, provide several keyboard shortcuts that make entering and editing commands easier.

Tab completion allows you to type just the first unique letters of a command or path. When you press the Tab key, the shell will complete the string. When you type a partial command and press the Tab key, but there are other commands or paths that start with the same letters, the shell will respond with a beep and wait for more input. For example, suppose you want to list the contents of your Documents folder.

You begin by typing

ls ~/Do

At that point, you press the Tab key and it completes the folder name to

ls ~/Documents/

because there is only one folder in your home directory that begins with "Do."

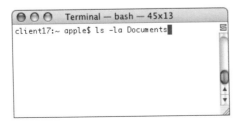

A quick way to enter a very long path is to drag the folder from the Finder into the Terminal window. The path appears after the cursor on the command line, with the correct path to that folder.

Shells interpret spaces in filenames as command, option, or argument separators. To get around this, you can either put the entire path in single or double quotes, or precede each individual space with a backslash (\). When a character is preceded by a backslash, it is called "escaping the character." This prevents the shell from doing anything special with the character. When a shell performs filename completion for you, it will escape spaces in filenames.

The shell maintains a list of previously entered commands. The up arrow and down arrow traverse the history list of commands. To execute a command again, press Return when it is visible at the command prompt.

Shells often provide a number of ways to speed the editing of commands. Use Ctrl-A to move quickly to the beginning of a line. Ctrl-E moves the cursor to the end of the line.

In addition to using the cursor keys to move the cursor forward and backward on the command line, Ctrl-F moves forward one character and Ctrl-B moves backward one character. To move forward and backward one word at a time, use Esc F and Esc B, respectively.

Use Ctrl-L or the clear command to clear the screen.

Ctrl-C terminates many commands in progress and will cause the shell to ignore any text currently being entered and return you to the command prompt.

The cursor does not need to be at the end of the line when you press Return. The shell interprets all of the text entered on the current line regardless of the cursor's location when your press Return.

File System Representations

Before you begin experimenting with some of the more useful command-line tools, make sure you understand how Unix represents the file system. Unix systems create a single hierarchy of folders and files (often described as an inverted tree) that includes all of the file systems available to the computer. The topmost directory is the root directory and is written as "/" (forward slash). Instead of attaching files and folders to specific hardware devices such as hard drives or network drives, each file system from an available disk appears as a directory within the larger file system tree.

Consequently, locating files via the command line often involves specifying a path starting at the root and descending through the tree to the required file or directory. For example, the Finder might present a network drive on your desktop with the name Troubleshooting. In the command-line interface, this corresponds to the directory /Volumes/Troubleshooting.

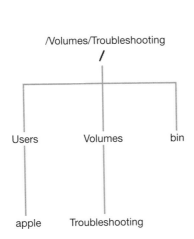

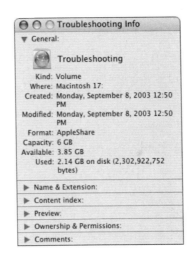

In Finder preferences, the General pane allows you to specify whether hard disks, removable media, and network volumes mounted with the Connect to Server command appear on your desktop. Volumes appearing on your desktop, however, are not really located in your Desktop folder. Therefore, they are not available to you on the command line with a path of the form ~/Desktop/*volume*. Instead, those volumes are available in the command line within the /Volumes directory.

Volumes dynamically automounted from a server (such as network home directories) appear in the command line within the /Network/Servers directory.

Network volumes mounted from the Network icon in the Sidebar at the left of the Finder windows are available within the /private/var/automount/Network directory.

Directories and Files Not Seen in the Finder

The Finder presents only a subset of the files that actually exist in any file system. Some files, such as the file system catalog and desktop database files, are marked as hidden. The Finder elects not to show some other files and directories, such as those that are used during system startup or are less likely to be of interest to general users.

The files and directories in the root directory of your startup volume that the Finder elects not to show are listed in the text file /.hidden. Following a long-standing Unix convention, the Finder does not display files with names starting with a period. However, using the command-line interface, you can list these hidden files. By typing the command *ls -la ~/*, for example, you can list all directories and files, including hidden files, located in your home directory.

Locating Files

Mac OS X introduces a number of predefined directories intended to contain files of particular types. Many applications depend on the name and location of these directories, and they should not be renamed or moved. Most applications in the Mac OS X graphical user interface reside in /Applications, and operating system files reside in /System.

By convention, Unix programs store their configuration information in the hidden directory /etc; most command-line tools are installed in the hidden directories /bin, /sbin, /usr/bin, or /usr/sbin. These four directories are the four locations that shells search to find the programs whose names you enter on the command line. If you want to manually add a new program for the command line, you could place the file in one of these hidden directories, but a better solution would be to store it in a visible folder. Programs in locations other than the four default directories may be executed by specifying an absolute or relative path to the executable. For example,

/Developer/Tools/GetFileInfo /.hidden

executes the GetFileInfo command installed by the Developer Tools.

Understanding Frequently Used Commands

Locating, creating, copying, and deleting files and directories are the main tasks that casual users will perform using the command line. The few commands described here allow you to complete such tasks many different ways. These commands are commonly used to administer and troubleshoot any Unix-based system.

Although the names of commands may appear cryptic at first glance, you will find that most shell commands have been given names that attempt to be mnemonic. Oftentimes the command name is a common word without the vowels.

ls

The ls command, used to list one or more files, is probably the most frequently used command. As a consequence of its frequent use, the ls command supports many options. For example, using ls with the -l option displays the file type, size, date, and permission attributes along with the name of the requested files.

The use of many commands is simplified by the use of a current directory. All shells maintain a current directory for ease of specifying filenames used as arguments to commands. For example, entering

ls

with no files or directories specified will list the contents of the current directory. A file specification that doesn't begin with a forward slash (to identify the root directory) refers to a file or directory referenced from the current directory.

cd

The cd command changes the current directory to the directory you specify.

pwd

Use the pwd command to display or "print" the working directory.

cp and mv

You can use the cp and mv commands to copy and move, respectively, items in the command-line interface. To copy a flat file from your Public folder to your Documents folder, you can use the cp command. For example:

*cp ~/Public/*file_name *~/Documents/*new_file_name

To move a file from the Shared folder to your Documents folder, type

*mv /Users/Shared/*file_name *~/Documents/*new_file_name

> **NOTE ▶** The cp and mv commands ignore resource forks. Use them only with flat files. Use the ditto command to copy files with resource forks (See the "Mac OS X–Specific Commands" later in this lesson.)

rm

The rm command removes (deletes) the files that you name. You can list multiple files in a single command, use filename wildcards (discussed later in this lesson), or use a combination of both to remove many files with a single command. The command

rm -i ~/Documents/.rtf ~/Documents/*.txt*

removes all of the files whose name ends in ".rtf" or ".txt" that reside in your Documents directory. The -i option used in the example has rm ask whether or not you want to delete each file that you specify.

Another commonly used option of the rm command is -R. This option requests that rm recurse though all of the files and directories in the named directories deleting all of the files and directories that it encounters. The command

rm -iR ~/Documents/Projects

removes the Projects directory and all of its contents, including other directories, from your Documents directory. Since the -i option also appears, rm will prompt you to confirm the deletion of each file or directory that it finds.

> **NOTE ▶** Trash is not involved when you use these standard shell commands to remove files or directories. The files and directories that you remove cannot be recovered once the command has finished executing.

mkdir and rmdir

Use mkdir and rmdir, respectively, to make and remove empty directories.

Using File-Related Commands

Many command-line commands and troubleshooting tasks involve manipulating files and their attributes.

The more command allows you to view text files a page at a time. The touch command allows you to create an empty file with the specified name or, if a file with that name exists already, touch will update the modification date.

The cat command allows you to concatenate the contents of one or more files and display them on the standard output device. For example, typing *cat file1 >> file2* causes the contents of file1 to be appended to the contents of file2.

To determine the directory containing a particular command, use the which command.

To display a file's type, issue the file command followed by the name of the file or files whose type you wish to determine.

Finding Files Using Locate and Find

You can use both the locate and find commands to search the file system for files matching certain criteria.

The locate command uses a database describing the known files on your system. The locate database is built and updated automatically as long as your system is running at the appropriate time. By default on a Mac OS X system, the locate database is updated at 4:30 am each Saturday. You can execute the script that updates the locate database using the command

sudo /etc/weekly

The locate command understands the wildcard characters used by the shell. In order to pass the wildcard character to the locate command, you must escape the character so that the shell doesn't process it. For example, the commands

locate ".rtf"*

or

locate *.rtf

will print a list of all files with names ending in ".rtf," but

*locate *.rtf*

results in an error.

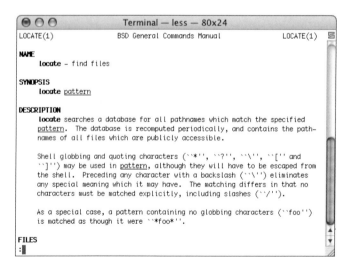

The syntax for the find command is more complex than for the locate command, but the possible uses of find are much broader. The command

find ~ -name ".rtf"*

starts a search of the files in your home directory and lists all of the files with names ending in ".rtf."

Using Shell Filename Wildcards

Shell filename wildcards provide a convenient way to specify a group of files based on a pattern. The wildcards supported by Unix shells are asterisk (*), question mark (?), and square brackets ([ ]).

The asterisk (*) wildcard matches any string of characters. For example, typing * matches all files, whereas typing *.rtf* matches all files ending in ".rtf."

The question mark (?) wildcard matches any single character. As such, it's more precise than the asterisk. For example, typing *b?ok* matches "book" but not "brook."

The [ ] wildcard matches a single character in the list of characters appearing within the square brackets.

A few examples will build your understanding of wildcards. Consider a collection of five files with the names ReadMe.rtf, ReadMe.txt, read.rtf, read.txt, and It's All About Me.rtf. Among these files:

- ▶ *.rtf matches ReadMe.rtf, read.rtf, and It's All About Me.rtf
- ▶ ????.* matches read.rtf and read.txt
- ▶ [Rr]*.rtf matches ReadMe.rtf and read.rtf
- ▶ [A-Z]* matches ReadMe.rtf, ReadMe.txt, and It's All About Me.rtf

To test your understanding of wildcards, use the touch command to create files with these names and then try these expressions, as well as some of your own creation, as a file specifier for the ls command.

Executing Commands as the System Administrator

The sudo command lets you run a command as another user. Typically, sudo without a user name argument is used to execute commands as the System Administrator. As configured initially on Mac OS X, only administrator users are permitted to execute this command. Precede the command you want to execute with sudo, as in

sudo chown -R apple:staff ~apple/*

and enter your password when prompted. In this way, you can run a command that must be executed as the System Administrator (root user) in order to complete successfully.

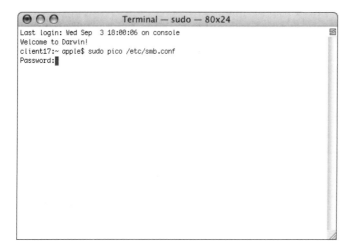

Two commands that you might need to run as root are chown and chmod. Use chown to change the ownership of an item and chmod to change the permissions of an item. These are discussed in the following section.

Changing File Attributes

When you change the ownership or permissions of an item using a command-line interface, the changes are reflected in that item's Info window in the Finder.

Likewise, when you change the permissions in the Info window, the changes can be seen when displaying the item in a command-line interface.

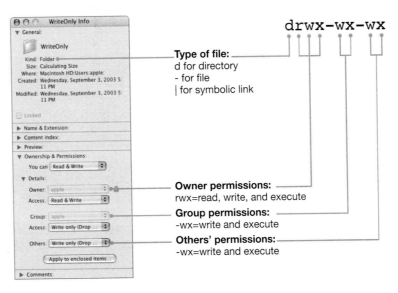

In this figure, the *d* in front of the permissions indicates that the file is a directory. The permissions for the owner, *rwx*, correspond to Read & Write in the Info window for that folder.

The *x*, or execute, permission on a file identifies a program that can be run. For a directory, the execute permission determines whether or not the directory can be searched. To access a file in a directory, you must have search permission for each directory from the root directory down to and including the directory containing the file.

Here are some examples of useful permissions you can set only from the command line:

▶ A user who has *x* but not *r* permission to a directory cannot list the directory's contents, but can access files in it if he or she knows the names of the files.

▶ If the "sticky bit" is set on a directory, along with *w*, anyone can write a file to it, but only the directory owner or a file's owner can remove a file.

The chown (change owner) and chmod (change mode) commands allow you to change the ownership and the permissions associated with one or more files. Use chown to change the owner or group assigned to a file. For example,

chown apple:staff /Users/Shared/ReadMe.rtf

assigns the user apple and the group staff to the file /Users/Shared/ReadMe.rtf. If you own a file, you can reassign the group for that file to another group as long as you are a member of the new group. You cannot, however, change the owner of a file unless you are the System Administrator.

The chmod command

chmod g+w,o-rw /Users/Shared/ReadMe.rtf

adds write permission for members of the group assigned to the file ReadMe.rtf and removes read and write permissions for other users.

Changing Ownership of a File

In this exercise, you will use a command-line interface to change ownership of a file.

1   Log in as Apple Admin.

2   Open Terminal (/Applications/Utilities).

3   Use the touch command to create a file called CMDTest.txt in ~/Documents:

    touch ./Documents/CMDTest.txt

4   At the prompt, use the cd command to navigate to ~/Documents:

    cd ~/Documents

5   Display a long list of the items in that folder:

    ls -l

6   Use the chown command to change the owner of the CMDTest.txt file
    to root:

    sudo chown root CMDTest.txt

    You can change who owns the file and the group that has access to it by
    entering

    owner:group

    after the chown command, where *owner* is the user you are changing owner-
    ship to and *group* is the name of the group you are giving permissions to.

7   When prompted, enter Apple Admin's password.

8   Display a long-format list of the items and verify that the CMDTest.txt file
    is owned by root:

    ls –l

Changing the Permissions of a File

In this exercise, you will use a command-line interface to change the permissions
of a file.

1   While still in Terminal, use the following command to change the permis-
    sions on CMDTest.txt so that group and everyone have no permissions:

    sudo chmod go-r CMDTest.txt

2   If prompted, type the password for the Apple Admin account.

3   Display a long-format list of the items and verify that owner has read and
    write permissions, and group and everyone have none:

    ls –l

4 In TextEdit, choose File > Open to open CMDTest.txt.

An Open Failed error message should appear. This is because the user Apple Admin no longer has read permissions for the file.

5 Using the chmod command, add read and write permissions to group and read permissions to everyone:

sudo chmod g+rw,o+r CMDTest.txt

6 Verify the change:

ls -l

7 Verify that you can now open CMDTest.txt with TextEdit.

8 Quit TextEdit.

Logging In Remotely

The ssh command allows you to log in to a remote computer and execute commands with a secure shell. All communication between the local and remote computer is encrypted when you log in via ssh.

To allow another user to access your computer remotely, you must enable Remote Login using the Services pane of Sharing preferences. Once Remote Login is enabled, a user can connect to your machine using ssh provided he or she knows a user name and password that is defined on your machine. The exact process is beyond the scope of this book.

When you're logged in remotely, the commands you type in that session are sent over the network by ssh and are executed on the remote machine. Remotely logging in to another user's computer is extremely useful for troubleshooting, but be aware that the ssh command can also be used for nefarious purposes. As such, do not enable Remote Login on your own computer unless instructed to do so by your system administrator.

Mac OS X–Specific Commands

Mac OS X systems have some important commands that you won't find on other Unix platforms.

The open command allows you to use the command line to open a file as if you had double-clicked it in the Finder.

The system_profiler command provides command-line access to the same information as the System Profiler application.

The ditto command is a copy command that works with flat files and files with resource forks. To copy a file and its resource forks, type the following command:

ditto -rsrcFork source_file destination_file

CpMac is not installed by default. It is installed as part of the Developer Tools package into the directory /Developer/Tools. It also allows you to copy files with resource forks. You use it like cp.

Additional Mac OS X–specific commands include pbcopy, pbpaste, and softwareupdate. These are located in the directory /usr/bin.

ls -lS ~/Documents | pbcopy

creates a listing on the Clipboard of all of the files in your Documents directory sorted by file size. You could then paste the listing into a TextEdit document or Mail message.

The softwareupdate command allows you to view the list of available updates and to install updates that you specify.

MvMac, GetFileInfo, and SetFile are installed into the directory /Developer/Tools as part of the Developer Tools package. They allow you to manipulate HFS files with resource forks, and to get and set file attributes (such as type and creator) associated with HFS files.

Managing Processes from the Command Line

Instead of using the Activity Monitor, you can determine the currently running processes from the command line using the ps or top commands.

Use top to view a regularly updated view of system utilization, including memory usage, page faults, and the set of currently executing processes.

```
● ● ●                 Terminal — top — 80x24
Processes:  37 total, 2 running, 35 sleeping... 93 threads        14:51:00
Load Avg:  0.20, 0.35, 0.18    CPU usage:  18.6% user, 9.7% sys, 71.7% idle
SharedLibs: num =   92, resident = 19.4M code, 2.34M data, 5.29M LinkEdit
MemRegions: num = 2461, resident = 16.2M + 5.80M private, 24.9M shared
PhysMem:  32.2M wired, 53.2M active, 39.8M inactive,  125M used,  258M free
VM: 1.68G + 58.6M   9998(0) pageins, 0(0) pageouts

  PID COMMAND      %CPU   TIME   #TH #PRTS #MREGS RPRVT  RSHRD  RSIZE  VSIZE
  331 screencapt   0.0% 0:00.08   1    24     33  316K   752K   964K  43.3M
  321 top          7.0% 0:18.85   1    17     26  236K   404K   600K  27.1M
  318 bash         0.0% 0:00.03   1    12     15  152K   848K   744K  18.2M
  317 login        0.0% 0:00.07   1    13     37  140K   396K   492K  26.9M
  316 Terminal     0.8% 0:03.00   3    61    120 1.16M  5.20M  5.14M  89.3M
  313 Finder       0.0% 0:01.72   1    85    118 2.10M  8.25M  8.34M  96.0M
  312 SystemUISe   0.0% 0:00.99   1   165    110  756K  4.84M  4.06M  88.4M
  310 Dock         0.0% 0:00.51   2    70    108  560K  7.18M  2.45M  78.0M
  305 pbs          0.0% 0:00.24   2    32     39  460K  1.11M  1.50M  43.7M
  272 automount    0.0% 0:00.02   2    25     27  228K   828K   916K  28.3M
  270 cupsd        0.0% 0:00.36   1    11     27  372K   880K   872K  28.3M
  266 automount    0.0% 0:00.29   3    70     41  408K   936K  1.23M  29.1M
  260 rpc.lockd    0.0% 0:00.01   1     9     16   84K   360K   140K  17.7M
  251 nfsiod       0.0% 0:00.00   5    29     23  100K   312K   156K  19.6M
  240 mDNSRespon   0.0% 0:00.03   2    39     28  236K   800K   808K  27.3M
  219 crashrepor   0.0% 0:00.00   1    16     18  108K   316K   140K  26.7M
```

In the leftmost column of top's tabular output, you will find the process identifier (PID) associated with that process. You can also use the ps command to determine the PID of a process in order to send that process a message using the kill command. The command

ps -auxww | grep TextEdit

prints the PID and other information for the TextEdit process.

You can send signals from the CLI to running processes requesting actions such as rereading a configuration file, logging additional information, or quitting. For example, with the kill command, you can send a signal to a process with a specified PID. The command

kill -TERM PID

asks the process with the given PID to terminate.

To force-quit a process from the command line, use the kill signal as follows:

kill -KILL PID

The killall command allows you to signal processes using the name of the process rather than the PID. The command

killall -KILL TextEdit

force-quits all processes that belong to you with the name TextEdit.

Monitoring System Usage

Many shell commands exist to help you monitor the system. The last command shows you which users have logged in most recently or when a specified user last logged in to your system.

The id command allows you to determine which groups a particular user has access to or to determine the short name for a user, given their UID.

Mac OS X systems maintain many log files. Viewing log files on your system or on another system using ssh can help you troubleshoot any number of problems. The command

tail -n 10 /Library/Logs/Software\ Update.log

displays the 10 most recently installed software updates. The command

tail -f /var/log/system.log

displays the current contents of the system log, then continues to print new lines as they are added to the file.

Managing Disks and Volumes

You can get all of the functionality available in Disk Utility with two commands accessible from the command-line interface. The first is hdiutil, which handles the image-management functionality. The second is diskutil, which handles the rest of the Disk Utility functionality. You can read man pages to learn how to use the different features, or you can type either command at the command line to read text describing the different options you can use.

You can use the command-line utilities df and du to determine free space and space utilization on a volume. The utility tar can create archives, but note that tar does not preserve resource forks.

Using the Command Line with the Graphical Environment

In Mac OS X, the command line and the graphical user interface work hand-in-hand. You can easily transfer data from one environment to the other and move between the two environments.

You can select a group of files in the Finder and drag them to a Terminal window to add their paths to a command.

The pbcopy and pbpaste commands allows you to copy and paste, respectively, data to and from the Clipboard.

The open command allows you to open files and URLs as if you had double-clicked them in the Finder. For example,

open ~/Documents/ReadMe.rtf

launches TextEdit (or your preferred application for dealing with RTF files) and opens the specified ReadMe.rtf file.

open http://www.apple.com

launches your preferred Web browser (set in Internet preferences) and opens the Apple home page.

Advanced Commands

Use the grep command to search the contents of the listed text file or files. In the example,

grep domain /etc/resolv.conf

the file resolv.conf is searched for the word "domain," and the lines containing that word are displayed.

The process status command, ps, displays information about the processes running on your computer, or on the remote computer if you are logged in remotely. The optional arguments to ps used in the command

ps -auxww

tell ps to list information about all of the processes on your computer in wide format.

The ps command displays the Process ID or PID of a process. Once you know the PID, you can use the kill command to terminate the process.

Often, the output of one command can be used as input for another command. The Unix pipe character (|) is used for this purpose. The command

ps -auxww | grep Finder

executes both the ps and grep commands. The output of the ps command is sent to the grep command as input that searches for the word "Finder" and displays any lines containing that word.

Command-Line Issues

The command line offers a very powerful tool for administering and trouble-shooting a Mac OS X system. Using the command line, however, calls for great attention to detail and involves fewer safety nets than interacting with the system using the graphical user interface.

Things to watch for when using the command line include the following:

▶ Commands like cp and mv, which don't handle files with resource forks correctly.

▶ Shells don't provide an undo feature, and you can't retrieve deleted files from the Trash.

▶ The numeral 0 (zero) and the uppercase letter O, and the numeral 1 (one) and the lowercase letter l often look the same but rarely mean the same thing to a shell.

▶ Spaces in filenames need to be escaped from the shell.

▶ The man pages come in numbered sections. Sometimes you have to specify the command and also the name section number to display the page you want.

▶ Occasionally you might find a man page that is out of date.

What You've Learned

▶ The command line gives you another way to execute commands in Mac OS X.

▶ Interfaces to the command line include console, ssh, single-user mode, and Terminal.

▶ The man pages provide online help.

▶ You can navigate around the file system and move, copy, and rename files from the command line.

▶ You can make changes to file ownership and permissions at a more granular level using a command-line interface.

▶ You can use locate and find to find files.

▶ The last command helps you keep track of user logins.

▶ The id command helps you keep track of user and group IDs.

▶ The tail command helps you view recent activity in a log file.

▶ The command-line interface gives you another way to force-quit applications and processes.

References

The following Knowledge Base articles (located at http://kbase.info.apple.com) will provide you with further information regarding using the command-line interface.

Open Firmware Password

▶   106482, "Setting up Open Firmware Password Protection in Mac OS X 10.1 or later"

Terminal

▶   25591, "Mac OS X 10.3: Terminal Commands That Require Authentication Unlock Other Applications"

▶   61357, "Mac OS X: About Entering Commands in Terminal"

▶   106712, "Troubleshooting Permissions Issues in Mac OS X"

Review Quiz

Use the following questions to review what you have learned:

1.   What are four ways to access the command-line interface in Mac OS X?

2.   What is sudo?

3.   Name some commands that require sudo if you are logged into Mac OS X as an administrator user.

Answers

1.   You can access the command line by logging in as >console, remotely logging in using ssh, putting Mac OS X into single-user mode, or using Terminal.

2.   The sudo command lets you run a command as if you were logged in as a different user.

     Most commonly, sudo is used to run commands as the System Administrator.

3.   The chown and chmod commands require that you used sudo to execute them if you are operating on files or directories that you do not own or have permission to modify.

6

Time

This lesson takes approximately 1 hour, 30 minutes to complete.

Goals

Describe basic networking concepts and terms

Use Network preferences to configure Mac OS X to receive an IP address from a DHCP server, communicate with other computers on the same network, and access network services

Use Internet Connect to connect a Mac OS X computer to connect to remote networks over PPP, PPPoE, or VPN

Use Network Utility and Network preferences to troubleshoot networking issues

Networking Configuration and Troubleshooting

One of the strengths of Mac OS X is its integration with network and Internet services. Network data storage, such as iDisks (one of the benefits of an optional .Mac subscription), can be mounted and accessed just as if it was a local disk drive. iCal and Address Book are able to seamlessly store and retrieve calendar and contact data over the network, allowing the data to be synchronized between multiple computers. With just one click, users can purchase a song online and have it downloaded and added to their iTunes Music Library. However, the key to accessing those services is the correct configuration of network hardware and software.

Network Configuration Applications

When working with Mac OS X 10.3, you will configure network settings using three applications:

▶ Network Setup Assistant—Guides you through configuring Mac OS X for the most common methods of connecting to the Internet. You can launch Network Setup Assistant by clicking the "Assist me" button in Network preferences. This lesson won't discuss the Network Setup Assistant in much detail because its step-by-step interface is self-explanatory.

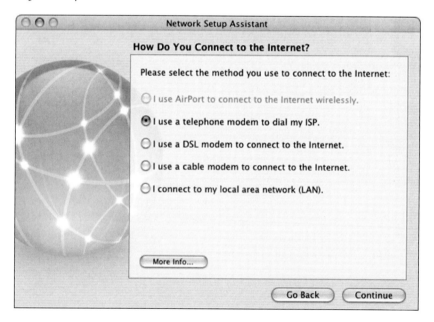

▶ Network preferences—The main utility for configuring the network settings beyond the basic configuration provided by the Network Setup Assistant. As such, this lesson focuses primarily on Network preferences.

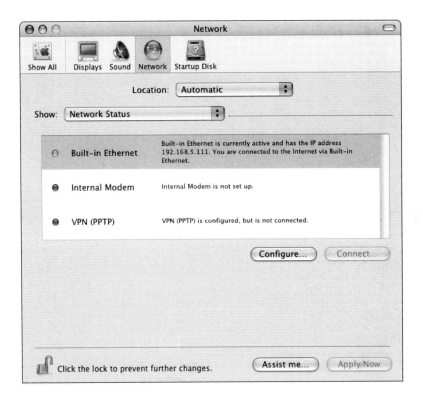

▶ Internet Connect—Establishes connections to remote networks. Most frequently it is used to establish an Internet connection with an Internet service provider (ISP) via Point-to-Point Protocol (PPP) or Point-to-Point Protocol over Ethernet (PPPoE), but it is also used to establish Virtual Private Network (VPN) connections and provide authentication for 802.1X-enabled networks.

You can also import and export Internet Connect configurations. This allows network administrators to create and distribute files that contain network-specific configurations that users can import and use.

Understanding Network Routing

How computers communicate with one another over networks can be difficult
to understand. In order to understand it better, try relating it to the postal
system. In many respects, this system is like a TCP/IP (Transmission Control
Protocol/Internet Protocol) network.

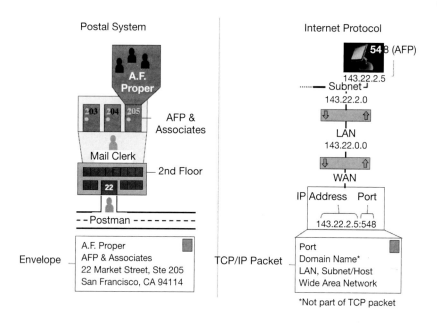

In postal terms, we send information in envelopes. In TCP/IP terms, we send
information in packets. When we address envelopes, it is important that we
include information to get the envelope to its intended recipient; information
such as name, address, city, state, and ZIP code are necessary to get the envelope to its destination. With TCP/IP packets, information such as IP address
and port are required for the packet of information to reach its destination.

For an envelope to travel through the postal system, sorters and deliverers are
required for routing the envelope to its destination. In a similar fashion, a
TCP/IP network uses routers to sort and deliver packets, routing them toward
their destination.

The largest IP networks are made up of smaller networks. Large networks, networks that span a large logical area, are called WANs, or wide area networks. As networks become smaller and more specific to an audience, they are called LANs or local area networks. Finally, these LANs can be divided into subnetworks or subnets.

Routing packets through larger and then smaller networks is like routing an envelope addressed to a business office. The envelope is routed to the destination city, then to the office building, and finally to the floor of the office building where the business has its suite.

A network uses an IP address for its unique identification. The IP address in a TCP/IP packet encodes the information necessary to deliver the packet through the network to the subnet of the recipient. An IPv4 address is a 32-bit number that is divided into four 8-bit parts called octets. These octets can have a value from 0 to 255. An example IP address would be 143.22.2.5.

Normal users need not concern themselves with how to parse an IP address, but administrators should have at least a passing familiarity with the subject. The first octet of an IP address tells you which parts of the IP address identify the network where the recipient resides. Depending on the range of the first octet, an IP address will be labeled with a class (A, B, or C), which then determines if the first; the first and second; or the first, second, and third octets are used to identify the network.

Class	First Octet Range	Network Range	Example
Class A	0–127	First octet	17.0.0.0
Class B	128–191	First and second octet	143.22.0.0
Class C	192–223	First, second, and third octet	220.143.23.0

Those octets that are not used to identify the network are used to identify the destination or host to which the TCP/IP packet is intended. As mentioned previously, a network can be divided into smaller portions called subnets to increase network performance and to make network administration easier. The network can be divided physically (the computers don't use the same networking hardware and wires) or logically (hardware is shared, but software maintains the separation between systems).

The TCP/IP protocol uses subnet masks to isolate the portion of an IP address that pertains to the intended recipient. Exactly how subnet masks work is beyond the scope of this book. Suffice to say, when you are given a subnet mask number by your ISP or system administrator, enter it into the appropriate field in Network preferences, and Mac OS X will manage everything else. In our postal analogy, the subnet mask is like a secret decoder that you place on top of the envelope to hide all addressing information except the recipient's floor and suite number.

Once the envelope reaches the correct floor, the office suite of the business is identified by its suite number, and the envelope is delivered, perhaps after a double-check that the name of the business on the envelope matches the name on the suite door. In the IP world, the office suite number would be the host IP address, and the business name is analogous to the domain name.

One more thing must occur for the envelope to reach its recipient. The business residing in the office suite has many employees. The envelope usually contains the name of the employee for whom it is intended. In the IP world, the IP address merely identifies the host to which the packet is bound. However, on the host, there are many potential recipients called processes. These processes communicate on IP ports. It is the combination of the host IP address and the port number that enables a TCP/IP packet to be delivered to the correct recipient process on the host.

Networking in Mac OS X

Configuring a Macintosh to use a network is rather easy, once you understand the three basic components as far as Mac OS X is concerned: locations, ports, and protocols.

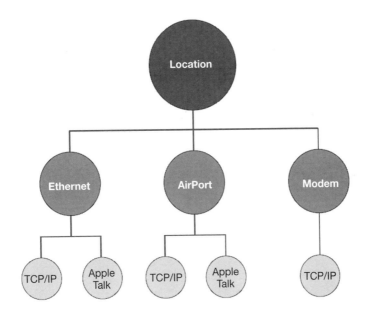

▶ Location—A set of configurations on the local Mac that describes the network ports and the protocols that run on those ports. It is meant primarily as an organizational tool to manage connectivity. Portable computer users frequently connect to the Internet or networks in different ways in different places, so the use of the term "location" reminds you that Mac OS X has the capability to store different sets of network preferences, which you may name for the location in which you use them. For example, you might have one location for your home, another for the office, and yet another for on the road.

▶ Port—A device (such as a network interface card) that serves as a common interface to various other devices within a local area network or as an interface that allows networked computers to connect to an outside network. The most common type of network interface card (NIC) is an Ethernet card, but modems and AirPort Cards are other common types of ports. There are also virtual ports, such as VPN, that don't match up directly to a physical interface. Rather, they route network data out through another port.

These pieces of hardware have a unique identifier called a Media Access Control (MAC) address. These addresses are used in the Media Access Control layer of the network to uniquely identify network ports (different from IP ports). One or more IP addresses may be associated with a single MAC address.

▶ Protocol—A special set of rules that control communication between systems. In Network preferences, you can configure two protocols: TCP/IP and AppleTalk. TCP/IP protocol supports File Transfer Protocol (FTP), Server Message Blocks (SMB), and Apple Filing Protocol (AFP) network connections, whereas AppleTalk is used for AFP and printer connections on the network. Some ports support only certain protocols. For instance, the AppleTalk protocol is not supported over PPP modem connections.

Mac OS X relies primarily upon Network preferences to configure locations, ports, and protocols. A location can have multiple ports, and different locations can contain ports of a similar nature. That is, one computer can have more than one modem configuration to connect to different ISPs or more than one Ethernet card to connect to different subnets.

Checking Network Status

To get a quick overview of the network connection status of your computer, open Network preferences. Then, from the Show pop-up menu, choose Network Status. A quick look at the Network Status pane tells you which ports are active and configured correctly, helping you determine where the problem is if you're experiencing network difficulties.

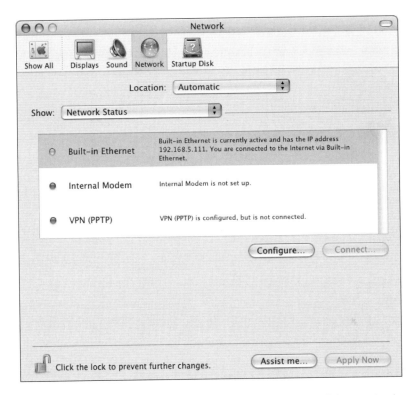

Network Status displays a list of the enabled ports configured for use in the chosen location. Colored indicators show the status of each network port configuration:

▶ Green—The port configuration is active and has been assigned an IP address, either manually or by a DHCP (Dynamic Host Configuration Protocol) server. (See "Using Dynamic IP Addresses" later in this lesson.)

▶ Yellow—The port configuration is active but may not be able to connect to the Internet.

▶ Red—The port configuration is not active.

In addition to these color codes, a message is displayed next to each port describing its configuration status.

The state of network connections is not static. As connections become active (such as when a PowerBook with an AirPort Card moves within range of a base station) or inactive (such as when an Ethernet cable is unplugged), Mac OS X automatically reconfigures and reprioritizes the network settings to reflect the changes. (See "Activating and Prioritizing Network Ports" later in this lesson.)

To go to the pane in Network preferences where you can configure a port, you can select a port and click the Configure button or choose a port from the Show pop-up menu. (See "Configuring Ports" later in this lesson.)

If a port is not connected, select the port and click Connect to launch Internet Connect. For example, if you have configured your modem settings in Network preferences but are not connected, select the modem and click the Connect button in the Network Status pane. When Internet Connect launches, click the modem's Connect button to connect to your ISP.

All network settings, including locations, are system-wide settings. You will need to be authenticated as an administrator in order to make changes. If necessary, you can do so by clicking the lock in the lower-left corner of the Network pane.

Using the Network Status Pane to Monitor Connectivity

To make the most of this lesson, you should have access to a Mac OS X 10.3 computer on a network. Ideally, the network provides Internet access, not just local file and printer sharing services. The exercises in this lesson explain how to set up such a computer, but it's not imperative that you actually do so. You should be able to follow along by reading the step-by-step instructions and examining the screen shots.

The Network Status pane in Network preferences provides a quick overview of the status of each of the enabled network interfaces.

1   Open System Preferences and click Network.

2   Choose Show > Network Status.

The Network Status pane lists each of the enabled network interfaces and the status of each one.

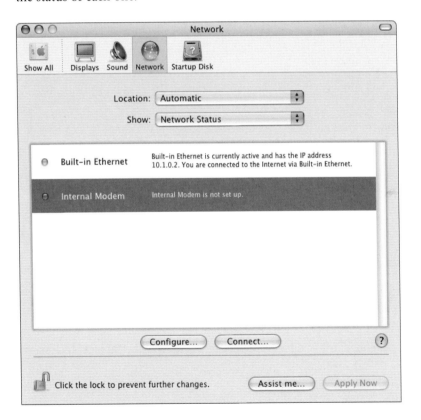

Assuming you are properly connected to an Ethernet network, the indicator next to Built-in Ethernet should be green, indicating that the interface is active and has an IP address assigned to it.

3   Unplug the Ethernet connector from your computer.

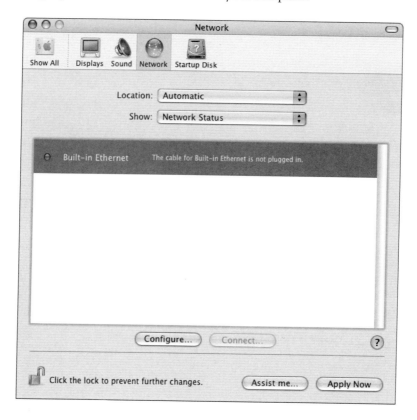

Notice that the indicator in the Network Status pane has changed to red, and the status text states that the cable is not plugged in. You would get the same message if the cable was plugged in, but the cable itself was broken or not plugged into an active port at the other end.

4   Plug the Ethernet connector back into your computer.

Notice that the indicator in the Network Status pane returns to green.

Creating and Choosing Locations

As explained previously in this lesson, a location is merely a way of organizing the configurations of network ports and the protocols that run on those ports. There must be at least one location on your Mac, and you can create as many additional locations as you need using Network preferences.

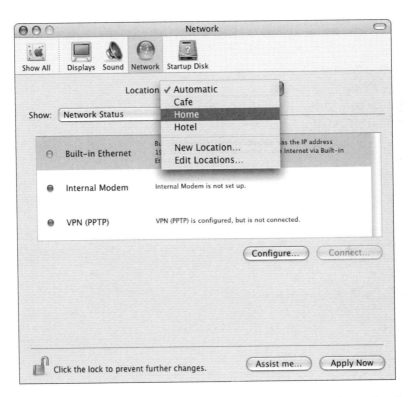

From the Location pop-up menu, you can choose a location with previously configured network settings. You can also use the Location menu to create new locations or edit existing ones. The Automatic location is the default configuration that was created when you went through Network Setup Assistant after installing Mac OS X. By default, all available ports are included and activated in the Automatic location.

To create a new location, choose Location > New Location. Enter a name for the location and click OK. The new location is listed in the Location menu. Changes made in Network preferences apply to whatever location is listed in that menu.

You can also use the Location submenu in the Apple menu to choose a location without having to open Network preferences. The Location submenu also provides an easy way to open Network preferences, where you can change settings directly and manage your locations.

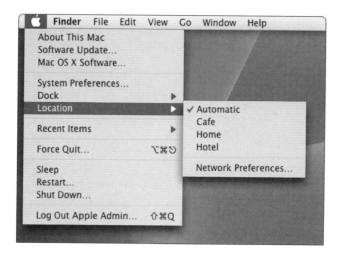

For more information on Locations, refer to Knowledge Base article #106653, "Using Network Locations in Mac OS X."

Managing Ports

You may have a Power Mac G5 fully loaded with ports such as Gigabit Ethernet, AirPort Extreme, Bluetooth, and internal modem, but it can't communicate over a network until you have properly activated and configured at least one of these ports. Fortunately, the Network Setup Assistant takes care of this after installing Mac OS X. But in case you need to alter the default settings, you should know how to manually manage your ports.

Activating and Prioritizing Network Ports

You can manage local network ports in Network preferences by choosing Show > Network Port Configurations.

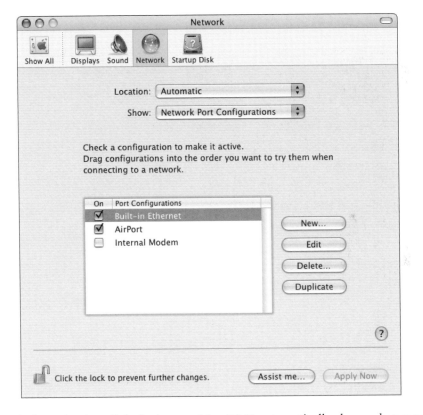

Begin by activating all desired ports. Mac OS X automatically chooses between the active ports in the currently chosen location to maintain the best possible network connection. For example, a single location could contain configurations for AirPort, Ethernet, and modem ports on an iBook. Suppose that iBook was plugged into an Ethernet router in an office that also had an AirPort Base Station and telephone line for the modem. Chances are that the iBook would connect to the network through the Ethernet port because that provides the fastest possible connection. Should someone turn off the router for maintenance, the iBook would switch over to use AirPort instead. Likewise it would fall back to the internal modem if the AirPort signal was lost.

To specify the order in which these ports will be accessed when you are trying to connect to a network, simply drag and drop them into their desired order, then click Apply Now.

The current priority of the ports is displayed in the Network Status pane. As ports become active or inactive, the listing in Network Status is reorganized based upon the status of the ports. The port at the top of the list is the primary port, the one used to access nonlocal networks.

Monitoring Port Prioritization in Network System Preferences

This demonstration is intended to be run on a Mac OS X computer that has been configured to access both an Ethernet and AirPort network. If you don't have such a setup, follow along anyway, but be aware that your results will be different.

1   Open Network preferences.

2   Choose Show > Network Port Configurations.

    Two port configurations are listed: Built-in Ethernet and AirPort.

3   If Built-in Ethernet is not listed first, drag the Built-in Ethernet port configuration entry up in the list until a line at the top of the list appears, and then drop.

    This should rearrange the entries so that Built-in Ethernet is listed first.

4   If you see any other entries, other than Built-in Ethernet and AirPort, turn them off.

5   Click Apply Now.

6   Choose Show > Network Status.

7   Unplug the Ethernet cable.

Built-in Ethernet's status changes to red and AirPort moves to the top of the list (assuming an active wireless network is in range), indicating that it now has highest priority.

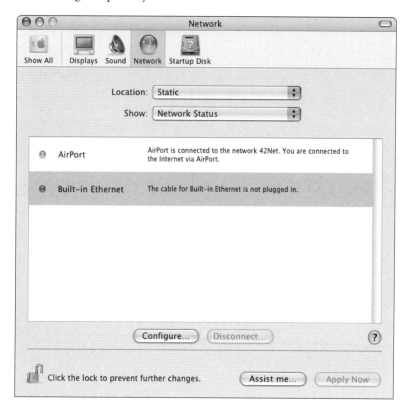

8   Plug the Ethernet cable back in.

Since the Built-in Ethernet is active again, it moves to the top of the list and is now the primary networking port.

Configuring Ports

When a port is activated, it is listed in the Show pop-up menu. Choosing a port from the Show pop-up menu allows you to configure the port. You can configure a single port with different connection information in this configuration pane.

Which Network configuration panes are available depends on which port you choose from the Show menu. When you choose an Ethernet port, five panes are available, although not all must be configured: TCP/IP, PPPoE, AppleTalk, Proxies, and Ethernet. When you choose AirPort, the four panes are TCP/IP, AppleTalk, Proxies, and AirPort. With modems, the available panes are TCP/IP, PPP, Proxies, and Modem. Each of the possible configuration panes is discussed in detail in this section. The configuration panes are designed to be simple enough for normal users to fill out and powerful enough to accommodate the needs of system administrators. Most users need not understand the various settings in these panes, as long as they correctly enter the information provided to them by their ISPs or system administrators. If you encounter an unfamiliar technical term or mysterious setting option, chances are you can safely ignore it.

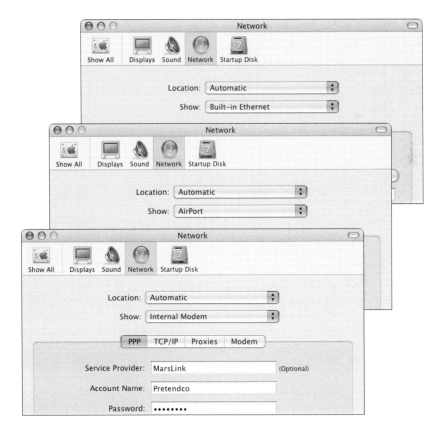

TCP/IP

In the TCP/IP pane, you can configure how the computer obtains IP address information, as well as specify the DNS (domain name system) servers to use.

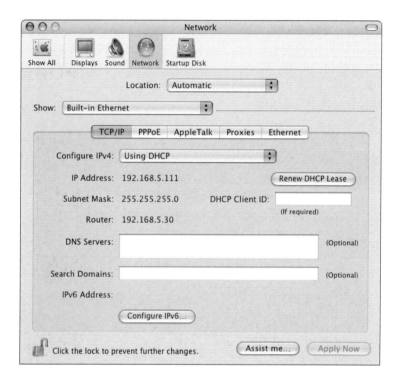

The methods for obtaining and setting the IP address vary depending on the network port.

The Ethernet and AirPort ports provide four configuration methods: Manually, "Using DHCP with manual IP address," Using DHCP, and Using BootP (Bootstrap Protocol). A fifth option, Off, turns the port off.

The Built-in Modem port also provides the Manually configuration method, but instead of the DHCP and BootP methods, it provides Using PPP and AOL Dialup.

The TCP/IP pane has a Configure IPv4 pop-up menu. IPv4 is short for Internet Protocol Version 4. It is the most widely used protocol.

Choosing Configure IPv4 > Manually means that you are assigning this computer a static IP address. (See "Using Static IP Addresses" later in this lesson.) You will need to enter the IP address, as well as subnet mask, router, and DNS information in the appropriate fields.

For networks where a DHCP server is used, choose either Using DHCP or "Using DHCP with manual IP address." The DHCP server assigns unique addresses from a range of available addresses, alleviating the need to assign one for each computer manually. The router (gateway) address, the DNS server addresses, and the subnet mask can also be assigned by the DHCP server. The administrator decides how much information is supplied by the DHCP server and how much is supplied by the user.

If you choose Using BootP, Mac OS X will obtain an IP address from a BootP server, similar to receiving an address from a DHCP server. However, unlike when using DHCP, a computer set to use BootP will receive the same address each time it requests one. BootP is rarely used, except for some managed networks.

When configuring TCP/IP for a modem port, the DHCP and BootP selections are not available. Instead, the PPP and AOL Dialup options are provided to use dynamic IP addresses provided by an ISP.

Always double-check the TCP/IP settings. After making changes, check to see if you can use a Web browser to access an external Web page or if you can access a file server. (Accessing file servers is covered in Lesson 7.)

IPv6 Support

In addition to supporting IPv4, Mac OS X natively supports Internet Protocol Version 6 (IPv6), the next generation protocol for the Internet.

IPv6 is a new protocol designed by the Internet Engineering Task Force (IETF) to replace the aging IPv4 protocol. The two protocols will coexist until IPv6 eventually replaces IPv4.

IPv6 addresses some of the limitations of IPv4, such as address size. The address size increases from 32 bits (current IPv4 standard) to 128 bits. Also, IPv6 improves the process of routing and network autoconfiguration.

By default, IPv6 is configured automatically in Mac OS X. However, if you need to configure IPv6 manually, click Configure IPv6 in the TCP/IP pane in Network preferences; choose Configure IPv6 > Manually; and enter the IPv6 address, router address, and prefix length that your system administrator supplied.

Using Static IP Addresses

One way to provide a device with an IP address is to manually configure it. In Mac OS X, for example, you use Network preferences to enter a static (or unchanging) IP address.

Static IP Address: 10.0.1.3   Static IP Address: 10.0.1.4

Setting a New Location with a Static IP Address

This exercise demonstrates how you configure a location that uses a static IP address. If you have a working network connection already, following these steps will disrupt your connection, so you may prefer simply to read along.

1   In Network preferences, note the name of your current location, then choose Location > New Location.

    A configuration sheet appears, asking you to name your new location.

2 Enter the name *Static* and click OK.

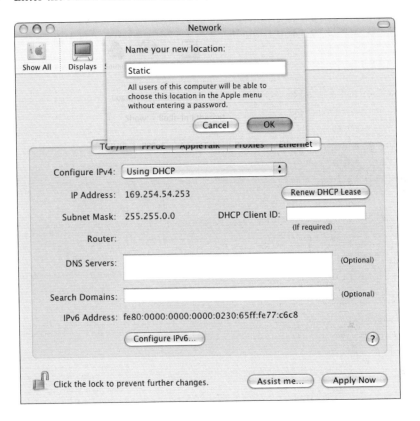

3 Choose Show > Network Port Configurations, then disable all network ports other than Built-in Ethernet.

4 Click Apply Now.

5 Choose Show > Built-in Ethernet.

6 Choose Configure IPv4 > Manually.

7 Enter the necessary information into the following fields:

  ▶ IP Address

  ▶ Subnet Mask

  ▶ Router

  ▶ DNS Servers

  ▶ Search Domains

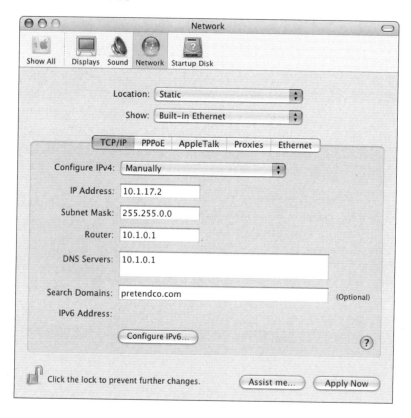

8 Click Apply Now, then choose Show > Network Status.

Mac OS X attempts to connect to the network using the settings entered in the previous step. If any of them are incorrect, Built-in Ethernet will not have a green light in the Network Status pane.

9   From the Location menu, choose your original setting noted in step 1 and then click Apply Now to restore your network connection.

Using Dynamic IP Addresses

Instead of manually entering a static IP address, a computer can be assigned a dynamic (or changing) IP address either by a Dynamic Host Configuration Protocol (DHCP) server or through Apple's Rendezvous, a feature that automatically configures and detects certain services that you can use on your local network, such as printers, iChat, and various types of sharing.

As you saw in the previous exercise, there are many different settings that must be entered in order to connect a host to a network. This configuration can become tedious and time consuming to administer, especially for mobile hosts. For this reason, DHCP was created to simplify the configuration of hosts. It allows the dynamic assignment of configuration information as hosts come on the network.

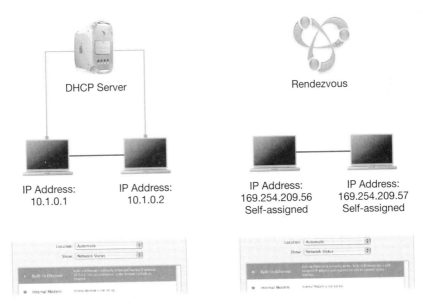

DHCP servers provide a unique IP address to each device on the network. The DHCP server can be something as big and powerful as a computer running special software such as Mac OS X Server or as small and simple as a wireless router with built-in DHCP capabilities.

DHCP servers work well, but sometimes you need to connect devices together on a network where a DHCP server isn't available. For example, you and a friend might have AirPort-equipped PowerBooks and just want to exchange some files. In cases where you don't have a DHCP server on your network, devices and Mac OS X computers on your network use the built-in Rendezvous protocol to configure self-assigned IP addresses automatically with no manual intervention.

On Mac OS X 10.3, the Network Status pane indicates when a computer is using a self-assigned address instead of receiving an address from a DHCP server. Self-assigned addresses begin with 169.254 and are known as link-local addresses. The link-local address corresponds with the Rendezvous name of the computer, which always ends in ".local". You set the Rendezvous name in Sharing preferences.

Understanding DNS Servers

Names are easier for humans to remember and relate to than numbers. If a business were to refer to itself by its business license number or the suite number on its door, people would have a hard time remembering or relating the number to the products or services of that business. For this reason, businesses usually identify themselves with a simple descriptive name such as Apple Computer.

Likewise, when setting up shop on the Internet, businesses usually choose a similar domain name that's easy for humans to remember such as apple.com. Although the domain name is all a Web surfer must remember to visit a site, it's actually associated with a numeric IP address, and, by extension, with a host. The system of mapping domain names to IP addresses is called the domain name system (DNS). Dedicated hosts that provide DNS services are called DNS servers. If DHCP doesn't configure your DNS servers automatically, you must manually enter the IP addresses of the DNS servers you wish to use, otherwise you will not be able to surf the Web using alphanumeric URLs. Your ISP or system administrator should be able to provide you with the appropriate DNS server addresses to enter in this field.

PPP

In the PPP pane, you enter the phone numbers and PPP login information for your dial-up connection. This information is normally included with the configuration information from your ISP. You can configure several modem ports, each with unique dial-up and IP address configurations.

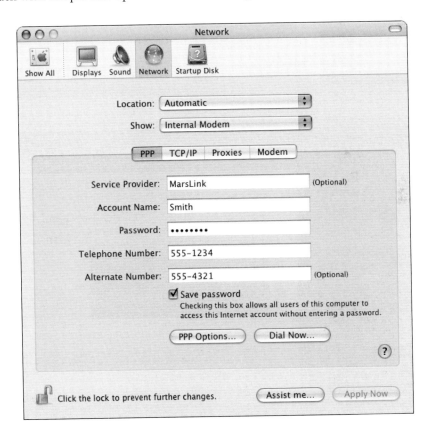

Click PPP Options if you want to configure PPP to connect automatically when starting a TCP/IP application such as a Web browser or mail application. You can also connect using a Terminal window for a command-line interface.

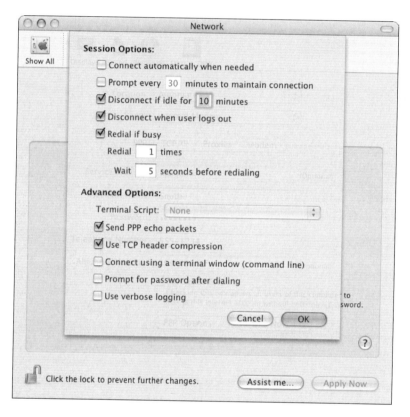

You may not want to enable "Connect automatically when needed." Many daemons and background services running in BSD may trigger an automatic connection, whether you want one or not.

If PPP is configured to not connect automatically, you can establish a connection manually by choosing Modem Status > Connect or by clicking Connect in the Internet Connect utility.

In the Modem pane, you choose the type of modem your computer uses and set the preferences for it. A long list of modems is included, but to use the internal modem provided in most Macintosh computers, choose Internal Modem. You can opt to display the modem status in the menu bar.

> **NOTE** ▶ If you choose AOL Dialup in the TCP/IP pane, the options in the PPP and Modem panes are inactive because connection and modem configuration is handled through AOL's own software.

PPPoE

If you are using an Ethernet connection to a digital subscriber line (DSL) modem, PPPoE may be required by your ISP. With an Ethernet port chosen in the Show pop-up menu, configure the account name and password in the PPPoE pane. You can also choose to display the PPPoE status in the menu bar.

You can configure additional PPPoE options by clicking the PPPoE Options button.

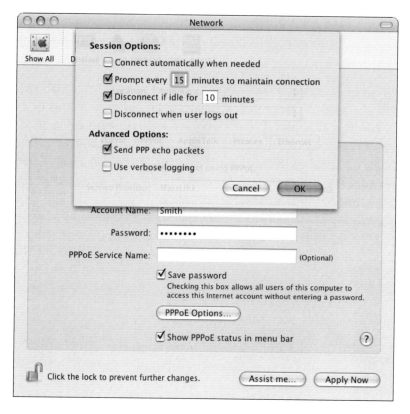

Just as with PPP, you can use Internet Connect to establish the connection to the ISP as well as enter the account information.

NOTE ▶ When PPPoE is configured on the Ethernet port, AppleTalk is disabled.

AppleTalk

The default network protocol in Mac OS X is TCP/IP. AppleTalk is disabled by default, but you may enable it to support AppleTalk printers and peer-to-peer networking on an AppleTalk network. Although AppleTalk was used extensively in Mac OS 9.*x* and earlier, TCP/IP is preferred because it is nonproprietary and works with non–Macintosh computers. However, TCP/IP and AppleTalk are not exclusive and can be active at the same time.

You can configure the AppleTalk protocol for an Ethernet or AirPort network port in the AppleTalk pane. The AppleTalk computer name is listed, and you can choose the AppleTalk zone if one is available. You can also configure the AppleTalk node ID and network ID manually, using the Configure pop-up menu. AppleTalk can be used for AFP connections (peer-to-peer file sharing) or network printer connections.

> **NOTE ▶** AppleTalk can be enabled on only one port at a time. If you attempt to enable AppleTalk on a second port, AppleTalk will be disabled automatically on the first port.

Configuring AppleTalk over Ethernet

This exercise will enable AppleTalk on the network so that you can access servers using the AppleTalk protocol.

1   Open Network preferences.

2   Choose Show > Built-in Ethernet.

3   Click the AppleTalk button.

4   Select Make AppleTalk Active.

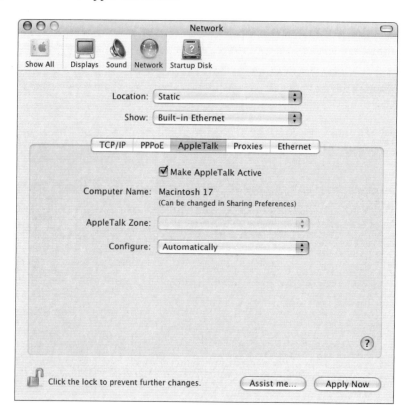

5   Choose Configure > Automatically.

6   Click Apply Now.

7   Quit System Preferences.

Proxies

All network port configurations have a Proxies pane. In this pane, you can configure Mac OS X to use any proxy servers that might be required by your network administrator. A proxy server is a host computer that acts as an intermediary between a client computer and the Internet. In this way, an enterprise can ensure security by limiting access and can provide administrative control and caching services. Just as enterprises use firewalls when they want to restrict what comes into their network, they use proxy servers when they want to restrict what goes out from their network. For example, a proxy server could block all Web surfing or selected sites.

In a proxy configuration, requests for information—such as Web pages or lists of files—are sent to the proxy server. The proxy server checks the request against a database of restricted servers and, if approved, forwards that request to the server that has the information you are requesting. When the request is answered, the proxy server receives the information, checks it against a database of restricted content, or caches the content for later use and passes it on to the requesting computer.

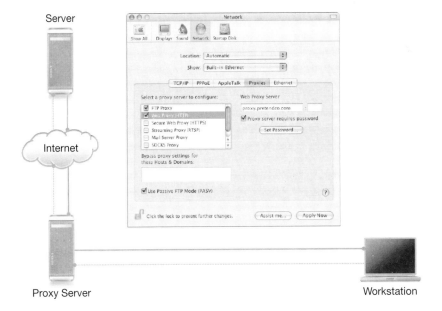

Proxies can be configured for file transfers using FTP, Gopher, the SOCKS Firewall protocol (which checks information while hiding the IP address of the client), the Real Time Streaming Protocol (RTSP) media streaming protocol (such as QuickTime streaming servers), Secure Web, or HyperText Transfer Protocol (HTTP).

You can safely ignore the Proxies pane unless specifically instructed to configure it by your network administrator. In the Proxies pane, you select the checkboxes for the type of proxy servers to use. Once the proxy server is enabled, you specify the address of the proxy server. You can also specify a user name and password to use if a proxy server requires one for security reasons.

In the Proxies pane, you can also configure FTP to use passive mode, which allows the client computer to make the data connection rather than the FTP server. You can also configure domains that you want the proxy servers to ignore.

Ethernet

In most cases, Mac OS X will correctly configure the Ethernet port to match the network configuration. However, in some cases, you may be required to manually override these settings. When you choose Manually (Advanced) from the Configure pop-up menu in the Ethernet pane in Network preferences, you can specify the speed, duplex, and packet size used when communicating via the Ethernet port.

> **NOTE ▶** You should only change these settings if instructed to do so by your network administrator. Incorrect settings can not only prevent your computer from communicating on the network but can also confuse network devices and prevent other computers from using the network.

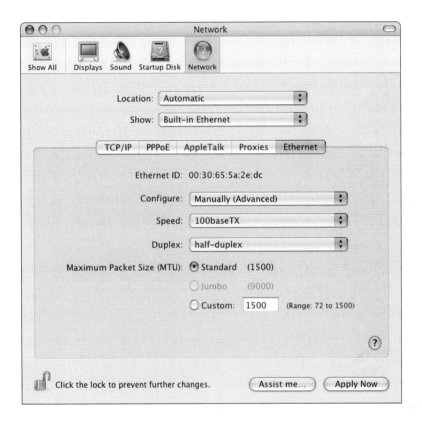

Configuring Virtual Private Networks

Mac OS X supports VPN technology, which lets IP traffic travel securely over a public TCP/IP network using "tunneling" to encrypt data between the client system and host network.

Mac OS X supports two VPN protocols over an existing Internet connection: Point-to-Point Tunneling Protocol (PPTP) and Layer Two Tunneling Protocol (L2TP) over IP Security (IPSec).

The PPTP protocol supports client-to-gateway and network-to-network connections. L2TP over IPSec supports network-to-network connections only and offers strong authentication using IPSec, Microsoft Challenge-Handshake Authentication Protocol (CHAP), or third-party solutions such as SecureID.

Use Internet Connect to connect to a VPN server that implements the L2TP and PPTP standards, such as the VPN server that comes with Mac OS X Server 10.3.

If the VPN server you want to connect to does not implement the L2TP and PPTP standards, you'll need to configure the appropriate TCP/IP settings in Network preferences and use a special VPN client software to connect to the network.

To configure your computer to connect to a virtual private network (VPN) follow these steps:

1   Obtain the VPN configuration and connection setting from your system administrator.

2   Configure VPN connection settings in Internet Connect.

3   Configure the TCP/IP and Proxies VPN settings in the VPN pane of
    Network preferences, using information from your system administrator.

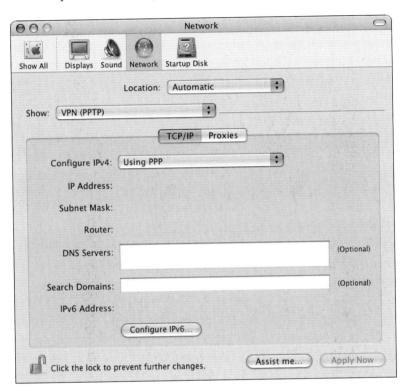

Configuring 802.1X

The Institute of Electrical and Electronics Engineers (IEEE) 802.1X standard is
intended to enhance network security by requiring a user to authenticate himself
or herself before accessing a network. Currently, 802.1X is primarily used with
wireless networks; however, it can also be implemented on a wired network.

When a user attempts to access a network through an access point, such as an AirPort Base Station or an Ethernet switch that has 802.1X enabled, the user must provide identity information that the access point forwards to an authentication server. If the authentication server is able to validate the user, the access point allows normal access to the network.

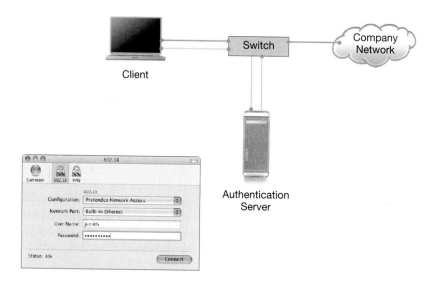

Your network administrator provides a user name and password that you enter in the 802.1X pane in Internet Connect. If required, you can create multiple configurations, each with unique user information, allowing the computer to connect to different networks.

Troubleshooting Network Issues

When troubleshooting networking issues, the first step is to determine if the problem is caused by misconfiguration of the computer or if the network or network services are not working correctly.

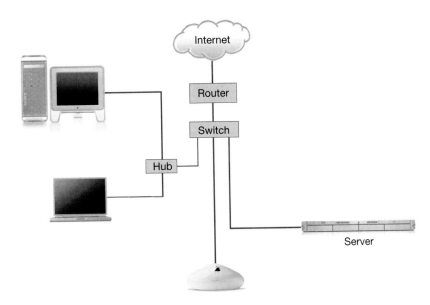

Check to make sure the settings in Network preferences are set correctly. The Network Status pane provides an overview of the enabled and active port configurations, allowing you to quickly determine which one is having problems. Check to make sure the port configurations are enabled and are configured correctly.

Next, you should be familiar with the physical topology of your network. Any computer, cable, hub, switch, or router can be a point of failure. When troubleshooting a network, try to isolate the problem by eliminating points of failure. If a computer can reach other computers through switches and hubs, that indicates that the physical network is functioning properly. If not, try to work backwards and see if you can reach computers on the same subnet. If not, check your Ethernet cable, and then your Ethernet card to make sure they're functioning properly.

Using Network Utility

If you have trouble accessing the network, double-check that all the information you entered earlier in Network preferences is correct. Verify that you have a valid IP address and subnet mask and that the DNS Servers entry is correct. Note that an IP address starting with 169.254 is a self-assigned link-local address that allows you to communicate with other computers on your local network only, but not with outside networks and the Internet at large.

With Network Utility (/Applications/Utilities), you can view network information and test basic network connectivity by using commands such as Ping, Traceroute, or Lookup. Because Network Utility uses BSD tools, the BSD Subsystem must be installed. (It is installed by default.)

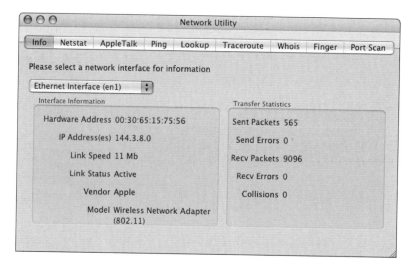

The rest of this lesson will consider the troubleshooting commands Ping, Traceroute, Lookup, and Port Scan. Network Utility has four other tools that are not necessarily concerned with troubleshooting:

▶ Netstat—An advanced command that system administrators use to monitor the network activity of their machines and the network.

▶ AppleTalk—Provides details and statistics for local and network AppleTalk configurations.

▶ Whois—Used to find out the registrant of a particular domain name.

▶ Finger—Used to get information about users on Unix-based machines.

Identifying the MAC Address Using Network Utility

The following steps will help you identify the MAC address of your machine. The MAC address, also known as the hardware address, can come in handy when setting up network services. For example, an AirPort Base Station can allow access only to a predetermined list of MAC addresses.

1   Open Network Utility (/Applications/Utilities).

2   Click Info.

3   Choose "Ethernet Interface (en0)" from the pop-up menu.

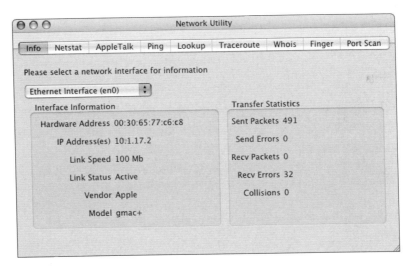

Identify the MAC address (Hardware Address) as well as your IP address for the built-in Ethernet Interface.

Identifying the MAC Address Using System Profiler

Here you will use System Profiler to retrieve the MAC address information.

1 Open System Profiler (/Applications/Utilities).

2 Select Network from the Contents pane on the left.

The upper-right pane lists each of the available network interface configurations. Currently, at least Built-in Ethernet should be available.

3 Select Built-in Ethernet from the list of configurations.

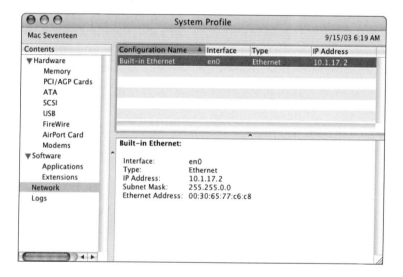

The pane beneath the configuration list provides details about the selected configuration.

4 Compare the values for Ethernet address and the IP address displayed in System Profiler to those obtained using Network Utility. They should be the same.

5 Quit System Profiler.

Ping

Ping, one of the tools in Network Utility, sends packets to the network interface of a computer on an IP network to see if the computer responds or echoes. If all the signals time out, the computer might be disconnected from the Internet or at least be unreachable from your computer.

Ping can be used to isolate a networking problem. Try pinging a server using its IP address. If that works, you've established that the server is up and your computer is able to reach it via the network. Use Ping with the server's domain name to find out if DNS is working correctly.

If you are unable to ping a server, try pinging another computer that is nearby (accessible through as few network devices such as routers as possible) to determine if the problem is with your local network or router settings. If this works, check to make sure the router entry in Network preferences is set correctly. See if the other computer is able to ping the same server.

Determining System Accessibility on an IP Network

This exercise walks you through the steps required to determine whether a machine is reachable on a given IP network. It assumes that your computer is properly configured for Internet access.

1   Open Network Utility.

2   Click Ping.

3   In the "Please enter the network address to ping" field, type *www.apple.com.*

4   Select Send only and set it to 2 pings.

5   Click Ping.

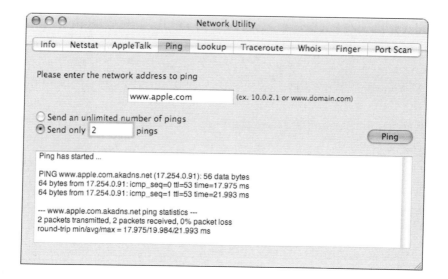

You should see information regarding the packets returned by Apple's server.

6   Scroll to the end of the results list.

7   Record the min/avg/max round-trip latency times that give you an indication as to how long it took for the server to respond, in milliseconds.

8   In the "Please enter the network address to ping" field, type *www.apple.com.au*, which is Apple's Australian server.

9   Click Ping.

If you are physically closer to Apple's main server in the United States, it shouldn't surprise you that the latency times are higher for Apple's Australian server.

Looking Up Internet Addresses

At times you want to make sure that you are accessing a valid DNS server or determine the IP address for a given domain name. You can query the DNS server with nslookup and dig, two more commands found in Network Utility.

Use nslookup (the default) to convert numerical IP addresses to domain names. You'll find that using nslookup will provide easier-to-read results than dig will when trying to convert a domain name into a numerical IP address, but the results may not always be accurate. Although dig provides a more complex response, its output is considered more accurate. You can also specify which information to look up such as the mail records in the DNS server and so on.

Using Lookup to Verify DNS Is Set Properly

Here you will use the Lookup tool and nslookup in Network Utility to compare known IP addresses to their domain names.

1   In Network Utility, click the Lookup button.

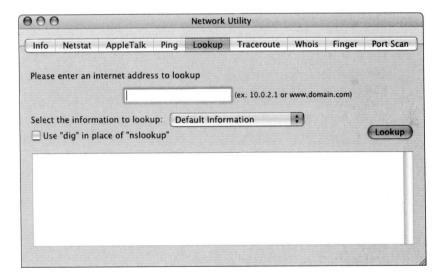

2   Enter Apple's domain:

www.apple.com

3   Deselect "Use 'dig' in place of 'nslookup.'"

4   Click Lookup.

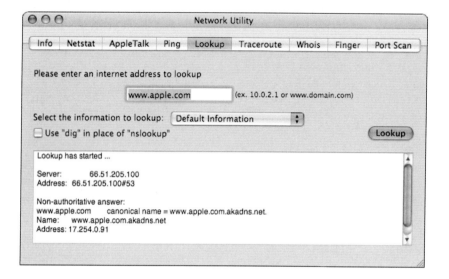

You should see the IP address for Apple in the lower window.

DNS also keeps track of mail records and aliases. You can get this information by choosing the different types of options from the "Select the information to lookup" pop-up menu.

Tracing Routes

The Traceroute command in Network Utility traces the route through an IP network from your computer to the destination computer and shows the hop count, the number of trips a packet took from one router or network device to another to make the journey. This information is useful in determining where network delays are occurring.

The output should look like the following:

```
traceroute to yahoo.com (66.218.71.198), 30 hops max, 40 byte packets

1 gweb.icg-sj.com (192.168.5.30) 4.693 ms 3.96 ms 0.547 ms

2 64.133.108.129 (64.133.108.129) 44.557 ms 45.87 ms 42.215 ms

3 63.169.238.193 (63.169.238.193) 47.455 ms 44.088 ms 42.073 ms
```

Each line represents a network hop on the way to the destination. The numbers on the beginning of the lines indicate the order in which the hops were traversed. The time in milliseconds (ms) indicates the time it took for the network device to respond.

Using Traceroute to Record the Path Between Two Systems

This exercise walks you through the process of determining the path between two networked systems.

1 In Network Utility, click the Traceroute button.

2 In the network address field, type the IP address for Apple's Web site:

   66.51.205.100

3 Click Trace.

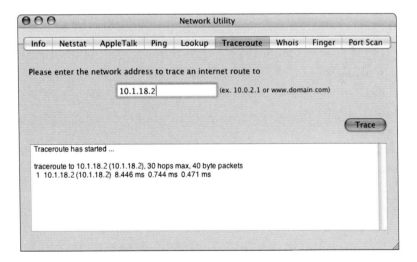

Network Utility shows you how many hops it takes for your packet to get to Apple's Web server. If you are using a firewall, it's possible that all you will see are asterisks. In that case, try using the IP address of another computer on your local network, if you have one. In that case, you should see only one hop since it takes only one hop for the packet to reach the other computer.

Scanning Ports

Port Scan is mainly used for security reasons. However, it can also be useful in troubleshooting. For example, if you are trying to connect to a Web server without success, you can scan the open ports on the Web server and ensure that the machine is running and, more importantly, that port 80, the HTTP port, is open. You can also do this with the FTP ports when trying to connect to an FTP server or the NFS (Network File System) port, and so on.

The output of Port Scan should look something like the following:

Port Scanning host: 192.168.5.30

Open Port: 21 ftp

Open Port: 139 netbios-ssn

Open Port: 427 svrloc

Open Port: 515 printer, spooler

Open Port: 548 afpovertcp

Open Port: 660

If Port Scan recognizes the use of the port, it will tell you what the port is being used for. The preceding example shows that port 21 is being used for FTP.

> **NOTE** ▶ Port Scan may look like a port attack to a system administrator. Do not use it on other people's machines without first notifying the system administrator. If you don't, you may find yourself the recipient of a visit from your company security department even though you were using the command for troubleshooting purposes.

Determining the Open Ports on a System Connected to the Network

In this exercise, you will use Port Scan to determine the open ports on a computer. You will need two Macintosh computers on the same local network.

1   On one computer, open Sharing preferences.

2   Click Services.

3   Note which services, if any, are already turned on.

4   Turn on all services.

5   Note the computer's local subnet address at the top of the window.

6   On the other computer, open Network Utility.

7   Click the Port Scan button.

8   In the IP address field, enter the other computer's local subnet address noted in step 5.

9   Click Scan.

This scan may take a few minutes.

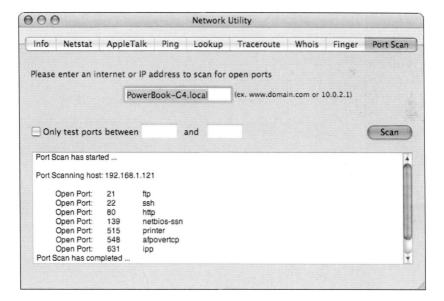

10 Review the ports that are open.

Port 21 is the FTP port, so if you want to test whether a machine is running an FTP server, you can run Port Scan on it and test whether port 21 is open or not. HTTP uses port 80, and HTTPS uses port 443.

NOTE ▶ You cannot scan the open ports on the system that you are using. You have to use Netstat to identify the open ports on your current system.

11 Quit Network Utility.

12 On the other computer, turn off all services that weren't originally on in Sharing preferences.

13 Quit System Preferences.

What You've Learned

▶ You need to understand the basics of IP networking to be able to configure and troubleshoot IP networks.

▶ In Mac OS X, simple networking configuration is done with the Network Setup Assistant, and additional configuration is done in Network preferences.

▶ You can configure different locations with different ports, configure TCP/IP settings for each of your different ports, enable AppleTalk, and configure proxies.

▶ To effectively troubleshoot your IP network, you need to be familiar with the network topology.

▶ Mac OS X provides you with a set of network tools that can aid you in troubleshooting. These tools (Ping, Lookup, Traceroute, and Port Scan) are in Network Utility.

References
The following Knowledge Base articles (located at http://kbase.info.apple.com) will provide you with further information regarding network configuration in Mac OS X.

Cable Modem/DSL/LAN

▶ 106747, "Mac OS X: Troubleshooting a PPPoE Internet Connection"

▶ 106749, "Mac OS X: Troubleshooting a Cable Modem, DSL, or LAN Internet Connection"

Dial-Up/PPP

▶ 106748, "Mac OS X: Troubleshooting a Dial-Up/PPP Internet Connection"

Internet and Networking

▶ 25270, "Mac OS X: Do Not Use Leading Zeros in IP Address"

▶ 106260, "Mac OS X: Computer Name Does Not Appear on Network"

▶ 106439, "'Well Known TCP and UDP Ports Used By Apple Software Products"

▶ 106796, "Mac OS X: Internet and Network Topics (Getting Connected, Troubleshooting)"

▶ 106797, "Mac OS X: Slow Startup, Pauses at 'Initializing Network' or 'Configuring Network Time'"

▶ 106653, "Using Network Locations in Mac OS X"

Network Utility

▶ 61426, "Mac OS X: About Network Utility"

Modem

▶ 24803, "Troubleshooting Phone Line Issues That Affect Modem Connections"

▶ 106446, "Mac OS X: Apple System Profiler Modem Information Incorrect or Missing"

▶ 106447, "Mac OS X: How to Gather Modem Troubleshooting Information"

Review Quiz

Use the following questions to review what you have learned:

1.   Where do you go to configure network settings?

2.   What is the difference between static and dynamic IP addressing?

3.   What is 802.1X?

4.   List four tools in Network Utility that are used for troubleshooting.

5.   How does Ping work?

6.   What does Traceroute do and what is it useful for?

7.   How can you use Port Scan for troubleshooting?

8.   What three quick fixes should you consider for troubleshooting a network problem?

Answers

1.   You can perform basic network configuration by using the Network Setup Assistant. You can use Network preferences for additional or advanced configuration. Use Internet Connect for configuration and connection to remote networks through PPP, PPPoE, and VPN.

2.   Static IP addresses are those that are manually set in Network preferences. The computer always uses the same address.

      Dynamic addresses are those that are either assigned by a DHCP server, or when a DHCP server is unavailable, created by the computer. Unlike static addresses, a dynamic address is not permanent and will change.

3.   802.1X is a standard that requires a user to authenticate before the computer is able to access the network. 802.1X configuration is done in Internet Connect.

4.   Port Scan, Ping, Lookup, and Traceroute aid in troubleshooting.

5.   Ping sends signals to another computer on the Internet to see if that computer echoes.

6. Traceroute traces the route through the Internet from your computer to the destination computer and shows the number of hops needed to make the journey. This is useful in determining where any network delays are occurring.

7. You can use Port Scan to determine if certain ports that should be open are in fact open.

8. Verify/adjust settings in Network preferences; familiarize yourself with topology; use Network Utility.

7

Time This lesson takes approximately 1 hour to complete.

Goals Describe how service discovery is implemented in Mac OS X

Configure Mac OS X using Directory Access to access network services via AppleTalk, SMB, SLP, NetInfo, and Rendezvous

Use the Finder to mount remote AFP, SMB, WebDAV, FTP, and NFS volumes so that files can be transferred between the local system and the server volume

Configure Mac OS X clients to bind to Network Directory hosted on Mac OS X Server

Use System Preferences to automatically mount a designated shared volume on login

Use Directory Access to configure Mac OS X to authenticate users using an LDAP or Active Directory server

Troubleshoot a Mac OS X computer that is not able to access a directory service parent

Configure Mac OS X to use single sign-on for network services

Troubleshoot single sign-on issues by verifying the Kerberos ticket

Lesson **7**
Accessing Network Services

To access a service on another computer on your network, you must find the service, make the connection, and prove your identity.

In the past, finding out where to connect was often haphazard and inefficient. Users had to get information from their system administrators or from other users, store it somewhere, then remember where they stored the information when they wanted to connect. Today, computer software does most of that work for you, especially on Mac OS X. Most of the time, you can browse a list of available servers.

Connecting to a service is also easy on Mac OS X. In most cases, you just select from the list and click. In a few cases, you might have to type a computer name or address.

Most network services require that you prove your identity, typically by providing a password. Mac OS X helps you manage your passwords so that you don't have to type them over and over again, and it uses modern security methods to protect computers against unauthorized access.

Discovering Services

Mac OS X has the capability to find computers and other devices that are offering services on the network. This feature is known as service discovery. These resources can be browsed by user-friendly names.

Service discovery is a component of Open Directory, a core Mac OS X feature that allows computers to obtain important configuration information locally or over the network. Open Directory can discover network services that make their existence and whereabouts known. Services make themselves known by means of standard service discovery protocols.

One application that uses service discovery information is the Finder, which displays a list of computers you can connect to when you click Network in the Sidebar at the left of the Finder window. Using the Finder window to connect to shared resources is useful when you want to browse what is available on the network and find resources by common names.

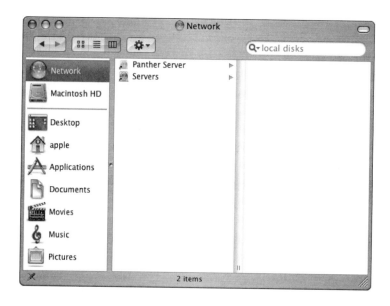

Another application that uses service discovery is Printer Setup Utility (/Applications/Utilities), which displays a list of shared printers in the Printer List window. Once a shared printer is discovered, you select and configure it.

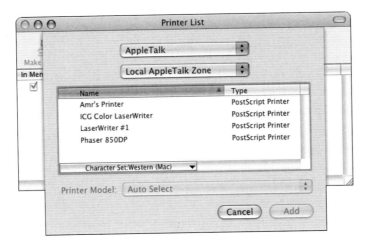

Connecting to a Volume from a Finder Window

These steps will lead you through the process of using the Finder to connect to a volume on a discovered server. This exercise assumes that your Mac is on a network with at least one shared volume. (Have another user enable Personal File Sharing in Sharing preferences on his or her Mac.)

1   Open a Finder window in column view and click Network in the Sidebar at the left of the window.

A list of file servers appears in the second column from the left.

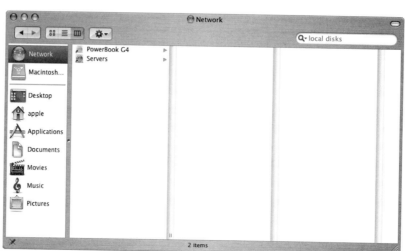

NOTE ▶ You can accomplish the same thing by choosing Go > Connect to Server (Cmd-K) and then clicking Browse.

2   Select the name of a file server.

An icon of the file server appears in the third column from the left.

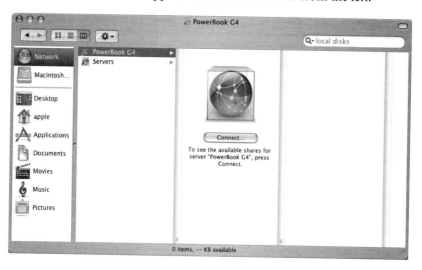

3 Click Connect (or double-click the name of the file server).

4 When prompted, specify that you want to connect as a registered user, then enter a user name and password for an account on the remote server.

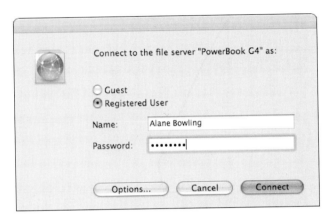

5 Click Connect.

A list of shared volumes to which you have access appears.

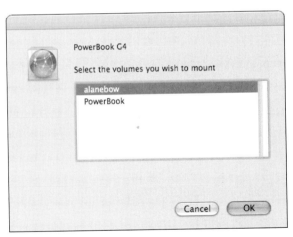

6   Select the volumes you wish to mount (Shift-click to select more than one), then click OK.

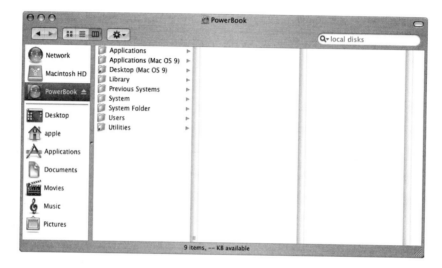

The shared volumes appear in the Sidebar in the Finder and can be used just like any other volume. Furthermore, the shared volumes appear on your desktop if Finder Preferences are set to show connected servers on your desktop.

Exchanging Files with a Shared Volume

In this exercise, you will use the Finder to exchange files with the shared volume you mounted in the previous exercise.

1   In the Sidebar at the left of the Finder window, select a shared volume and view its contents.

2   Select a small file on the shared volume and drag it to your desktop.

3   Change the name of the copied file on your desktop.

4   Select the renamed file on your desktop and drag it back to the shared volume.

5   If a dialog informs you that you do not have permission to see the results, click OK.

6   Unmount the shared volume by selecting it and then choosing File > Eject (Cmd-E).

Methods of Service Discovery

Mac OS X can display available services in two general ways:

▶   Querying a static directory of services

▶   Using a dynamic service discovery protocol

When using a static directory, Mac OS X queries a network server for a list of services that the server knows about. They are called static because the server has to be explicitly requeried to show any changes to its list. Static directories usually are not used for printers or servers. If they were, each time a printer or a server was added to the network, the administrator would have to manually edit the static list of services.

Dynamic service discovery protocols more accurately reflect the current state of the network because they update whenever new services appear or disappear on the network. The protocols usually work without the need of a dedicated server. Dynamic service discovery is what most people associate with service discovery.

▶   Rendezvous is Apple's implementation of an emerging industry standard called Zeroconf. Rendezvous provides more features than other service discovery protocols. In addition to discovering file, print, and other services on IP networks, it will assign IP addresses and map IP addresses to computer names.

▶   AppleTalk is the legacy Mac OS protocol for file and print services. Open Directory uses AppleTalk to discover services provided by Mac OS 9 or AppleShare IP. To discover AppleTalk printers in the Printer Setup Utility, it is not necessary to enable AppleTalk in Directory Access or in the Network pane of System Preferences.

▶ SLP (Service Location Protocol) was used for service discovery in earlier versions of Mac OS X. It has been superseded by Rendezvous but is still supported.

▶ SMB (Server Message Block), the file sharing protocol for Microsoft Windows computers, is a service discovery protocol for file and print services. It can be used as a hybrid system with dynamic discovery on the local network and a server-based lookup for clients on nearby networks. Because of this architecture, SMB clients can take several minutes to appear on the network.

Configuring Service Discovery

Directory Access (/Applications/Utilities) determines which directory services a Mac OS X computer uses and how it connects to specific directory domains. The Services pane of the Directory Access application enables you to select and configure the services that Mac OS X uses to obtain information, including the service discovery protocols.

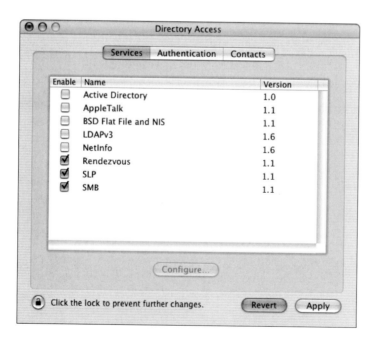

To make changes to the Open Directory service discovery protocols, you must first click the lock icon in the lower left and then authenticate by typing the name and password of an administrator. Then you can select the checkbox next to the protocol you want to enable or disable. Some Open Directory services (Active Directory, BSD Flat File and NIS, LDAPv3, NetInfo, and SMB) are configurable. You can tell a service is configurable if the Configure button becomes active when you select that service. We discuss how to configure these services later in this lesson. When you have finished selecting and configuring service protocols, click Apply.

If you know that you don't need a particular protocol, you can disable it in Directory Access. If you disable a protocol, Open Directory does not use it for service discovery on the computer. Other network services may still use the protocol, however. For example, if you disable the AppleTalk protocol, Open Directory does not use AppleTalk to discover file servers, but you can still connect to an AppleTalk file server if you know its name.

Authenticating in Directory Access

Before you can make any changes in Directory Access, you must authenticate as an administrative user.

1   Open Directory Access (/Applications/Utilities).

2   Click Services.

If you have not yet authenticated as an administrator user, the list of services is dimmed.

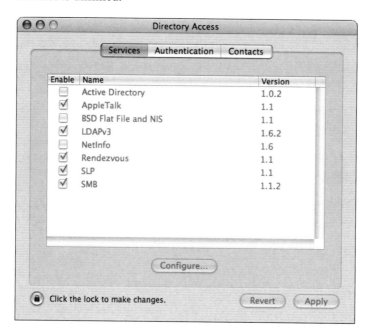

3   Click the lock icon in the lower-left corner.

You will be prompted for a user name and password.

4   Use your administrator user name and password and click OK.

The list entries are no longer dimmed, indicating that you are authenticated as an administrator capable of configuring the services.

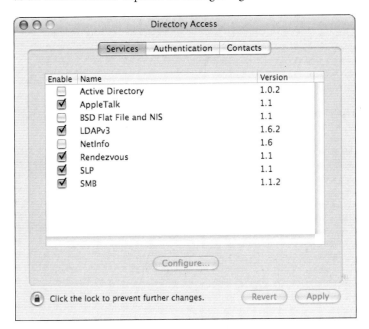

Viewing Configuration Options

You can configure a variety of directory service options with Directory Access.

1   In the Services pane of Directory Access window, select Rendezvous.

Notice that the Configure button is dimmed. This is because Rendezvous has no configuration options.

2   Select NetInfo.

Note that the Configure button is active for this service because it has configuration options.

3   Click Configure.

A configuration sheet appears.

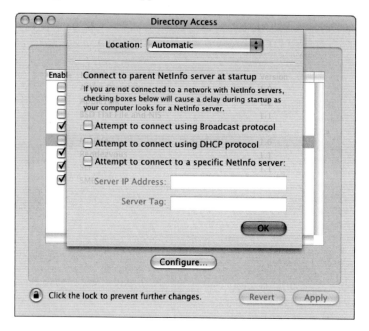

NOTE ▶ Depending upon your system configuration, your NetInfo settings may differ.

4   Read the text on the configuration pane, then click OK.

5   Disable the NetInfo service.

6   Click SMB.

Notice that the Configure button is active.

7   Click Configure.

A configuration sheet appears. This allows you to enter the workgroup name and WINS server for SMB discovery.

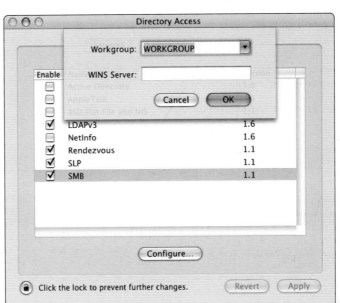

You can configure your computer to use a specific WINS server for SMB service discovery. WINS is a Microsoft NetBIOS name server. WINS servers maintain a name-to-address mapping for networks of Windows computers, which reduces traffic on the network. If no WINS server is available to the client, names are looked up on a network through broadcasts.

8 Click Cancel unless you really want to configure your computer to use SMB.

Disabling Discovery Services

In this exercise, you will turn off all discovery services in Directory Access and observe the impact of this change. This exercise assumes that your Mac is on a network with at least one shared volume. (Have another user enable Personal File Sharing in Sharing preferences on his or her Mac.)

1 Open a Finder window in column view and click Network in the Sidebar at the left of the window.

A list of file servers appears in the second column from the left.

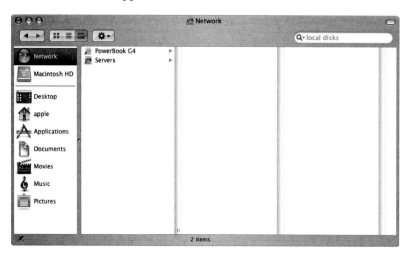

2   Open Directory Access and authenticate as an administrator, if necessary.

3   Disable all discovery services.

4   Click Apply.

5   If prompted, supply an administrator's user name and password.

6   Go back to the Finder and click Network in the Sidebar.

Now that your computer is no longer using discovery services, you will not see the file server that was previously listed. (It might not disappear right away due to caching.)

7   Choose Go > Connect to Server (Cmd-K).

Even though you cannot see the file server as an available Network service, you can still connect to it using Connect to Server.

8   Enter the server's local subnet address (found at the top of the server's Sharing preferences window):

afp://PowerBook-G4.local

9 Enter a user name and password for an account on the server and click Connect.

A window appears listing the volumes you have access to.

10 Click Cancel unless you really want to connect to a shared volume.

11 Return to the Directory Access window.

12 Enable all of the discovery services you intend to use.

13 Click Apply and supply your administrator password if prompted.

14 Quit Directory Access.

Connecting to Servers

From time to time, you might need to connect to a server that does not appear when you click the Network icon in the Sidebar at the left of the Finder window. You might want to connect to a server across the Internet that would not show up via Service Discovery protocols. Or you might want to connect to a local server that does not support service discovery, such as a Linux NFS (Network File System) server. To connect to these servers, in the Finder choose Go > Connect to Server (Cmd-K).

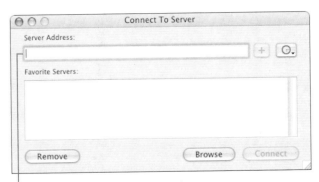

afp://pantherserver.pretendco.com/
smb://pantherserver.pretendco.com/
nfs://pantherserver.pretendco.com/shared/
ftp://pantherserver.pretendco.com/

Using Connect to Server

When you choose Go > Connect to Server, the Finder prompts you for an address. You can use either an IP address or a valid name for the computer. The prefix (afp:// or ftp://, for example) to the address tells Mac OS X which file sharing protocol to use. When you connect to a shared volume in this manner, the volume is mounted in the hidden directory /Volumes and appears on the desktop and in the Finder with other network and local volumes.

In addition to manually mounting a network volume, you can configure your user preferences to mount that shared volume automatically. Once the shared volume is mounted on the desktop, open Accounts preferences. Select the current user account and click Startup Items. You will be presented with a list of items that will open automatically when you log in. (The list may be empty.) Drag the icon for the shared volume from the Finder into the list, then quit System Preferences. The next time this user logs in, the volume will be mounted automatically. (The user may be asked to authenticate at login if the password was not saved when the volume was originally mounted.)

To unmount a shared volume, you either drag it to the Trash (which changes to an Eject icon labeled Disconnect) or select the volume and then choose File > Eject (Cmd-E). This action breaks the connection with the shared resource.

If you are connected to a network volume, and the server or network goes down, an alert will appear, indicating that Mac OS X is ejecting the volume because it cannot be used or is unavailable. Depending on the operating system on the computer offering the service, you might also get an alert that explains what happened to the service or network volume.

Using Connect to Server, you can connect to the following types of servers:

- Apple Filing Protocol (AFP)
- Server Message Block (SMB)
- WebDAV
- File Transfer Protocol (FTP)
- Network File System (NFS)

The following sections explain how to connect to the various types of servers. Since few readers have access to a computer with all types of servers, you are not expected to actually perform these step-by-step instructions. Simply read along to understand the procedures.

Connecting to Apple Filing Protocol (AFP)

The file sharing protocol most commonly used on Mac OS X is Apple Filing Protocol (AFP). This protocol allows you to mount volumes from computers running Mac OS 9 or earlier, as well as computers running Mac OS X.

These steps demonstrate the process of using Connect to Server to mount an AFP volume.

1   Choose Go > Connect to Server (Cmd-K).

The Connect to Server window appears.

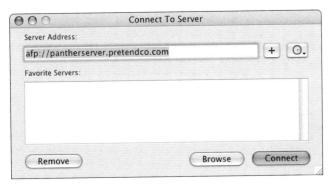

2   In the Server Address field, type

afp://

followed by the local subnet name or IP address of the computer, option-ally followed by a trailing slash.

NOTE ▶ Connect To Server assumes that you want an AFP volume if you do not specify a protocol.

3   Click Connect.

4   When prompted, specify that you want to connect as a registered user, then enter a user name and password for an account on the server.

NOTE ▶ If the account doesn't have a password, you won't be prompted for one.

5   Click Connect.

A list of shared volumes to which you have access appears.

6   Select the volumes you wish to mount (Shift-click to select more than one), then click OK.

The shared volumes appear in the Sidebar at the left of the Finder window.

Connecting to Server Message Block (SMB)

Another common file sharing protocol is Server Message Block (SMB). Computers running Microsoft Windows use this protocol to share files. Use it on Mac OS X to access files shared by computers running Windows.

These steps demonstrate the process of using Connect to Server to mount an SMB volume.

1   Choose Go > Connect to Server (Cmd-K).

The Connect to Server window appears.

2   In the Server Address field, type

smb://

followed by the name or IP address of the computer, optionally followed by a trailing slash.

NOTE ▶ When browsing for SMB servers in the Connect to Server browsing window on a network where DNS provides reverse lookups, the domain name will be displayed instead of the computer name. For details, refer to Knowledge Base article #107085, "Mac OS X 10.2: Expected, User-Defined Windows (SMB) Computer Name Does Not Appear in Connect to Server Dialog."

3   Click Connect.

The SMB Mount dialog appears.

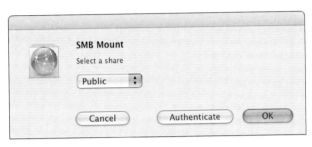

A Connecting To Server status dialog also appears.

4   In the SMB dialog, from the "Select a share" pop-up menu, choose the desired item.

Shared items are sometimes called share points, because you don't necessarily have to share an entire volume. You can choose to share only a particular folder on a volume, if you wish.

5   Click OK.

The SMB/CIFS (Common Internet File System) Filesystem Authentication dialog appears.

6   Enter the workgroup/domain, username, and password for an account on the server.

The administrator of the Windows computer can provide you with the name of the workgroup. The default is WORKGROUP.

NOTE ▶ SMB won't let you log in to an account without entering a password. For accounts with no password, the user can type anything.

7   Click OK.

The shared volume appears in the Sidebar at the left of the Finder window.

Connecting to WebDAV

WebDAV is a tool used for editing Web content. WebDAV uses the Hypertext Transfer Protocol (HTTP). This is the same protocol you use when you access pages on the Web with a browser. With WebDAV, however, you mount the Web site as a volume, and you can add and modify files as well as read them.

These steps demonstrate the process of using Connect to Server to mount a WebDAV volume.

1   Choose Go > Connect to Server (Cmd-K).

The Connect to Server window appears.

2   In the Server Address field, type

http://

followed by the name or IP address of the computer, optionally followed by a trailing slash.

3   Click Connect.

4   If a WebDAV File System Security Notice appears, click Continue.

5   If prompted, enter a user name and password for an account on the server, then click OK.

The shared volume appears in the Sidebar at the left of the Finder window.

Connecting to File Transfer Protocol (FTP)

FTP is important primarily because it is widely used on the Internet for transferring files. Most Unix-like operating systems provide FTP services, and FTP clients are available for nearly every computer operating system.

These steps demonstrate the process of using Connect to Server to mount an FTP volume.

1   Choose Go > Connect to Server (Cmd-K).

The Connect to Server window appears.

2   In the Server Address field, type

ftp://

followed by the name or IP address of the computer, optionally followed by a trailing slash.

3   Click Connect.

4   When prompted, enter a user name and password for an account on the server.

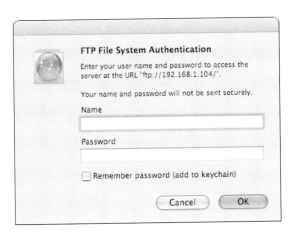

NOTE ▶ FTP won't let you log in to an account without entering a password. For accounts with no password, the user can type anything. FTP transmits all data, including the user name and password, in the clear, and is not a secure method of exchange.

5   Click OK.

The shared volume appears in the Sidebar at the left of the Finder window.

NOTE ▶ In Mac OS X 10.3, you can download files after mounting an FTP volume using Connect to Server, but you cannot upload files over FTP using the Finder. Uploading files to an FTP server can be accomplished only within an FTP client such as Fetch (www.fetchsoftworks.com) or Transmit (www.panic.com). This may be changed in a future release of Mac OS X.

Connecting to Network File System (NFS)

NFS is the file-sharing protocol used by most Unix systems. These steps demonstrate the process of using Connect to Server to mount an NFS volume.

1   Choose Go > Connect to Server (Cmd-K).

The Connect to Server window appears.

2   In the Server Address field, type

nfs://

followed by the name or IP address of the computer, optionally followed by a trailing slash.

3   Click Connect.

The shared volume appears in the Sidebar at the left of the Finder window.

Troubleshooting Network Service Problems

When troubleshooting network service problems, try the following strategies:

▶ If you are unable to locate printers or file servers on the network:

  ▶ Check to make sure Network preferences is configured correctly.

  ▶ Make sure that you have a working network connection.

  ▶ Use the network troubleshooting techniques covered in Lesson 6, to verify that you have network connectivity from the computer to the server.

▶ Computers using an address in a valid subnet can browse computers using a Rendezvous-assigned link-local address. Computers using a link-local address can only browse other computers using a link-local address.

▶ Check the log files located in /Library/Logs/DirectoryService. The two log files, DirectoryService.error.log and DirectoryService.server.log, will list which plug-ins loaded successfully and which ones failed.

▶ If you are unable to locate AppleTalk services, make sure AppleTalk is enabled on the primary port in Network preferences. Since AppleTalk can only be enabled on one network interface, you need to decide which interface will be used to access AppleTalk services. For example, if you enable AppleTalk on the AirPort Card, you won't be able to browse for AppleTalk services on the Ethernet port.

▶ If you are unable to browse for a Windows server, remember that you can only browse SMB servers that are in the same subnet. To connect to SMB servers outside the subnet, you need to provide the address for the server. Also, if an SMB server just started up, it can take 10 minutes or more for Connect to Server to locate it on the network. (See http://support.microsoft.com/default.aspx?scid=kb;en-us;188001 for more information.)

▶ When Connect to Server cannot connect to a server, it may display an error code with no explanation. For details, refer to Knowledge Base article #9804, "Mac OS System Error Codes: −299 to −5553." Also, be aware that sometimes the Console (/Applications/Utilities) has helpful information in its logs.

Authenticating Your Identity

As you go about your daily routine using your computer, a number of applications will need to know who you are. Authentication is the process whereby you prove your identity to the computer system. Common instances when Mac OS X requires authentication include the following:

▶   Login window

▶   Mail

▶   AFP login

Each of these applications needs to know your identity so that you can access some resource. In the case of the Login window, your identity is needed to verify that you have an account on the computer. If you do have an account and enter the correct password, you are given access to the Finder and all of your files.

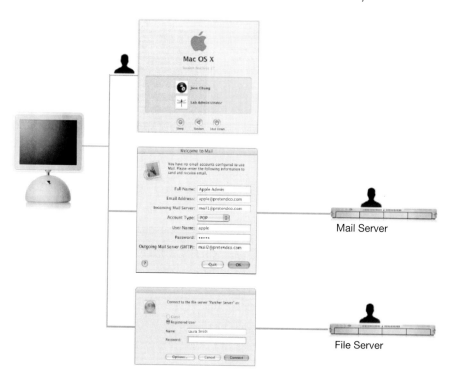

Often, it is another computer on the network that needs to know who you are. The mail server may need to know your identity in order to know which mailbox holds your messages. The AFP server needs to know your identity to know which volumes you can mount and which files you can access.

You can see how names and passwords quickly add up. Imagine if there were a dozen different servers you needed to access. You might have a dozen different passwords. Even if you did have the same name and password on every one of them, when you change your password you would have to change it 12 times if you wanted to keep all of your passwords the same.

One method of addressing this issue in Mac OS X is through the use of keychains, which provide a way to store your many passwords in a secure file format. Depending on your site, the keychain may be your only way to address this issue because other solutions may rely on changes in the configuration of servers on the network beyond your control.

Managing Accounts with Directory Services

Managing multiple user accounts and associated passwords becomes an issue when you access several services, each with its own system to authenticate users. For example, when you check your mail, the mail server doesn't know what user name and password you used to log in to your computer. Mac OS X checked the user name and password entered in the Login window against its own local users list. The mail server checks its own local users list for authentication. The login name and password for one service isn't necessarily related to the login name and password for another service.

One way to approach this problem is to make one list of users available to all of these different systems. If the Login window, the mail server, and the AFP server all look to the same list of users, they can all accept the same user name and password. If your password is changed on that master list, all of those services will recognize the change at once and use your new password.

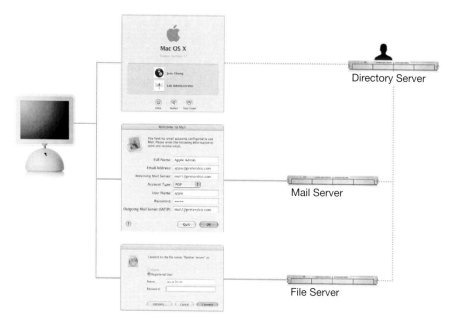

A directory service provides account information to a number of systems. There are several ways to implement a directory service, but the industry has, by and large, settled on a standard called LDAP (Lightweight Directory Access Protocol). Closely related to LDAP is Microsoft's Active Directory, a method based on LDAP, with some additional extensions that are specific to Microsoft clients.

Setting up a directory service is a job for the server administrator and is beyond the scope of this book. However, in the following sections you will learn how to set up Directory Access to connect to the directory services that you are most likely to encounter.

Authenticating with LDAP

LDAP is an industry-standard method for communicating directory information over a network. Unfortunately, there is much variation in the organization of that information. The configuration options range from very easy to very difficult. Begin by opening Directory Access, selecting LDAP, then clicking Configure, which opens a configuration sheet with a Location pop-up menu at the top.

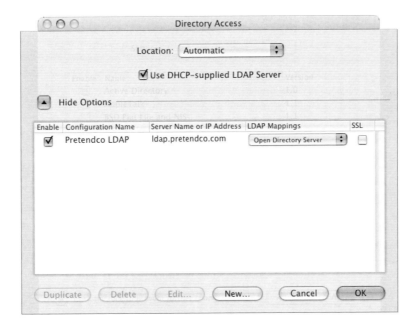

▶ Automatically configure with DHCP

Choose Location > Automatic, then select the "Use DHCP-supplied LDAP Server" checkbox. DHCP provides a standardized way to distribute LDAP locations to clients. If your site is running Mac OS X Server, the odds are good that this simple checkbox is all you need for your computers to find and use a directory server. Since this option is on by default, it is possible to find and use a directory server on a newly installed computer without any additional configuration.

▶ Manually configure for specific directory servers

If your site doesn't use DHCP to distribute LDAP information, you'll have to add some information so that the client can find and use the directory information. The information you'll need to get from your administrator includes the following:

   ▶ The address of the LDAP server

- ► The type of server you are connecting to: Open Directory (for Mac OS X Server), RFC 2307 (for many Unix servers), or Active Directory. For Active Directory Servers, you'll normally want to use the Active Directory plug-in explained shortly in "Authenticating with Active Directory."

- ► The search base of the LDAP server

  The search base is a string of text that will be different for every site. It will look something like "dc=pretendco, dc=com".

- ► Manually configure for custom directory server

  This is an advanced configuration that will not be covered in this book. This allows a very flexible but complex configuration that enables you to work with a customized LDAP server. This configuration is covered in the Apple Certified System Administrator classes.

Finally, after you have configured Mac OS X to use your LDAP server, you need to tell Mac OS X to look to this LDAP server for all authentication attempts. You do this in Directory Access by clicking Authentication, choosing Search > Custom path, clicking Add, then specifying the LDAP server.

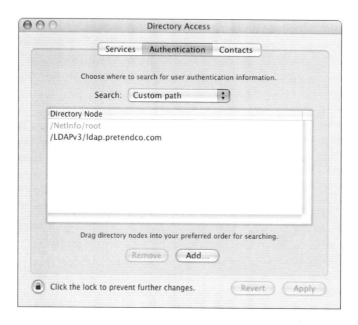

Authenticating with Active Directory

In addition to LDAP, Mac OS X can use Active Directory for authentication information. Begin by opening Directory Access, selecting Active Directory, then clicking Configure, which opens a configuration sheet with three text fields.

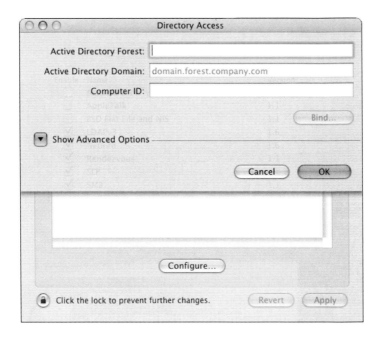

You must fill in all three text fields with information you obtain from your system administrator:

▶   Active Directory Forest address

▶   Active Directory Domain address

▶   Computer ID

Again, after you have configured Active Directory, you need to configure t' authentication search path to include Active Directory. You do this in D:

Access by clicking the Authentication button, choosing Search > Custom path, clicking Add, then specifying the Active Directory server.

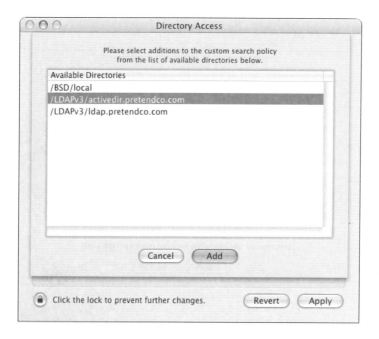

Authenticating with Kerberos

Another way to deal with the problem of multiple login accounts is through the use of tickets. Rather than proving your identity to network services by presenting a user name and password, you prove your identity by presenting a piece of data (the ticket). The service verifies your ticket and, if you have a valid ticket, you are granted access. The name of the system that implements this ticket architecture is Kerberos.

A directory service solves the multiple account problem by coordinating all of its associated servers to use a single list of users. Kerberos simplifies this by keeping the list of users on one computer only. The ticket mechanism ensures that the rest of the services don't need your name and password; they only need a valid ticket.

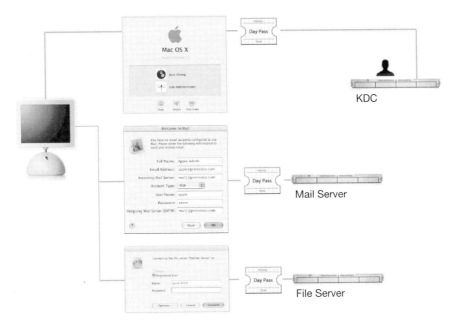

Using Kerberos, you negotiate with one system on the network called a Key Distribution Center (KDC). When the KDC is satisfied that you have authenticated (typically by entering the correct user name and password), it will give you the ticket required to access other servers on the network. In Mac OS X, this is integrated with the Login window, so the initial login will result in the user obtaining a ticket that can be used for the duration of the login session.

Tickets are encoded in such a way that each one is unique. Each service can inspect the ticket and verify that the ticket is valid. To prove your identity to a server, you send your ticket instead of sending a name and password.

A ticket is not something an end user normally will work with directly. If the system is working correctly, a user's system will acquire tickets and present them when required to access a server, all in the background. A properly configured Kerberos system is not only very secure, it is also very user-friendly.

Kerberos was developed at MIT and is widely accepted as one of the most secure ways to perform authentication. However, using tickets is a fundamental change from the more familiar method of requiring a user name and password.

A service that has been modified to work with Kerberos ticket authentication is said to be Kerberized. It requires modification of both the client software and the server software so that they present and accept tickets, respectively.

If your site is using Mac OS X Server 10.3 for the directory server, your clients automatically will be using Kerberos when you configure Mac OS X to connect to an Open Directory server.

Kerberos can work on other types of servers such as Unix or Linux servers running the standard MIT Kerberos. Such configurations are complex and often are customized for each individual site. Details of this configuration are beyond the scope of this book.

In either case, if your site is configured for Kerberos, your users may use the Kerberos applications on Mac OS X. In a perfect Kerberos configuration, Kerberos is integrated with the Login window, and the Kerberos login is not exposed to the user.

The Kerberos tickets are visible in the Kerberos application, which is found in /System/Library/CoreServices/Kerberos.

Here are the tasks you can perform with the Kerberos application:

▶ View the tickets.

Remember that with Kerberos the client is presenting a ticket to the network services. If the client never received a ticket, it will not be able to connect to Kerberized services. You can use the application to view the tickets received from the KDC. If the window is blank, there might be a problem with the KDC, which should provide the ticket to the client.

▶ Get tickets.

If you notice that you don't have any Kerberos tickets, you can force login to the KDC and attempt to get a ticket.

▶ Destroy tickets.

You can destroy your Kerberos tickets as a security measure. Future access to Kerberized services will require you to re-enter your name and password to get a new ticket from the KDC.

▶ Renew tickets.

Kerberos tickets are only good for a specified period of time (usually 8 to 10 hours). Renewing a ticket will reset its expiration time.

▶ Change password.

Change your password on the KDC.

Troubleshooting Authentication

Troubleshooting authentication can be tricky. Try these suggestions if you have difficulty proving your identity:

► View the Kerberos ticket using the Kerberos application and check to see if the ticket has expired. Also, be sure the clocks on your computers are synchronized within five minutes. (Using a network time server is a good idea.)

► Use the Console utility to view the error and server logs that may contain useful information.

► To locate the source of an authentication problem, try logging in locally on the server or from other clients.

What You've Learned

► Mac OS X uses service discovery protocols to find out what network services are available.

► You use Directory Access to configure service discovery protocols.

► The Finder's Connect to Server feature allows you to access another computer using the protocols AFP, FTP, NFS, SMB, and WebDAV.

► If you use a directory service or Kerberos, users don't have to remember passwords for each network service.

References

The following Knowledge Base articles (located at http://kbase.info.apple.com) will provide you with further information regarding service discovery in Mac OS X.

AppleTalk

▶ 106298, "Mac OS X: Using AppleTalk With PPPoE"

▶ 106613, "Mac OS X: 'No AppleTalk Printers Are Available' Message"

Rendezvous

▶ 107346, "Mac OS X 10.2: Rendezvous Name Fails to Save"

▶ 106472, "Mac OS X: FTP, Internet Sharing, Rendezvous, SSH, and Telnet Require the BSD Subsystem"

▶ 106964, "Mac OS X 10.2: About Your Computer's Rendezvous Name"

▶ 107174, "Mac OS X 10.2: About Multicast DNS"

Windows (SMB)

▶ 107085, "Mac OS X 10.2: Expected, User-Defined Windows (SMB) Computer Name Does Not Appear in Connect to Server Dialog"

▶ 107117, "Mac OS X 10.2: Windows File Sharing (SMB) Computers Beyond Your Subnet Do Not Appear in Connect to Server Dialog"

▶ 19652, "Networking with a Windows PC"

▶ 61646, "Mac OS X 10.1: About Improving SMB File Transfer Speed with cp or CpMac"

▶ 106471, "Mac OS X 10.1 or Later: How to Connect to Windows File Sharing (SMB)"

URLs

Visit the following Web site for more information:

▶ Description of the Microsoft Computer Browser Service: http://support.microsoft.com/default.aspx?scid=kb;en-us;188001

Books

Locate the following books for more information:

▶ LDAP overview: Carter, Gerald, *LDAP System Administration*, Sebastopol, CA: O'Reilly and Associates, March 2003.

▶ Kerberos overview: Garman, Jason, *Kerberos: The Definitive Guide*, Sebastopol, CA: O'Reilly and Associates, August 2003.

Review Quiz

Use the following questions to review what you have learned:

1. What is meant by the term "service discovery?"

2. What are some applications that use service discovery information?

3. What are four protocols Mac OS X can use for service discovery? How do you enable or disable them?

4. What is the impact of disabling a service discovery protocol? Does it mean the computer cannot use that protocol at all?

5. Which files should you check for service directory errors?

6. Can the computer discover SMB servers beyond the local subnet?

7. What protocol would you use to share files with computers running Microsoft Windows?

Answers

1. It is the capability of a computer to find out about computers and other devices that are offering services on the network.

2. One is the Finder, which displays a list of computers you can connect to when you choose Go > Connect to Server. Another is Printer Setup Utility, which displays a list of available printers in the Printer List window.

3. They are AppleTalk, Rendezvous, SLP, and SMB. Use Directory Access to enable or disable the protocols the computer uses for services discovery.

4. If you disable a protocol, Open Directory does not use it for service discovery on the computer. Other network services may still use the protocol, however.

5. DirectoryService.error.log and DirectoryService.server.log.

6. No, SMB browsing in Mac OS X is limited to discovering workgroups and shared computers on the subnet.

7. Server Message Block (SMB).

8

Time

This lesson takes approximately 1 hour to complete.

Goals

Use Network preferences and Sharing preferences to configure a Mac OS X computer so that remote clients can locate shared volumes via AppleTalk and IP

Use Sharing preferences to enable file sharing, Web sharing, and FTP services

Enable file sharing on Mac OS X over AFP

Locate the files that correspond with the computer's main Web site, as well as the user's Web site

Turn on the firewall in Sharing preferences so that access through IP ports for inactive services is blocked

Perform quick fixes to file sharing issues

Lesson 8
File and Internet Sharing

As you learned in the previous lesson, Mac OS X allows you to connect to AFP, FTP, and SMB servers by browsing for them in the Finder or by choosing Go > Connect to Server (Cmd-K). These connection methods give you easy access to the most common types of file servers.

Mac OS X also uses these protocols to allow you to share files on your computer. In addition to sharing files, Mac OS X allows you to share an Internet connection with other computers. This lesson explains how to enable file and Internet sharing, as well as how to protect your computer using Mac OS X's built-in firewall.

> **NOTE** ▸ Mac OS X does not provide WebDAV serving capabilities, but it does allow other users to access Web pages on your computer using a Web browser, as explained in this lesson.

Sharing Services

Sharing preferences, as its name implies, controls file sharing and Internet sharing, but it also controls several other useful services. Click the Services button in Sharing preferences to see the complete list of available services.

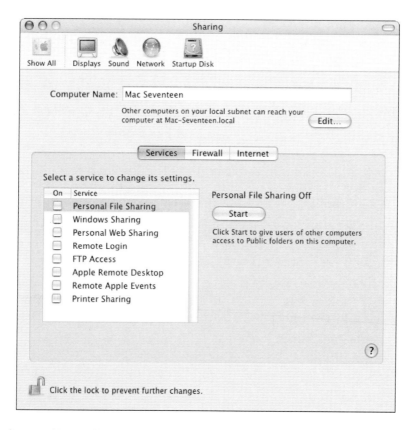

Before we discuss file and Internet sharing, let's first consider two other services, Remote Login and Remote Apple Events, because they have serious security implications.

By enabling Remote Login or Remote Apple Events, you potentially give control of your computer to other users on both the local network and beyond. Remote Login allows users to log in to your computer from another computer using the secure shell (ssh) command-line utility to run applications remotely, which is less secure than requiring a user to physically access the computer. Remote Apple Events allows applications on other computers to control Mac OS X applications on your computer using Apple events. If you don't have a specific reason to enable Remote Login or Remote Apple Events, leave them turned off.

With the exception of Printer Sharing and Apple Remote Desktop, all other services in Sharing preference are covered in this lesson.

Using AFP File Sharing

To make the most of this lesson, you should have access to at least two Mac OS X 10.3 computers on the same network. Ideally, they should be physically close so you can make changes on one computer and see the effect on the other. The computer that is sharing files is called the local computer, or server. The computer that is accessing the shared files on the server is called the remote computer, or client. This section explains how to set up these computers, but it's not imperative that you actually do so. You should be able to follow along by reading the step-by-step instructions and examining the screen shots.

> **NOTE ►** The screen shots in this book were taken on computers running Mac OS X 10.3. However, client computers attempting to connect to your file sharing services need not be running Mac OS X 10.3. Users with older versions of the operating system can connect as well, though the interfaces and procedures may be slightly different.

In this exercise, you will enable Personal File Sharing (using the AFP protocol) on your server.

1   Open Sharing preferences.

2   Click Services.

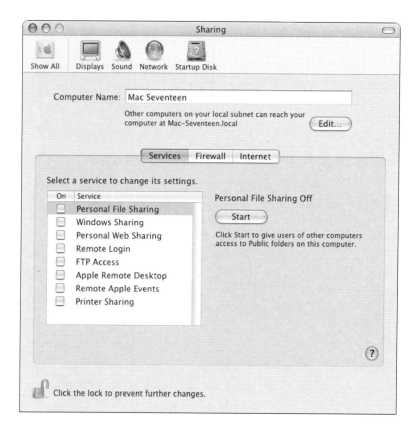

3   Select Personal File Sharing, then click Start, or turn on Personal File Sharing by selecting its checkbox.

It may take a moment for Personal File Sharing to start. When it does, the Start button changes to Stop, and the top of the window explains how other computers on your local subnet can access your computer. At the bottom of the window are similar instructions that are also applicable to local users, but intended primarily for users outside your local subnet. For these instructions to work properly, it may be necessary to enable port forwarding on your router, and that's beyond the scope of this book.

4   Note the address given to your computer at the bottom of the window.

It should be afp:// followed by the IP address of your server, such as

afp://192.168.1.100/

NOTE ▶ When attempting to share files over AFP with a Mac OS 9 client
on which IP is disabled, you need to enable AppleTalk in Network preferences on your server.

Verifying AFP File Sharing

In this exercise, you use your client to connect to a server over AFP using a
variety of methods.

1   Choose Go > Connect to Server (Cmd-K).

The Connect to Server window appears.

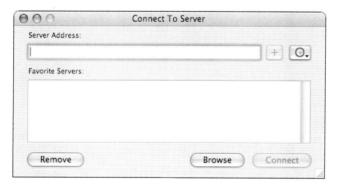

2   In the Server Address field, type

afp://

followed by the IP address of the server, optionally followed by a forward
slash (in this example, you should type *afp://192.168.1.100/*).

3 Click Connect.

An authentication dialog appears.

4 Specify that you want to connect as a registered user, then enter a user name and password for an account on the server.

> **NOTE** ▶ If the sharing user's account doesn't have a password, you won't be prompted for one.

5 Click Connect.

A list of shared volumes to which you have access appears.

If you connected as a user with a normal (non-admin) account on the server or as a guest, the volumes listed are the users' home directories on the server. If you connected as an administrator, the volumes listed are your own home directory plus each mounted file system (hard drive, CD-ROM, disk image, and so on) on the server. Although an administrator can navigate to any user's home directory, access to that directory is restricted based upon file and folder permissions (more on this later in the lesson).

Non-administrator

Administrator

6   Select the volumes you wish to mount (Shift-click to select more than one), then click OK.

The shared volumes appear in the Sidebar at the left of the Finder window.

7   Eject any volumes mounted in the previous step by clicking the Eject icon next to the volume icon in the Sidebar.

8   If your server has a DNS name, choose Go > Connect to Server again, but this time specify the server's DNS name instead of its IP address.

For example:

afp://imac

You should be able to connect, log in, and mount volumes as you did before.

You can use either uppercase or lowercase letters in the server name, but *afp* must be lowercase.

9   Eject any mounted volumes again.

10 Choose Go > Connect to Server again, but this time specify the server's Rendezvous name instead of its IP address.

For example:

afp://iMac.local

You should be able to connect, log in, and mount volumes as you did before.

11 Eject any mounted volumes again.

12 Click the Network icon in the Sidebar in the Finder.

You should see the server listed as a network service.

13 Select the server and click Connect.

You should be able to connect, log in, and mount volumes as you did before.

14 Leave the shared volume mounted on your client for now.

Disabling AFP File Sharing

If sharing your files with other users increases productivity, imagine how disruptive it can be when you break the connection. Fortunately Mac OS X provides a way to let connected users know when you plan to disable Personal File Sharing.

1   On the server, open Sharing preferences.

2   Click Services.

Personal File Sharing should still be turned on.

3   Select Personal File Sharing and click Stop.

If a client computer still has one of your shared volumes mounted, a dialog appears.

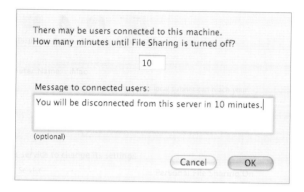

4   Specify how many minutes before the service is turned off and enter an optional message to connected users, then click OK.

If you enter a message, it is immediately sent to all connected users. Otherwise, a default warning is sent, and it repeats frequently as time runs out, allowing connected users the opportunity to close shared files and disconnect before sharing is disabled.

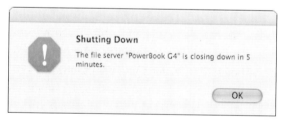

Setting Permissions for AFP File Sharing

When you enable Personal File Sharing, users who have accounts on your server (or know the user name and password of an account) can log in over the network and access files and directories on your computer. Exactly which files and directories they can access is determined by permissions. File permissions set in the Info window not only protect your files and directories from unauthorized access by local users, as explained in Lesson 2, they also restrict access by remote users.

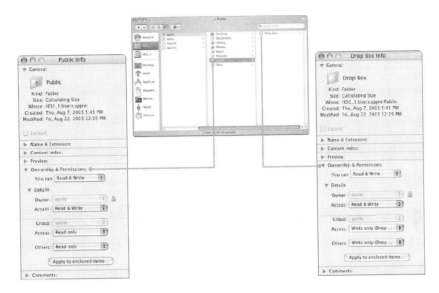

Mac OS X Server can configure arbitrary share points, but Mac OS X is more limited. When you create a user account, Mac OS X automatically configures folder permissions in the home directory to allow only certain types of access.

Normal (non-admin) users can mount the home directories of other users, but they have full access only to the files and folders in their own home directories. Administrators can mount the entire volume because they may need to make changes outside their own home directories, such as installing new applications or deleting preference files. However, that doesn't mean administrators can access all the folders within all users' home directories. The default permissions allow access to only the Public and Sites folders, whether you're authenticated as a normal user or as an administrator.

The Public and Drop Box folders are useful for sharing files with other users. The permissions for the Public and Sites folders in each user's home directory allow read-only access to Group and Others. This allows users to view and open the folder contents, but not to change the contents. Within each Public directory is a Drop Box folder with the permissions for Group and Others set to Write Only. This allows users to copy files into the Drop Box, but not to view the files in the folder.

Using SMB File Sharing

To allow Windows users to connect to your Mac OS X computer and print to shared printers, enable Windows Sharing. Since this uses the SMB protocol supported in Mac OS X, other Macintosh users can also use these services.

Enabling SMB File Sharing

In this exercise, you enable Windows Sharing (SMB) on your server.

1   Open Sharing preferences and click Services.

2   Select Windows Sharing, then click Start, or turn on Windows Sharing by selecting its checkbox.

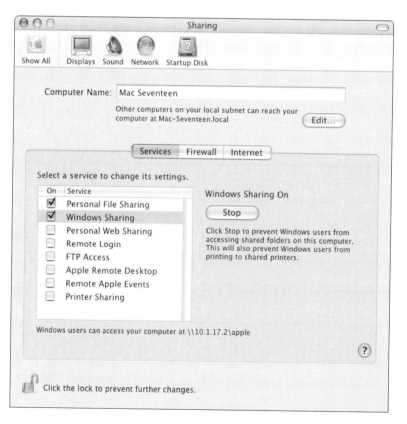

It may take a moment for Windows Sharing to start. When it does, the Start button changes to Stop, and the top of the window explains how other computers on your local subnet can access your computer. At the bottom of the window are similar instructions that are also applicable to local users, but intended primarily for users outside your local subnet. For these instructions to work properly, it may be necessary to enable port forwarding on your router, and that's beyond the scope of this book.

3 Note the address given to your server at the bottom of the window.

It should be \\ followed by the IP address of your server, followed by your short user name, such as

\\10.1.17.2\apple

NOTE ▶ Windows uses the backslash (\) as a pathname separator. Unix-like systems use the forward slash (/).

Verifying SMB File Sharing

In this exercise, you use your client to connect to a server over SMB.

1 In the Finder, choose Go > Connect to Server (Cmd-K).

2 In the address field, type

smb://

followed by your server's IP address, DNS name, or Rendezvous name.

For example:

smb://192.168.1.100

smb://imac

smb://imac.local

3 Click Connect.

An authentication dialog appears.

4 Enter the server's user name and password, as well as workgroup name. The default workgroup name is WORKGROUP, although it may have been changed in Directory Access, discussed in Lesson 7.

An SMB Mount window appears.

5 Choose the desired share point from the pop-up menu, then click OK.

Users connecting to a Mac OS X computer over SMB have access to their own home directories only, regardless of whether they authenticated as a normal user or administrator.

6 Eject the volume.

Enabling FTP Access

Enabling FTP Access allows users to exchange files with your server using FTP client applications that are available for practically every operating system. Mac OS X users also enjoy limited access over FTP using the Finder and full access using an FTP client.

In this exercise, you will enable FTP Access on your server.

1 Open Sharing preferences.

2 Click Services.

3 Select FTP Access, then click Start, or turn on FTP Access by selecting its checkbox.

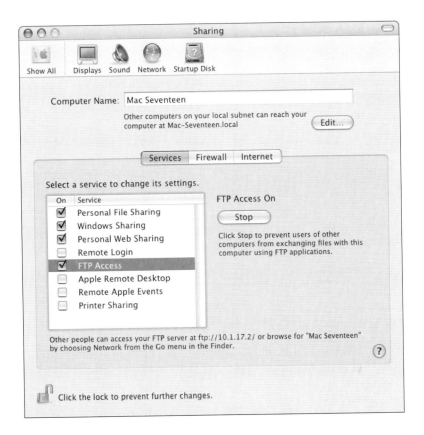

It may take a moment for FTP Access to start. When it does, the Start button changes to Stop, and the top of the window explains how other computers on your local subnet can access your computer. At the bottom of the window are similar instructions that are also applicable to local users, but intended primarily for users outside your local subnet. For these instructions to work properly, it may be necessary to enable port forwarding on your router, and that's beyond the scope of this book.

4   Note the address given to your server at the bottom of the window.

It should be ftp:// followed by the IP address of your server, optionally followed by a forward slash, such as

ftp://198.165.1.100/

Verifying FTP Access

In this exercise, you will connect to a server over FTP.

1   In the Finder, choose Go > Connect to Server (Cmd-K).

2   In the address field, type

ftp://

followed by your server's IP address, DNS name, or Rendezvous name.

For example:

ftp://192.168.1.100

ftp://imac

ftp://imac.local

3   Click Connect.

An authentication dialog appears.

4   Enter a user name and password of an account on the server.

You need a valid user account with a password to log in over FTP. Mac OS X has the capability to allow anonymous FTP login, but setting it up to do so is beyond the scope of this book. Also note that FTP transmits all data, including passwords, in the clear and, as such, is not recommended when security is a priority.

5   Click OK.

When a client logs in to an FTP server using the Finder, his or her home directory is accessible, but regardless of the actual permissions for items, the user has Read Only access. If you want access to all files and folders on the server with their proper permissions respected, you must log in using an FTP client such as Fetch (www.fetchsoftworks.com) or Transmit (www.panic.com). Keep in mind that regardless of how you log in using FTP, items that are normally hidden by the Finder are visible, and information exchanged between the client and the server is not encrypted.

Troubleshooting File Sharing

If users are unable to connect to your computer, use the following troubleshooting techniques:

▶   Verify that the appropriate file sharing protocol is enabled in Sharing preferences.

▶   If the protocol is enabled, but users are still unable to connect, there could be a networking problem such as a misconfigured setting in Network preferences or a broken physical connection in the network.

    ▶   Check the IP address and DNS settings in Network preferences. Remember that if an IP address starts with 169.254, it was self-assigned and therefore is accessible only to computers on the local subnet.

    ▶   Use Network Utility to check whether the two computers are able to communicate.

▶   If users are able to connect but not authenticate, verify that they are entering a valid user account for the sharing computer and that they are entering the correct password. (Make sure the Caps Lock key is not on—passwords are case-sensitive.)

▶   If users are able to connect and authenticate but are unable to access files, make sure that permissions for the files and all folders the user is trying to access are set to allow access. If just one encompassing folder doesn't have at least Read permission for the user, he or she will be blocked from accessing the files, regardless of how the files' permissions are set.

▶   If users have problems connecting to a file server, use the network trouble-shooting techniques covered in previous lessons to verify that you have network connectivity from the computer to the server.

▶   Remember that when a Windows server joins an SMB network, it can take 10 minutes or more to broadcast its availability for sharing. (See http://support.microsoft.com/default.aspx?scid=kb;en-us;188001 for more information.)

▶   When Mac OS X systems on the same local network use identical computer names, Rendezvous will add a unique number hyphenated to each computer's .local name. For example: if three Macintosh systems all running on the same local network are named "Mac," one system's .local name will be "Mac," and the second and third systems automatically would be named "Mac-2" and "Mac-3" to maintain unique IDs on the network.

Understanding Personal Web Sharing

When you perform a default installation of Mac OS X, the industry-standard Apache Web server software is installed. This powerful software allows you to host Web sites on your Mac, serving HTML pages to remote users across the Internet or to local users on an intranet.

By default, Mac OS X creates a single main Web site for the computer and separate Web sites for each user with an account on that computer. These aren't full-blown sites like you find when you surf the Web; they are placeholders for sites that you can create.

If you choose to create your own sites, which is completely optional, you need to understand how to create HTML documents, which is beyond the scope of this lesson. However, you can find many books on the subject, as well as programs, such as Adobe GoLive and Macromedia Dreamweaver, that make the process simple enough for non-professionals.

Mac OS X Main Web Site

Your computer's main Web page is located in /Library/WebServer/Documents, and the default "home page" is index.html.en, assuming you selected English as your language during the installation of Mac OS X. (The two-character extension identifies the document's language.)

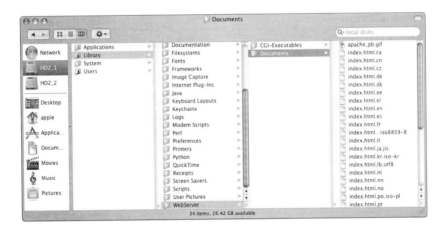

NOTE ▶ This description of file locations assumes the default Apache configuration that installs with Mac OS X. It is possible to reconfigure Apache by editing configuration files, but that topic is beyond the scope of this lesson.

You can modify or replace the files in /Library/WebServer/Documents with the actual content you want to present.

To access the main Web page of your computer, open a Web browser such as Safari, and in the address field, type the URL followed by the IP address of your computer, such as

http://192.168.1.100/

Mac OS X User Web Sites

Whenever a new user account is created, Mac OS X creates a ~/Sites folder containing a file called index.html and an images folder.

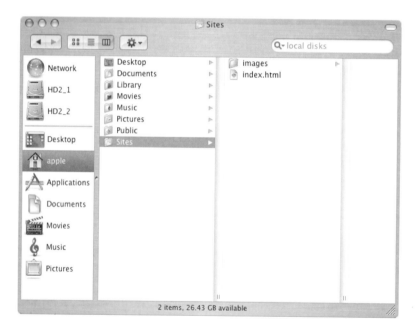

If you want to create and display a personal Web page, you can replace this file and folder with whatever you need.

To access your personal Web page on your computer, open a Web browser such as Safari, and in the address field, type the URL followed by the IP address of your computer, followed by a slash (/), a tilde (~), and your short user name, such as

http://192.168.1.100/~wpeece/

Enabling Personal Web Sharing

To allow users to view Web pages on your Mac OS X computer, enable Personal Web Sharing. When you do so, Sharing preferences displays the URLs for your main Web page and for user Web pages. Users should enter these URLs into the address field of their Web browsers to connect to this computer.

Follow these steps to enable Personal Web Sharing on your computer:

1   Open Sharing preferences.

2   Click Services.

3   Select Personal Web Sharing, then click Start, or turn on Personal Web Sharing by selecting its checkbox.

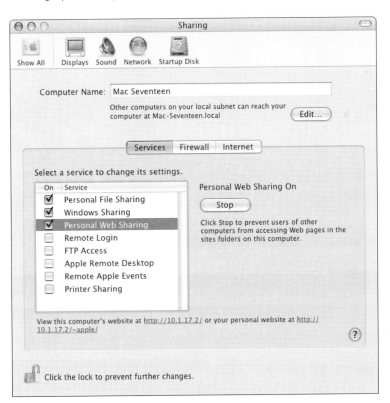

It may take a moment for Personal Web Sharing to start. When it does, the Start button changes to Stop, and the top of the window explains how other computers on your local subnet can access your computer. At the bottom of the window are similar instructions that are also applicable to local users, but intended primarily for users outside your local subnet. For these instructions to work properly, it may be necessary to enable port forwarding on your router, and that's beyond the scope of this book.

4   Note the Web address given to your server at the bottom of the window.

It should be http:// followed by the IP address of your server, followed by a slash, such as

http://198.165.1.100/

Append a tilde (~) and your short user name to enter the address for your personal Web site, such as

http://198.165.1.100/~apple/

Verifying Personal Web Sharing

In this exercise, you will view the Web pages on your server.

1   Open Safari (/Applications).

When using Safari on a network that is not connected to the Internet, you can ignore the error message "The specified server could not be found" when Safari attempts to load a default Web page.

2   To view the server's main Web site, in the browser's address field, type *http://* followed by your server's IP address, DNS name, or Rendezvous name, then press Return.

For example:

http://192.168.1.100

http://imac

http://imac.local

You should see a Web page that looks something like this.

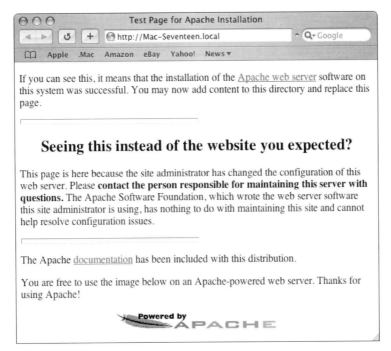

Note that the window title is "Test Page for Apache Installation."

3   Try using the other address formats.

All of them should work.

4   To view a user's personal Web site, in the browser's address field, type *http://* followed by your server's IP address, DNS name, or Rendezvous name, followed by a slash, a tilde, and the user's short name, then press Return.

For example:

http://192.168.1.100/~apple/

http://imac/~apple/

http://imac.local/~apple/

You should see a Web page that looks something like this.

Note that the window title is "Mac OS X Personal Web Sharing."

5   Try using the other address formats.

All of them should display the same page.

Modifying the Home Page Files

As mentioned previously, editing and creating HTML is beyond the scope of this book, but the basic concept is presented here to show the results of simple changes to the default Web pages.

To edit the main and user Web pages, follow these steps:

1   In the Finder on your computer, drag TextEdit from the Applications folder to the Dock.

This action adds an icon for TextEdit to the Dock.

2   Click the TextEdit icon in the Dock to open it.

An empty window appears.

3   Choose TextEdit > Preferences.

The Preferences window appears.

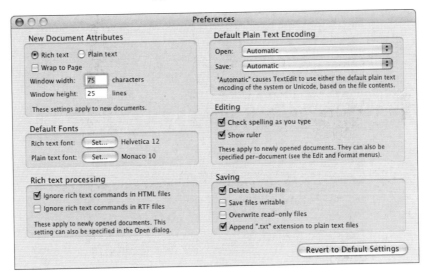

4   Select the "Ignore rich text commands in HTML files" checkbox in the "Rich text processing" pane.

This setting will allow you to edit HTML files as text.

5   Close the Preferences window.

6   Close the blank document.

7   In the Finder, navigate to /Library/WebServer/Documents.

8   Open the index.html.en file by dragging and dropping the file onto the TextEdit icon in the Dock.

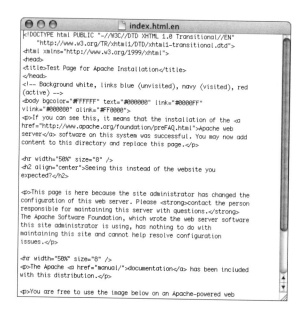

```
●●●                        index.html.en
<!DOCTYPE html PUBLIC "-//W3C//DTD XHTML 1.0 Transitional//EN"
    "http://www.w3.org/TR/xhtml1/DTD/xhtml1-transitional.dtd">
<html xmlns="http://www.w3.org/1999/xhtml">
<head>
<title>Test Page for Apache Installation</title>
</head>
<!-- Background white, links blue (unvisited), navy (visited), red
(active) -->
<body bgcolor="#FFFFFF" text="#000000" link="#0000FF"
vlink="#000080" alink="#FF0000">
<p>If you can see this, it means that the installation of the <a
href="http://www.apache.org/foundation/preFAQ.html">Apache web
server</a> software on this system was successful. You may now add
content to this directory and replace this page.</p>

<hr width="50%" size="8" />
<h2 align="center">Seeing this instead of the website you
expected?</h2>

<p>This page is here because the site administrator has changed the
configuration of this web server. Please <strong>contact the person
responsible for maintaining this server with questions.</strong>
The Apache Software Foundation, which wrote the web server software
this site administrator is using, has nothing to do with
maintaining this site and cannot help resolve configuration
issues.</p>

<hr width="50%" size="8" />
<p>The Apache <a href="manual/">documentation</a> has been included
with this distribution.</p>

<p>You are free to use the image below on an Apache-powered web
```

9 Change the line that says

<title>Test Page for Apache Installation</title>

to say

<title>Test Page for Reader</title>

10 Save and close the document.

11 Navigate to /Users/apple/Sites/ in the Finder.

12 Open the file index.html by dragging it to the TextEdit icon in the Dock.

13 Change the line that says

<BODY BGCOLOR=#FFFFFF>

to say

<BODY BGCOLOR=#FFFF00>

14 Save the file.

15 Quit TextEdit.

Testing the Modified Home Page Files

To verify the changes you made, follow these steps:

1   Open Safari on the client.

2   In the Address field, type the Web address of your server's main Web site, for example:

    http://imac.local

    The title at the top of the page should now reflect the change you just made.

3   Enter the Web address of your computer's personal Web site for the user Apple Admin and verify that the page's color has changed.

Sharing Your Internet Connection

If you have an Internet connection, the Internet button in Sharing preferences allows you to share your Internet connection with other Macintosh computers on your local network.

For example, if your computer accesses the Internet using a DSL (digital subscriber line) modem connected to Ethernet, and your Macintosh also has an AirPort Card installed, you can share the DSL connection with other AirPort-equipped computers. Complete instructions for doing so are included with AirPort products.

When you select the checkbox to share your Internet connection using Built-in Ethernet, a warning appears about the possibility of causing a network problem. If your network already has a DHCP server, enabling Internet sharing will add a second DHCP server, confusing other computers on the network and creating network problems.

> **NOTE** ▶ Exercise extreme care if your Internet connection and your local network use the same port (Built-in Ethernet, for example.) Thoroughly investigate possible side effects before you turn on Internet sharing. In some cases, (if you use a cable modem, for example), you might unintentionally affect the network settings of other ISP customers, and your ISP might terminate your service to prevent you from disrupting its network.

Protecting Your Mac with the Firewall

Mac OS X includes firewall software you can use to block unwanted network connections and prevent unauthorized network access to your computer. The firewall uses the BSD utility ipfw (IP Firewall) to block network traffic on specific IP ports. To enable the firewall, click Firewall in Sharing preferences and then click the Start button. When you enable the firewall, all ports other than the ones checked in the list will be blocked. Blocking ports may disrupt services such as iChat Rendezvous browsing and iTunes music sharing, so be sure to block only those ports you know are not in use.

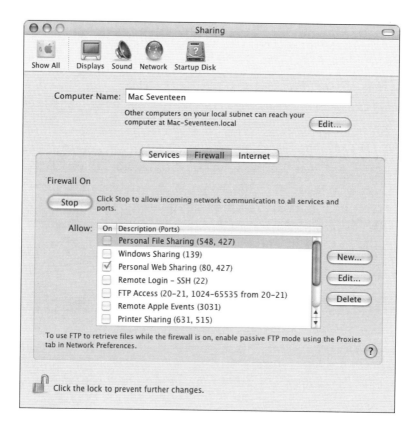

When you turn on a service in the Services pane of Sharing preferences, Mac OS X automatically allows that service in the Firewall pane. This allows authorized traffic to pass and other traffic to continue to be blocked.

You cannot change the settings for the default ports listed in the Firewall pane; however, you can specify additional ports to be opened as follows:

1   Click New.

A configuration sheet appears.

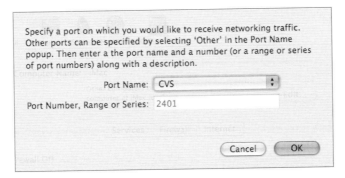

Specify a port on which you would like to receive networking traffic. Other ports can be specified by selecting 'Other' in the Port Name popup. Then enter a the port name and a number (or a range or series of port numbers) along with a description.

Port Name: CVS

Port Number, Range or Series: 2401

Cancel   OK

2   From the Port Name pop-up menu, choose one of the defaults and click OK, or choose Other.

Defaults have port numbers already assigned. If you choose Other, you must specify the port number to use.

3   Enter a port number, range, or series to open.

4   Enter a description of the port.

5   Click OK.

What You've Learned

▶ Users can connect to your computer using Connect to Server, an FTP client, or a Web browser.

▶ File permissions protect your files and directories from unauthorized access by network users as well as local users.

▶ You enable AFP, FTP, SMB, and Web file sharing in Sharing preferences.

▶ You also enable Remote Login and Remote Apple Events in Sharing preferences. These services have significant security implications.

▶ Volumes available over AFP depend on whether you log in as an administrator or normal user.

▶ Personal Web Sharing allows users with a Web browser to connect to your computer's main Web site and to users' Web sites.

▶ FTP Sharing on Mac OS X requires users to log in with a user name and password.

References

The following Knowledge Base articles (located at http://kbase.info.apple.com) will provide you with further information regarding file and Internet sharing in Mac OS X.

File Sharing

▶ 106461, "Mac OS X: File Sharing"

▶ 107086, "Mac OS X 10.2: Windows File Sharing Will Not Start, Stay On, or Allow Workgroup Name Change"

Windows (SMB)

▶ 106660, "Mac OS X: Sharing With Non-Apple Operating Systems"

Review Quiz

Use the following questions to review what you have learned:

1. What are the preconfigured share points on Mac OS X?

2. Where do you enable AFP, FTP, SMB, and Web file sharing?

3. Where is your computer's main Web page located?

4. What URL would you use to access the Web page for user nancy on the computer client.example.com?

5. If users are unable to access files on your computer over the network, what should you check?

Answers

1. A normal user can mount only user home directories. Administrators can mount the whole volume.

2. You enable AFP, FTP, SMB, and Web file sharing in the Services pane of Sharing preferences.

3. Your computer's main Web page is located in /Library/WebServer/ Documents. If you selected English as your language during installation, the name of the file is index.html.en.

4. You would type the URL *http://client.example.com/~nancy/*.

5. Verify that the appropriate file sharing protocol is enabled; verify network connection between the two computers; if using Windows, verify that the account is allowed to log in; check permissions.

9

Time
This lesson takes approximately 1 hour to complete.

Goals
Use System Profiler to identify what USB and FireWire devices are connected to and recognized by the system

Connect a FireWire storage device to a Mac OS X computer

Use System Profiler to identify what storage devices are connected, how many partitions each storage device has, and the size of each partition

Use Bluetooth preferences and the Bluetooth File Exchange utility to transfer files between two Bluetooth-enabled systems

Perform basic peripheral troubleshooting

Configure Universal Access preferences to facilitate use of peripherals by users with special needs

Peripherals

Macintosh computers come from the factory with a wide range of necessary and useful hardware components, from internal hard disks and optical drives to keyboards and mice. In addition, Macintosh computers have options for adding internal and external peripherals such as expansion cards, printers, and scanners.

Mac OS X provides a robust, extensible method of supporting peripherals by identifying how devices connect to a computer (known as a *bus*) or the functionality they provide (known as *device class*). Included with Mac OS X are applications, such as Disk Utility, iPhoto, and Image Capture, that interact with and manage the connected devices.

Understanding Buses

In a computing context, a bus is the way devices are added to and communicate with a computer. Typically, a bus combines a hardware connector or communication device with a protocol. Mac OS X includes support for a variety of industry-standard buses. Different types of buses have evolved over the years to meet the changing needs of computer users. Some buses are most appropriate for desktop computers, and others are designed primarily for the small form factor and reduced power consumption of laptop computers. Some are designed for high-speed data throughput, and others sacrifice speed for lower component costs. This section looks at some common buses in use on the Macintosh, and then details several of the more complicated buses.

Bluetooth

FireWire 400/800
IEEE 1394/1394b

PCI
Peripheral Component Interconnect

PCI-X
Peripheral Component
Interconnect Extended

SCSI
Small Computer System Interface

USB 1.1/2.0
Universal Serial Bus

PCI and PCI-X

Peripheral Component Interconnect (PCI) cards are expansion cards that are installed inside desktop computers after turning off power. Typically, PCI cards add display capabilities (almost all Power Macintosh systems use a PCI display card to connect a monitor), hardware RAID (Redundant Array of Independent Disks) data storage, or high-end analog video capture and compression. PCI cards are available to add a SCSI bus as well as additional USB and FireWire buses. PCI supports bus speeds up to 66 MHz, and PCI-X supports bus speeds up to 133 MHz. Note that PCI buses are present even in Macintosh models that lack slots, such as the iBook and PowerBook.

PC Card

Also known as CardBus or PCMCIA (Personal Computer Memory Card International Association), the PC Card bus is used primarily on laptop systems. The thickness of PC Cards is indicated as Type I, Type II, or Type III. Although support for PC Cards was included in Mac OS 9, the use of PC Cards in Mac OS X requires a version higher than 10.0.3.

ATA and Serial ATA

Advanced Technology Attachment (ATA), also referred to as Parallel ATA, is an internal bus commonly used to connect storage devices such as hard disks and CD-ROM drives. Most Mac OS X-compatible computers prior to the Power Mac G5 used ATA for internal storage devices.

The Power Mac G5 was the first Apple computer with Serial ATA, the industry-standard storage interface designed to replace the Parallel ATA interface. Serial ATA supports 1.5 Gbit/s throughput (equivalent to a 150 Mb/s data rate). Since each Serial ATA drive is on an independent bus, there's no competition for bandwidth as with Parallel ATA.

Note that computers with Serial ATA buses still may include an ATA bus to connect slower storage devices such as optical media drives.

SCSI

Small Computer System Interface (SCSI) is a high-speed bus used mostly for storage devices. Due to the comparatively higher cost of SCSI drives and interfaces, ATA drives are used more commonly for internal storage. SCSI bus devices usually are reserved for systems that require high-performance data transfer. Current Macintosh systems do not have SCSI built-in, and they require the addition of a PCI card to connect SCSI devices.

USB 1.1/2.0

Universal Serial Bus (USB) is a plug-and-play interface for external add-on devices such as audio players, joysticks, keyboards, telephones, scanners, and printers.

Although still considered to be low speed, USB 1.1 supports a data speed of up to 12 Mbit/s, much faster than Apple Desktop Bus (ADB) and serial bus (the bus types it replaced in the Macintosh product line). USB 1.1 accommodates a wide range of peripherals, including MPEG video devices, data gloves, and digitizers.

The more recent USB 2.0 supports data transfer speeds of up to 480 Mbit/s, and is better suited for high-speed peripherals, such as storage devices and digital cameras. USB 2.0 devices can be plugged into a USB 1.1 bus but will operate at the slower USB 1.1 bus speed. Similarly, USB 1.1 devices can be plugged into a USB 2.0 bus, but will operate at the slower USB 1.1 speed.

USB ports provide electricity to attached peripherals, but the maximum power is very low (5 volts and .5 amps). Additionally, only USB ports and hubs with their own power source, called powered USB ports or hubs, can provide the maximum amount of power. Although a low-power device, such as a mouse or keyboard, can be plugged into any USB port, a device that requires more power, such as a scanner, needs to be plugged into a powered USB port, directly to the computer, or to a powered USB hub.

The Classic environment provides support for USB devices. If you have an older USB device, such as a scanner, that doesn't have a Mac OS X driver, try installing the Mac OS 9 software for the device and running it from within the Classic environment. Also, if you need to print to a USB printer from a Classic application, you will still need to install the Mac OS 9 printer driver, even if you have a Mac OS X printer driver installed.

FireWire 400/800

FireWire is a high-performance bus that, like USB, enables you to plug devices into your Macintosh computer without needing to turn off or restart your system (a feature called *hot plugging*). It is most popular for connecting digital video cameras and storage devices such as hard drives. It is also used to connect scanners, speakers, and printers.

The first version of FireWire, now referred to as FireWire 400, is the industry standard known as IEEE 1394 that provides data transfer speeds up to 400 MBit/s. Sony-branded digital devices, such as cameras, often include iLink, Sony's implementation of FireWire using a 4-pin connector. FireWire 400 devices that require bus power use a 6-pin connector. The maximum cable length for FireWire 400 is 4.5 meters.

FireWire 800 is an implementation of the IEEE 1394b standard that provides data transfer speeds up to 800 Mbit/s. When using professional-grade glass optical fiber, FireWire 800 can burst data across 100-meter cables. FireWire 800 devices use 9-pin connectors that are different than those used by FireWire 400 devices, but adapters allow the use of any FireWire device on any FireWire bus.

Like USB, FireWire ports provide power; however, the amount is much greater: a maximum of 30 volts and 1.5 amps. Many dual-bus devices, such as disk drives, that require their own power source when connected to USB, can operate without a separate power source when connected via FireWire.

Starting in FireWire Target Disk Mode

Most Mac OS X 10.3–compatible computers that have built-in FireWire have the capability to start up in FireWire target disk mode (TDM). Instead of booting the operating system, the computer (target) in disk mode acts as a hard drive that can be used by the host Macintosh with a FireWire connection. Essentially, this gives the host computer full access to the master internal ATA drive of the target computer. This is especially useful when a computer is unable to boot. The computer can be placed into target disk mode and connected to another computer, allowing files to be copied from the nonbooting computer. For more information on using target disk mode, see Knowledge Base article #58583, "How to Use FireWire Target Disk Mode."

FireWire target disk mode can be a big security risk. There are multiple ways to use TDM to access a system without knowing the system's password. If someone has physical access to a system, he or she can access files on the system. One method to lock out TDM is to use the Open Firmware Password utility (which you can download from Apple) and give the hardware itself a password.

To experiment with FireWire target disk mode, you need two Macintosh computers with FireWire ports and a single FireWire cable. If you don't have access to the necessary hardware, you can still follow along with these instructions:

1   Unplug all other FireWire devices from the target computer (the one whose hard drive you want to access) prior to using FireWire target disk mode. Do not plug in any FireWire devices until after you have disconnected the two computers from each other, or have stopped using target disk mode.

2   Shut down the target computer.

3   Start up the target computer and immediately press and hold down the T key until the FireWire icon appears, indicating that the target computer is now in FireWire target disk mode.

NOTE ▸ If you are using a laptop as the target computer and battery power becomes completely drained during this process, disk corruption can occur. For this reason, it's highly recommended to use an AC adapter whenever in target disk mode.

For the rest of this exercise, the target computer will be referred to as a Fire-Wire hard drive. Alternately, you can use a real external FireWire hard drive (or iPod configured for use as a hard drive) instead of the computer in target disk mode to complete the exercise.

Connecting a FireWire Hard Drive

To connect the FireWire drive (the computer running in target disk mode) to a running Mac OS X system, follow these steps:

1 Make sure the host computer is fully booted into the Finder in Mac OS X.

2 Connect the target computer and the host computer using a FireWire cable.

   After a few seconds, Mac OS X adds the FireWire hard drive to the Sidebar. In some cases, the hard drive may not appear right away because the operating system may be busy verifying the disk.

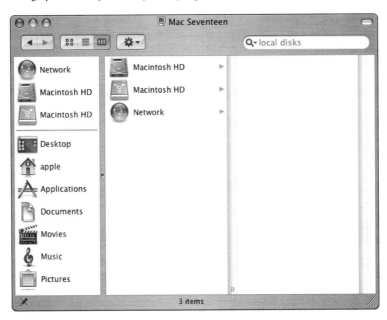

3 Open System Profiler.

4 Choose FireWire from the Contents pane.

System Profiler displays the FireWire device tree.

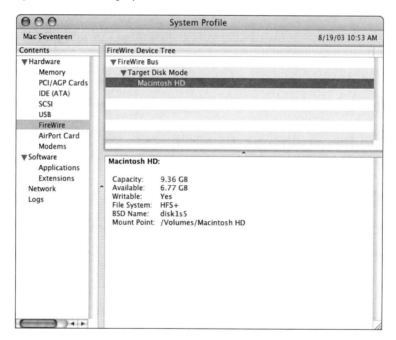

If the computer in target disk mode does not show up in the list of FireWire devices, quit and reopen System Profiler.

5 Select a partition from the Target Disk Mode item to see its capacity, available space, and file system.

6 Quit System Profiler.

7 Open Disk Utility.

8 Select a partition from the FireWire hard drive in the list of disks and volumes.

9 Click the Info button.

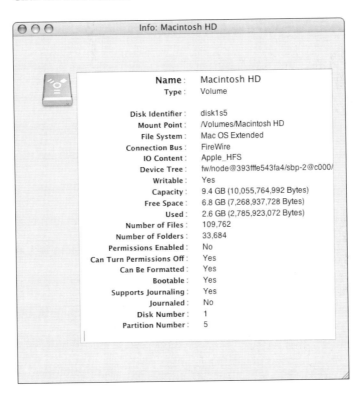

Notice that compared to System Profiler, Disk Utility provides more details, including the number of files and folders on a partition.

10 Quit Disk Utility.

11 In the Finder, select the FireWire drive and choose File > Get Info (Cmd-I) to view the permissions.

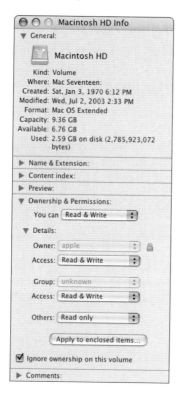

Because a FireWire drive is considered removable media, the Info window has the "Ignore ownership on this volume" option selected, and the owner of the file will be identified as the current user.

12 Unmount the FireWire drive from the host computer.

13 Disconnect the FireWire cable from the host computer and the FireWire hard drive (target computer).

14 Press and hold the power button to turn off the target computer.

15 Turn on the target computer without pressing any keys at startup to return it to normal operation.

Bluetooth

Bluetooth is an open specification for a technology that enables short-range wireless connections between desktop and laptop computers, personal digital assistants (PDAs), cellular phones, printers, scanners, digital cameras, and even home appliances on a globally available band (2.4 GHz) for worldwide compatibility. Because Bluetooth uses radio frequencies to transmit data, Bluetooth devices do not need to be in line-of-sight contact in order to communicate, as is the case for IrDA (Infrared Data Association). Although Bluetooth occupies the same bandwidth as AirPort, interference between the two is minimal, and users should not notice degradation of either when both are used in the same area.

With Bluetooth, within a 30-foot range you can wirelessly pair your Palm OS-based handheld device, Bluetooth-enabled cell phone, and other peripherals to your Macintosh computer. After the devices are paired, you can synchronize data, such as contacts and schedules, between your Macintosh and Bluetooth-enabled cell phones and PDAs. Though Bluetooth is not intended as a replacement for AirPort, it can be used for simple computer-to-computer communication. Mac OS X includes Bluetooth File Exchange (/Applications/ Utilities) to allow you to transfer files between two Bluetooth-enabled computers.

To take advantage of the Bluetooth support in Mac OS X, you must have a computer with Bluetooth pre-installed or install a Bluetooth adapter to act as a Bluetooth transmitter and receiver. To communicate with another device, you use Bluetooth preferences to pair with an available device and set a passkey to authenticate connections. Bluetooth preferences presents a list of all Bluetooth devices within range that are configured to be discoverable. Once you select the Bluetooth device on the list and click the Pair button, you're connected.

Configuring Bluetooth Devices

To experiment with Bluetooth devices, you need two Macintosh computers, both with built-in Bluetooth or with Bluetooth adapters. If you don't have access to the necessary hardware, you can still follow along with these instructions.

Before you can use Bluetooth to connect your computer to another Bluetooth device, you must perform some configuration, including setting a unique name for your computer:

1   Log in to your computer as Apple Admin.

2   If you are using a computer that does not have built-in Bluetooth support, plug a Bluetooth USB dongle into a free USB port.

3   Open System Preferences.

You should see a Bluetooth icon in the Hardware section.

Bluetooth preferences

4 If you do not see the Bluetooth icon, quit System Preferences and reopen it.

5 Click the Bluetooth icon to open Bluetooth preferences.

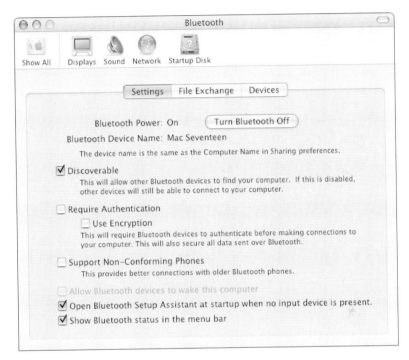

The Bluetooth Device Name is the computer name set in Sharing preferences.

6 Click the Settings button.

7 If Bluetooth Power is off, click Turn Bluetooth On.

8 Select "Show Bluetooth status in the menu bar."

This adds a Bluetooth menu on the right of the menu bar.

9 If it is not already enabled, select Discoverable.

10 Repeat steps 1 through 9 on a second Bluetooth-capable Macintosh, making sure that its computer name set in Sharing preferences is unique.

Pairing Two Computers Using Bluetooth

For two Bluetooth devices to communicate with each other, they must be paired so they can identify and authenticate each other. Normally you would pair your computer with a Bluetooth device such as a phone or PDA, however, this exercise has you pair two computers together to provide some Bluetooth experience without having to have a Bluetooth-enabled phone or PDA.

1 On your computer, in Bluetooth preferences, click Devices.

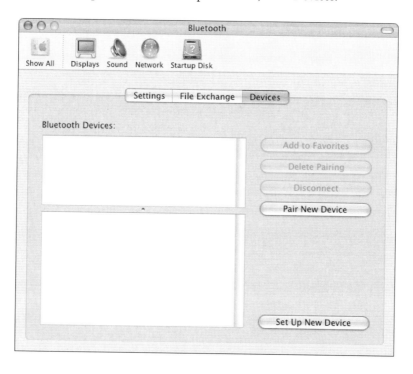

2   Click Pair New Device.

Bluetooth searches for Bluetooth-enabled devices within range.

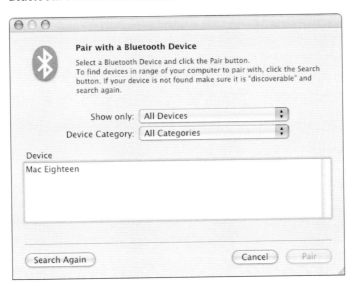

At first all other in-range Bluetooth-enabled devices are displayed as their MAC addresses, but after a few seconds, these numbers are replaced with their Rendezvous names.

3   If you do not see your other computer listed, click Search Again.

4   Select the device (your other computer) that you want to pair with and click Pair.

You will be prompted to enter a passkey.

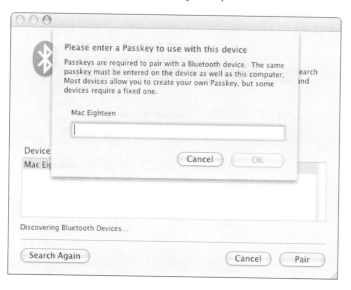

5   Enter a passkey on your computer and click OK.

A pairing request alert appears on the other computer.

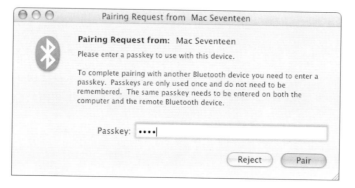

6   Enter the same passkey you specified on your computer, then click Pair.

If you enter an incorrect passkey, no error appears, and you will have to try again. If you enter the correct passkey, the Bluetooth pair is created and remembered, and the paired computers appear in each other's Bluetooth Devices lists in the Devices pane.

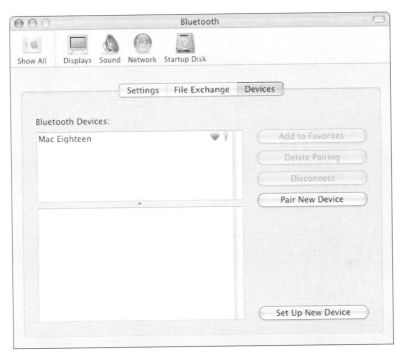

Exchanging Files Using Bluetooth

To use the Bluetooth File Exchange application to exchange files between Bluetooth-enabled computers, follow these steps:

1   In Bluetooth preferences on your computer, click File Exchange.

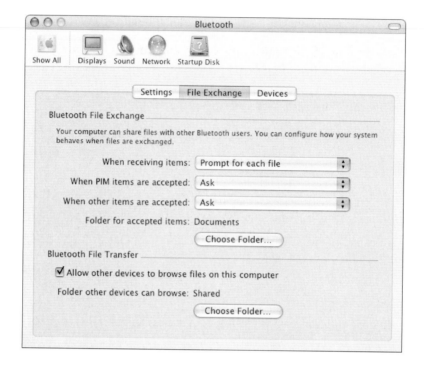

The File Exchange pane determines how files are transferred using Bluetooth. Use the default values shown in this screen shot for this exercise.

2   From the Bluetooth menu, choose Send File.

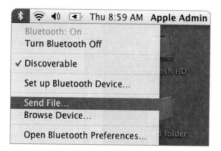

3 Select a small sample file on your computer, then click Send.

The Bluetooth File Exchange application opens and displays the Send File window.

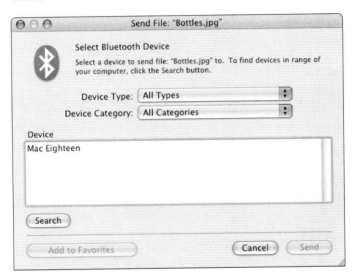

The previously-paired devices are listed.

4 Click Search to find the Bluetooth-enabled computers within range.

You might have to click Search multiple times to find your other computer.

5 Select the name of the computer you want to send files to from the list and then click Send.

Your computer displays a dialog that shows the progress of sending the file. This dialog disappears once the transfer is completed. If the transfer is declined, an alert message appears.

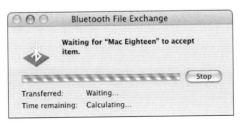

On the other computer, a dialog appears, asking if it is acceptable to receive the file.

6   Click Accept.

A progress dialog appears on the receiving computer as the file is sent.

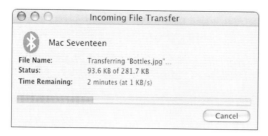

When the file transfer is completed, the receiving computer displays a dialog listing the file transferred.

7   Click the Find button (the magnifying glass) to open the folder containing the sent file. The default location for accepted items is specified in the File Exchange pane of Bluetooth preferences.

8   Quit Bluetooth File Exchange.

Viewing Peripherals with System Profiler

The Hardware section of the Contents pane in System Profiler displays reports for various hardware components, including buses supported by Mac OS X (for example, USB, FireWire, and PCI). After clicking a bus type, the upper-right pane of System Profiler displays a hierarchical view of the bus and devices connected to the bus. Clicking a device in the upper-right pane displays information about the device in the lower pane.

If you find that a connected peripheral is not functioning, use the Hardware section of the Contents pane in System Profiler to see if the device is recognized by the system. If the device is not listed, there may be a physical problem with the device or its connection to the system. If the device is listed in System Profiler, the hardware is working, and you are probably encountering a software issue, such as an incorrectly installed or configured device driver and/or support software.

System Profiler can generate reports of all the devices connected to a computer. To see what devices are connected to your computer, follow these steps:

1   Open System Profiler (/Applications/Utilities).

The System Profiler window displays the Hardware Overview.

The Contents pane on the left lists the types of reports that System Profiler can generate.

2   If the Hardware item in the Contents pane is not expanded, click the disclosure triangle to list all of the hardware reports.

Unlike the versions of Apple System Profiler that shipped with Mac OS X 10.2 and earlier, System Profiler has separate reports for each supported bus type.

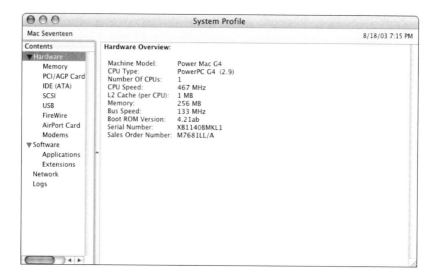

3 Select USB in the Contents pane.

Hierarchical lists representing the USB buses are displayed in the upper-right pane. The built-in Bluetooth port, if available, appears on the USB bus.

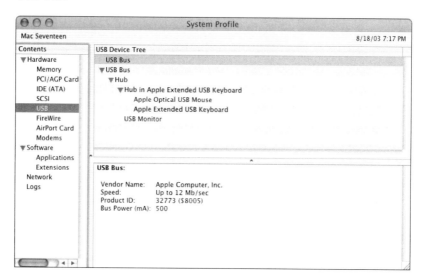

Devices connected to a bus are listed beneath the bus and indented. In the preceding screenshot, nothing is connected to the first USB bus, and a hub is connected to the second bus. The lower-right pane displays details about the currently selected bus or device.

If a device is connected to a hub, it is listed beneath the hub and indented. In this example, a USB monitor and the hub in the Apple keyboard are connected to the first hub. The mouse and keyboard are connected to the keyboard's hub.

NOTE ▶ Do not be confused by the fact that the keyboard is listed under a hub, which is located inside the keyboard itself. If a device allows other devices to be connected to it, it is actually a hub with the device (the keyboard in this case) connected to that hub.

The outermost Hub item under the USB Bus represents the hub that is part of the monitor casing. Both the monitor itself and the keyboard hub are attached to the monitor's hub. If you were to plug a mouse into the monitor's hub, the mouse would be listed as a peer to the keyboard hub.

4   Locate and select the mouse in the USB report for your computer.

   Details about the mouse are displayed in the lower-right pane.

5   Being careful not to click the mouse, unplug the mouse and move it to a different USB port, such as to a different free port on the computer, keyboard, or monitor.

6   Choose View > Refresh (Cmd-R).

7   Locate the mouse in the report to verify that it has changed places.

8   Move the mouse to yet another free USB port and refresh the report.

   If you are using a monitor with built-in USB ports, try moving the mouse to one of them or try plugging the mouse into a free USB port on the back of the computer.

9 Locate the mouse in the report.

10 Plug the mouse back into its original USB port.

11 Select the IDE or ATA item in the Contents pane.

12 The report window now lists all of the ATA buses in the computer and any devices connected to each bus.

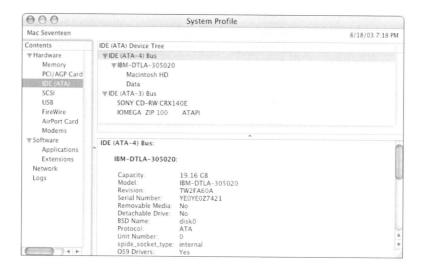

In this example, there are two ATA buses. The first bus has one device connected to it—an IBM hard drive; the second has two devices—a Sony CD-RW drive and an Iomega Zip drive.

13 Select the hard disk in the report.

The lower pane lists details about the disk drive, including the drive's capacity, serial number, and model number. It also lists the disk drive's partitions and details about each partition.

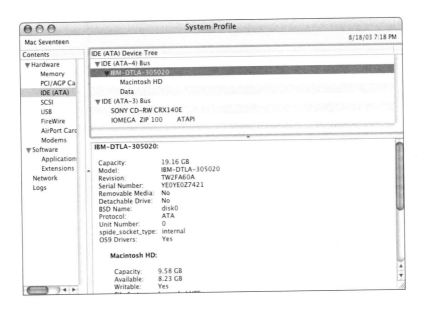

14 Select SCSI in the Contents pane.

Unless a SCSI card has been installed in your computer, the report pane displays "No information found."

15 Select PCI/AGP Cards in the Contents pane.

If you are using a laptop computer, you may be surprised to find that you still have a PCI device. Even though the display card is built-in, it is integrated into the system through the computer's integrated PCI bus.

Understanding Device Classes

Mac OS X groups devices into device classes, or types, to determine how to interact and support the devices' functionality.

Most applications do not care what buses' devices are connected. All they need to know are the types of devices connected. The operating system handles interaction across the various buses. For example, when using the Finder, you are able to retrieve files from a storage device whether the device is connected via FireWire, USB, or ATA.

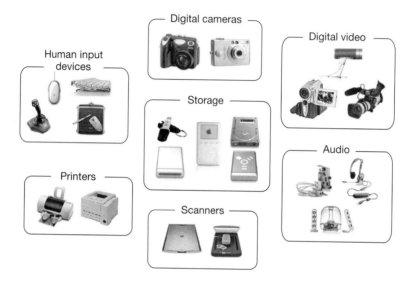

The three most common types of devices are human input devices, digital cameras and scanners, and storage devices.

Human Input Devices

One of the most common device types connected to a Macintosh computer is a human input device, part of the human interface device (HID) class. The HID class includes all of the devices that allow you to input data or control the computer. Some of the devices in this class include mice, keyboards, joysticks, and graphics tablets.

Digital Cameras and Scanners

To support digital cameras and scanners, Mac OS X includes the Image Capture framework. When you plug in a supported digital camera, or press a scanner's

Scan button, Mac OS X detects the action and opens an appropriate application to handle the camera or scanner. By default, iPhoto (/Applications) opens for cameras, and Image Capture (/Applications) opens for scanners. You can specify alternate applications in the Preferences menu item in the Image Capture utility.

Mac OS X supports digital cameras in three ways: it directly supports those that implement Photo Transfer Protocol (PTP); it uses the mass storage driver to access those that emulate a storage device and mount automatically on the desktop; and the Image Capture utility connects to cameras that have an Image Capture plug-in (/Library/Image Capture/Devices).

The Image Capture application also supports scanners that have installed either an Image Capture or TWAIN plug-in or module. In either case, the plug-in acts like a driver, providing software to allow the application to control the scanner. Image Capture modules for scanners also are installed in /Library/Image Capture/Devices, and TWAIN modules are stored in /Library/Image Capture/ TWAIN Data Sources.

Storage Devices

Mac OS X includes support for a wide variety of storage devices from hard disks to floppy drives to flash drives. In most cases, no additional drivers are required. If the device complies with ATA, FireWire, SCSI, or USB storage specifications, Mac OS X supports it. Some devices may provide a specialized driver or software to provide additional functionality such as password protection and encryption.

When removable drives or media are mounted, Mac OS X needs to make the file contained on the media accessible to the user. To accomplish this, the ownership of all the items on the disk is changed to the user who is currently logged in. For more information on how Mac OS X assigns permissions to removable media, see Lesson 2.

Ejecting Storage Volumes

Before unplugging a storage device from your computer, you should eject or unmount its volumes to avoid losing or corrupting data. This is true even for hot-pluggable devices connected via USB or FireWire.

To eject a volume, select the volume in the Finder and choose File > Eject. You can also use the Eject command in the Action pop-up menu. Removable media, such as CDs and FireWire hard drives, will have an eject button next to their icons in the Sidebar.

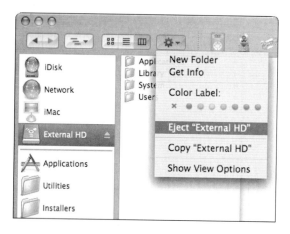

Disk Utility also includes commands for ejecting media and unmounting and mounting storage devices.

NOTE ▶ If you eject one volume from a drive that has multiple partitions, the system will also attempt to unmount the other partitions on the same drive.

Understanding Device Drivers

Drivers are programs that enable a computer to access and interact with hardware devices. Traditionally, drivers are thought of as existing at the lowest levels of the operating system. However, Mac OS X has three distinct types of drivers: kernel extensions, plug-ins or modules, and applications.

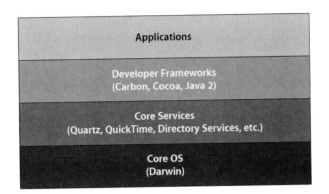

Kernel extensions (KEXTs) are pieces of software, provided in .kext files, that add functionality to the operating system kernel (Darwin). They are not the same thing as extensions in Mac OS 9. By default, kernel extensions are stored in /System/Library/Extensions. One type of kernel extension is a device driver. Mac OS X uses device drivers to provide system-wide or low-level functionality for a connected device, such as being able to read and write storage devices or read mouse movements.

Mac OS X includes a wide range of kernel extensions, allowing many devices to be used without installing extra software. However, if a device supports device-specific functionality, such as a disk drive providing password protection, you may need to install an extension provided by the developer of that device.

Some drivers are provided as plug-ins or modules for frameworks in Mac OS X. For example, support for cameras and scanners is provided with Image Capture modules. Printer drivers are provided as plug-ins to the printing architecture.

For some devices, a driver is not provided as an addition to the operating system; rather, it is included as part of an application. For example, a backup utility could include a driver to control a tape drive, since Mac OS X doesn't include native support for it.

Viewing Extensions with System Profiler

Because kernel extensions can be stored in several different Library folders, System Profiler provides the Extensions item under the Software section of the Contents pane. Clicking the Extensions item lists all of the installed kernel extensions available in the system, along with other information such as their version numbers and modification dates in the upper-right pane of the System Profiler window. Clicking a kernel extension in the upper-right pane displays the Info strings (additional text that is displayed in the Finder's Info window) in the lower-right pane of the window.

Not all kernel extensions are drivers. In addition to controlling devices, kernel extensions provide other low-level services such as file system and networking support. Unfortunately, aside from the name and possibly the Get Info string, there is no way to distinguish between the different types of kernel extensions in either the Finder or System Profiler.

To use System Profiler to generate a list of all installed kernel extensions:

1   Select the Extensions item beneath the Software item in the Contents pane.

System Profiler scans the system and generates a list of all installed kernel extensions.

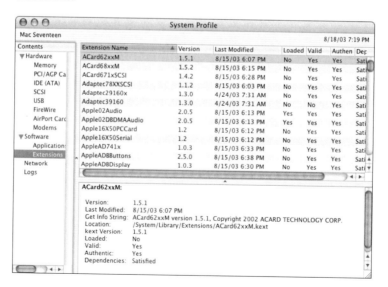

2   Scroll down to locate the driver for the iPod.

Note that the name of the extension is iPodDriver.

3   Quit System Profiler.

Configuring Universal Access

Some users have difficulty operating the basic user I/O devices included with Mac OS X computers, such as the display, keyboard, and mouse. For them, Universal Access preferences allows easier access to these peripherals.

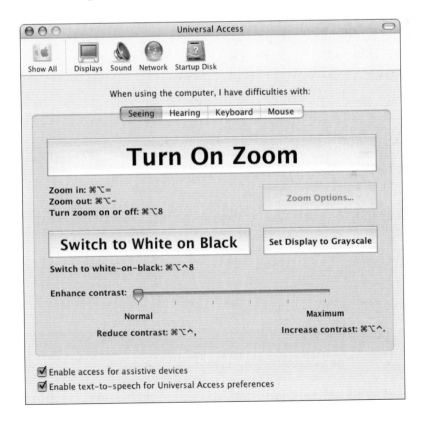

Universal Access preferences is divided into four panes:

▶ Seeing—Provides options to modify the display view. You can configure the display to zoom in wherever the pointer is, providing a magnified view of the screen. You can also set the screen to white on black for users sensitive to brightness.

▶ Hearing—Allows the screen to flash when an alert sound occurs.

▶ Keyboard—Provides options to lessen difficulties using the keyboard, such as pressing multiple keys simultaneously.

▶ Mouse—Allows the keypad, instead of the mouse, to be used for controlling the pointer.

If a user requires special equipment to control the computer, select the "Enable access for assistive devices" checkbox.

To help those with difficulty reading the screen to configure preferences, select the "Enable text-to-speech for Universal Access preferences" checkbox. With this selected, Mac OS X speaks the text pointed to in Universal Access preferences. (Turning on the "Text under the mouse" option in the Spoken User Interface pane of Speech preferences provides the same functionality in other System Preference panes, the Finder, and the Dock.)

Troubleshooting Peripherals

Here are some strategies for identifying and fixing problems with peripherals connected to your computer:

▶ Verify that the operating system recognizes that the device is connected. Use System Profiler's Hardware section of the Contents pane to locate the device. If you cannot find the device listed, you probably have a hardware problem, such as a broken device or loose connection.

▶ Unplug and reconnect the cables, making sure the connections are tight. Be sure the cables are not too long. USB 1.1 cables, for example, should be a maximum of 4.5 meters long. Try a different cable to connect the device to make sure the cable isn't defective.

▶ Try plugging the device into a different port. If the device doesn't have a power cord and is plugged into another USB device that doesn't have a power cord, try plugging the device directly into your computer or to a USB device that does have a power cord.

▶ Try unplugging all other devices to make sure that there isn't a conflict between devices.

▶ If you are able to find the device listed in System Profiler, you probably have a software problem. Check with the manufacturer and install the latest version of the drivers.

What You've Learned

▶ Buses, such as USB and FireWire, are used to connect devices to the computer.

▶ Devices are categorized into classes based upon their functionality.

▶ Drivers are pieces of code that allow the system or a user to interact with a device. Drivers can be kernel extensions that provide functionality at a very low level in Mac OS X (such as plug-ins), higher-level system components (such as the printing and Image Capture frameworks), or applications that are used to control specific devices.

▶ System Profiler provides information about connected devices and available drivers. The Hardware section of the Contents pane in System Profiler lists the buses built into your computer. For each bus, System Profiler lists the connected devices. The Extensions item in the Software section of the Contents pane lists all of the kernel extensions installed on your system.

▶ Universal Access preferences provides options to allow easier access for users with difficulties using I/O devices such as keyboards, mice, and monitors.

▶ To troubleshoot issues with peripherals, use System Profiler to determine whether a device is connected, plug the device into a different port, unplug other devices, or update drivers.

References

The following Knowledge Base articles (located at http://kbase.info.apple.com) will provide you with further information regarding peripherals in Mac OS X.

External Devices

▶ 58648, "Mac OS X: Do Not Connect USB Printer to Apple Pro Keyboard"

▶ 106403, "Mac OS X: 'No Driver for This Platform' Message"

USB

▶ 31116, "USB Cable: Maximum Cable Length"

▶ 43005, "USB: Hub Description"

▶ 61237, "What to Do if a USB Device Isn't Working"

▶ 86455, "Macintosh: USB 2.0 Specifications and Information"

▶ 93007, "About the Universal Serial Bus (USB)"

FireWire

▶ 30520, "About FireWire 400 Technology"

▶ 58583, "How to Use FireWire Target Disk Mode"

▶ 75471, "About FireWire 800 Technology"

ATFA

▶ 30510, "ATA, IDE, EIDE and ATAPI Defined"

▶ 88409, "Ultra ATA/100: A Brief Description"

Bluetooth

▶ 52080, "Apple Bluetooth Manuals"

Review Quiz

Use the following questions to review what you have learned:

1. What is the difference between a bus and a device class?

2. What can you use to determine if a device's nonfunctionality is caused by software in the operating system or by a bad physical connection?

3. What is FireWire?

4. What is USB?

5. What is Bluetooth?

6. What quick fixes are particularly useful to consider when troubleshooting peripherals issues?

7. What is the function of Universal Access preferences?

8. What are the three types of drivers discussed in this lesson?

Answers

1. A bus is what connects a device to a computer and carries data between the device and the computer. A device class is a grouping of devices by their functionality.

2. System Profiler will list all devices that are connected to a bus. If a device is not listed, there is a physical connection problem between the device and the computer.

3. FireWire is a high-speed bus most frequently used to connect external digital video cameras and storage devices.

4. USB is a low-speed bus, most frequently used to connect external input devices and printers.

5. Bluetooth is a wireless bus used to connect between a computer and cell phones, PDAs, and other computers.

6. Use System Profiler to locate the device; try a different port; disconnect other peripherals; update drivers.

7. Universal Access preferences allow the system to be configured to allow easier access to the computer for those that have difficulties using the mouse or keyboard, with hearing, or viewing the screen.

8. Kernel extensions, which reside in the kernel; plug-ins or modules; and drivers included as part of an application.

10

Time

This lesson takes approximately 1 hour to complete.

Goals

Use Printer Setup Utility to add local printers, network printers, and print servers

Use Printer Setup Utility to troubleshoot printing issues, including printer sharing

Use System Preferences to configure Mac OS X to receive faxes and allow other users to send faxes through your computer

Use the standard print dialog to send a fax from Mac OS X

Configure a printer connected to a Mac OS X computer so that it can be shared by Windows computers

Install and troubleshoot a PDF Workflow solution

Print a PostScript file to a raster printer

Describe how to configure printing under Classic

Print and manage print jobs from the command line

Lesson **10**

Printing

The printing architecture of Mac OS X includes the Printer Setup Utility; the print dialogs of printing applications; and the Common Unix Printing System (CUPS), a cross-platform, open-source printing solution. In addition to providing printing capabilities for applications in the Mac OS X graphical user interface, CUPS provides command-line printing services for PostScript and raster printers.

Using CUPS

When you print from an application within the Mac OS X graphical user interface, the Mac OS X imaging frameworks are used to create a Portable Document Format (PDF) spool file that is passed to CUPS. When you print from the command line, the spool file might be in a non-PDF format such as text or PostScript. CUPS allows you to print any of these document types to PostScript and raster printers, whether they are connected directly to your computer or shared over a network.

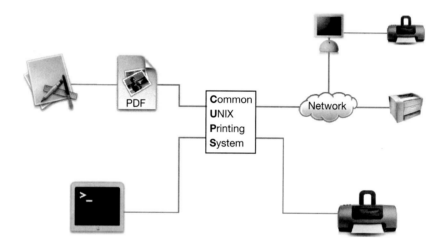

Spool files created by Mac OS X applications or by command-line utilities are placed in the hidden directory /var/spool/cups. The CUPS daemon then finds each spool file and passes it through a set of filters known as the print chain. These processes convert the file to a format that the printer understands, then they send the output file to the printer.

CUPS contains many features that are beyond the scope of this lesson. You can find more information about CUPS in Knowledge Base article #75413, "Mac OS X Server 10.2: How to Set Up Print Load Balancing Using CUPS." You can also learn more about CUPS by accessing online help in the built-in CUPS Web server by entering the following URL in a Web browser running on Mac OS X 10.3: *http://127.0.0.1:631.*

Managing Printers

You use Printer Setup Utility (/Applications/Utilities) to configure local and network printers in Mac OS X.

You can customize the toolbar in Printer Setup Utility by choosing View > Customize Toolbar. Drag icons from the configuration sheet to Printer Setup Utility's toolbar, then click Done.

Adding a Printer

The first time you open Printer Setup Utility, it prompts you to add a printer. When you click Add, a configuration sheet appears, and Printer Setup Utility searches for all available printing devices. The standard Mac OS X installation includes printer modules for Canon, Epson, Hewlett-Packard, Lexmark, and Xerox printers. It also includes GimpPrint, an open-source print driver that supports many older printer models that might not have Mac OS X drivers.

> **NOTE** ▶ GimpPrint drivers vary in quality. Some GimpPrint drivers are better than the vendor's and use less disk space. More often, the vendor-supplied drivers offer more functionality. GimpPrint drivers are most useful for customers who have very old printers or printers not supported by the vendor, and for customers who do custom, high-end printing.

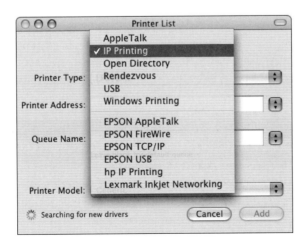

The topmost pop-up menu in the configuration sheet lets you specify the method your computer uses to access the printer. Choices include the following:

▶ AppleTalk—For a network printer that uses the AppleTalk protocol.

▶ IP Printing—For a network printer that is configured by its IP address. Quite often, IP printers are part of a printer queue, or print server, that provides printing services for a small or large network. IP printing allows you to add printers using the LPR/LPD (Line Printer Request/Line Printer Daemon), IPP (Internet Printing Protocol), and Socket/HP direct protocols.

▶ Open Directory—For a network printer or printer queue that is available statically through a directory service such as Lightweight Directory Access Protocol (LDAP).

▶ Rendezvous—For a network printer that uses Rendezvous.

▶ USB—For a printer connected to your computer's USB port. When you connect a USB printer, Mac OS X typically detects it, locates the driver, and adds the printer to the Printer List. If Mac OS X does not detect it, or if you want to add a USB printer and manually select the driver, you can click the Add button in the Printer List window.

▶ Windows Printing—For printers shared using the SMB protocol.

> **NOTE ▶** Other types of printers, such as FireWire and Bluetooth, might appear in the menu if you have added additional devices or drivers to your computer.

The configuration choices available depend upon the printer type you chose. For all types, once you have selected the printer and configured all settings, you click Add. The Printer List window will display the new printer.

When you add a printer, a PostScript Printer Description (PPD) file, describing the features of the printer, is created in the hidden directory /etc/cups/ppd regardless of whether or not the printer uses PostScript. The PPD file is copied or generated from files that were installed with the printer driver. PPD files for standard CUPS and GimpPrint drivers reside in /usr/share/cups/model and /usr/share/cups/model/C, respectively.

PPD files for Mac-specific drivers provided by third-party printer manufacturers are in subdirectories of /Library/Printers/PPD. The PPD files provided by printer manufacturers usually include more printer features than those provided with CUPS or GimpPrint.

In this exercise, you'll add a local USB printer to the Printer List for use with Mac OS X applications. If you don't have a USB printer, just read these steps so that you understand the procedure:

1   Open Printer Setup Utility (/Applications/Utilities).

Click Cancel if an alert appears with the message "You have no printers available."

2   Whenever you open Printer Setup Utility, the Printer List window appears.

The contents of your Printer List will differ from the screen shots in this book. If any printers are listed, and you have not connected and turned on your printer yet, Mac OS X probably found shared network printers. For this exercise, disregard these printers. The only one you are concerned with is the one connected directly to your computer.

3 Attach the printer to the computer with a USB cable and turn on the printer.

After a few seconds, if the printer is supported by Mac OS X, it will be automatically added to the list of printers in Printer Setup Utility. The name displayed will vary depending upon the model of the printer.

4 Select the printer and then click the Show Info button.

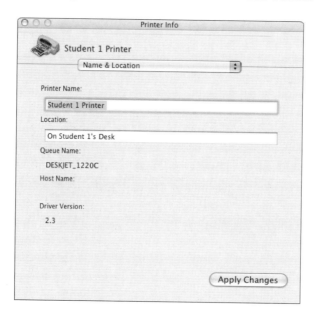

5   In the Printer Name field, enter a descriptive name for the printer.

6   In the Location field, enter the physical location of the printer.

7   Click Apply Changes and close the window.

Notice that the name of the printer in the Printer Setup Utility's list has been updated. You are now ready to print.

Printing to a Local Printer

To test that the USB printer added in the previous exercise is properly configured, follow these steps:

1   In Printer Setup Utility, open the print queue for your printer by double-clicking the printer in the list or by selecting the printer and choosing Printers > Show Jobs.

This step is not required for printing; you are doing it so that you can monitor the printing process.

2   Open TextEdit (/Applications) and in the untitled document that appears, type a few lines of text, such as *This is a test of the printer.*

3   Choose File > Print.

A Print dialog appears.

4   From the Printer pop-up menu, choose the newly added printer.

5   Click Print.

TextEdit prints your document by creating a spool file that is added to the queue for your printer.

You can monitor the progress of printing in the queue window that you opened in step 1.

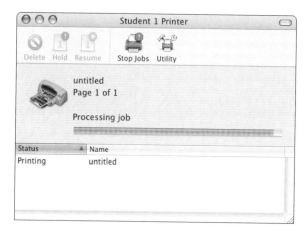

When the queue is done processing your job, the printer prints your document.

6   In TextEdit, close the untitled document, saving it to the desktop as *Print Tester.rtf*.

7   Quit TextEdit.

8   Quit Printer Setup Utility.

Sharing Printers

As explained in Lesson 7, Mac OS X can share many services and resources. In addition to sharing files and Internet access, you can share printers with networked users. You can turn on printer sharing multiple ways.

One place you can turn on printer sharing is in the Services pane of Sharing preferences. Select Printer Sharing from the list of services, then click Start.

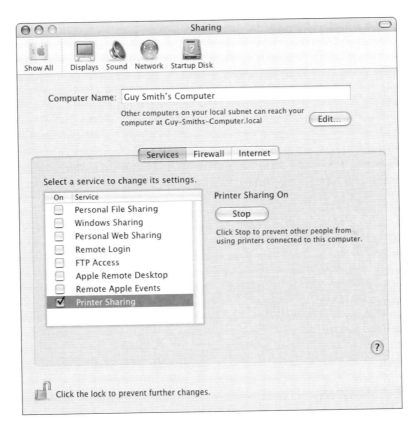

You can also turn on printer sharing in the Printing pane of Print & Fax preferences. Once you select the "Share my printers with other computers" checkbox, other Mac OS X and Windows users on the network can use printers connected to your system.

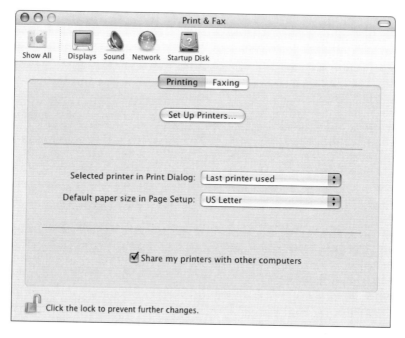

You can also share USB printers connected to an AirPort Extreme Base Station, but that is beyond the scope of this book.

Once you turn on Printer Sharing, all printers configured on your computer will appear in two places on other Mac OS X systems on the local network:

▶   In the Printer List in Printer Setup Utility

▶   In the Shared Printers menu item in the Printers pop-up menu in most applications' print dialogs

NOTE ▶ You can also reshare network printers so you are able to monitor and manage jobs sent to a network printer (if users printing to it go through your computer instead of printing directly to that network printer). There are two disadvantages to resharing network printers:

▶ You increase network traffic. Instead of users sending the print jobs directly to the printer, they send it to your machine and then your machine sends it to the printer.

▶ Your machine assumes the increased load of processing all print jobs sent to that network printer.

Printing to a Shared USB Printer

Not only does Mac OS X allow you to share printers that have been added to the Printer List in Printer Setup Utility, it also allows you to use printers that other users are sharing.

Any printer shared by another computer on your local network automatically appears in your computer's Printer List and in applications' print dialogs. If you do not want to use shared printers, you can disable the listing on your computer by deselecting the In Menu checkbox next to the printer name in the Printer List.

Your computer might not have the print driver required for a particular shared printer. In this case, Mac OS X will download the PPD file of the printer from the computer sharing the printer and provide your computer with details on the shared printer's capabilities. This process happens automatically and does not require any action on your part, but it may cause a slight delay when you first select the printer.

In this exercise, you'll add a shared USB printer to the Printer List. If you don't have a second Macintosh with a USB printer on your network, just read these steps so that you understand the procedure:

1   On the remote Macintosh, open Printer Setup Utility.

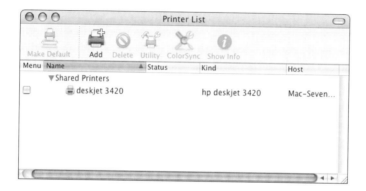

You should find your printer listed because Mac OS X scans the local network for any shared USB printers and automatically adds them to the list. As in the previous exercise, you may find printers other than your own listed. For now, disregard any other printers.

2   Select the printer that is connected to your computer.

3   Choose View > Columns > Location.

Printer Setup Utility adds a Location column displaying the location information. When sharing printers, you should always provide physical location information to let users know where to find their printouts.

4   Open any text document in TextEdit, then choose File > Print.

The Print dialog appears.

5   From the Printer pop-up window, choose Shared Printers. Then, choose the name of the printer connected to your computer.

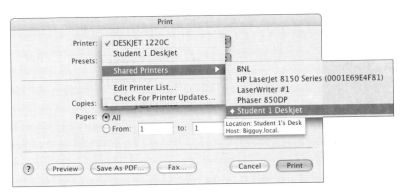

Notice that if you hold the pointer over the printer name, a small window appears, displaying information about the shared printer.

6   Click Print.

The document will be printed on the USB printer connected to your computer.

7   Close the sample print document.

8   Quit TextEdit.

9   Don't save changes if requested.

10   Quit Printer Setup Utility.

11   On your computer, turn off Printer Sharing.

Adding a Networked PostScript Printer

Unlike shared USB printers that are discovered and added to the list of available printers automatically, you manually add networked PostScript printers in Printer Setup Utility.

1 Open Printer Setup Utility.

The Printer List will already contain entries if you completed the USB printing exercise or if there are shared printers on the network. During this exercise, you can disregard these printers.

2 Click the Add button.

Printer Setup Utility displays a configuration sheet that allows you to specify information about which printer to add to your printer list.

3 Choose IP Printing from the topmost pop-up menu.

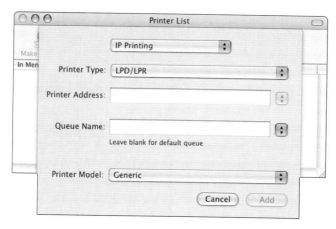

4 In the Printer Address field, enter the networked printer's URL or IP (Internet Protocol) address.

To obtain this address, you may need to contact your network administrator or check the printer's documentation to determine how to generate a configuration page.

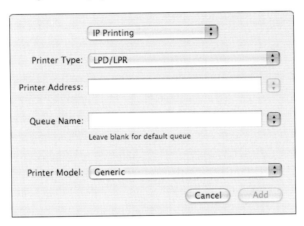

5 Leave the other settings at their default values and click Add.

Printer Setup Utility will redisplay the printer list with your network printer added.

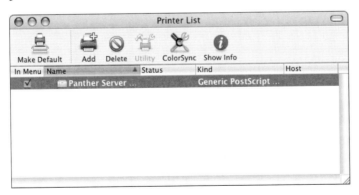

A URL or IP address does not help a typical user identify a printer. You can change the local name of the printer in the Printer Info dialog.

6 In the Printer List window, select the printer you just added.

7 Press Cmd-I to display the Printer Info dialog.

8 Change the Printer Name to something a bit more descriptive.

9 Click Apply Changes and close the Printer Info dialog.

10 Quit Printer Setup Utility.

Printing to a Networked Printer
Now that you have added a printer in Printer Setup Utility, make sure you can print to it.

1 Open any text document in TextEdit, then choose File > Print.

The print dialog appears.

2 From the Printer pop-up menu, choose the printer that you named in step 8 of the previous exercise.

3 Click Print.

4 Quit TextEdit.

Sharing Printers with Windows

Mac OS X 10.3 supports printer sharing over the SMB protocol commonly used in Microsoft Windows. This means two things:

▶ A Mac OS X computer can print to a printer shared by a Windows computer over the network.

▶ Windows computers can print to a Mac OS X computer's shared printer.

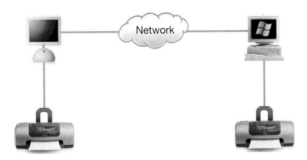

Printing to a Windows Shared Printer

With Mac OS X 10.3, you can print to printers shared by Windows computers. To add Windows-shared printers from the Printer Setup Utility, click Add, then from the topmost pop-up menu, choose Windows Printing. You can list printers by Windows workgroup or domain.

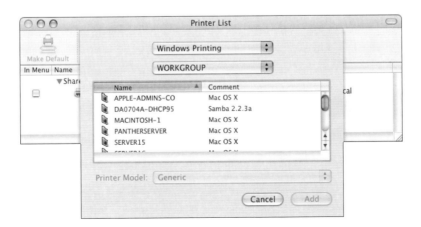

Printing from Windows

If you turn on Windows Sharing in the Services pane of Sharing preferences, Windows computers will see your Mac OS X computer in their Network Neighborhoods. On a Windows computer, you can browse for a Mac OS X computer under its workgroup. (You can change the workgroup of your Mac OS X computer in Directory Access.) If you double-click the Mac OS X computer's icon in Network Neighborhood, you will be able to see the shared printers. You can double-click a shared printer to use it. An alert will prompt you for the driver, which you can usually download from the Internet.

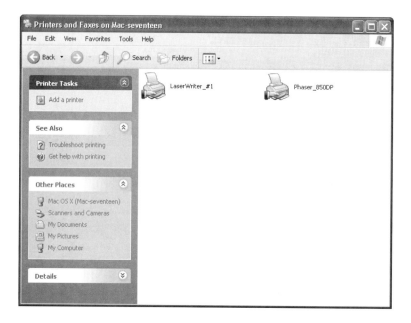

Managing Print Queues

Each printer you set up has a print queue associated with it. When you share a printer, all jobs sent to that printer are sent to that printer's queue on your computer, so it's important not to shut down your computer or put it to sleep.

You can view and manage a printer's queue from within Printer Setup Utility by double-clicking the printer's name in the Printer List. A window opens displaying the printer's queue and the current print status.

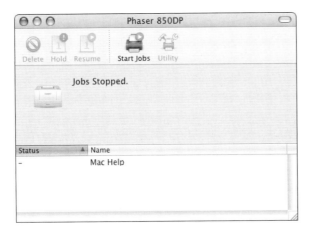

Individual print jobs can be paused, restarted, or deleted from the queue by selecting the print job and clicking the Hold, Resume, or Delete buttons, respectively. The Stop Jobs button stops the print queue completely until you click the Start Jobs button, after which the print jobs in the queue resume printing.

If a queue is stopped and someone tries to print to it, a dialog asks them to add the job to the queue and wait for the queue's owner to turn it on, or to restart the queue and print the job.

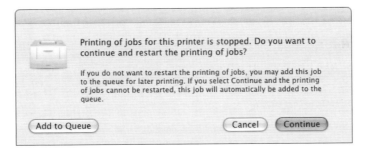

If you are resharing a network printer, you can conveniently monitor and
manage what is being sent to the printer by using the network printer's queue.
The queue can also be managed from the command line by using Terminal
(/Applications/Utilities), although doing so is not discussed in this lesson.

Setting Printer Info

The default names in the Printer List in Printer Setup Utility might not be
intuitive, especially for IP printers that display only an IP address. You can,
however, modify the entry and change the name to something more descriptive and useful. You can also provide location information to help others find
where the printer is physically located. To modify printer information, select
a printer from Printer List and choose Printers > Show Info (Cmd-I).

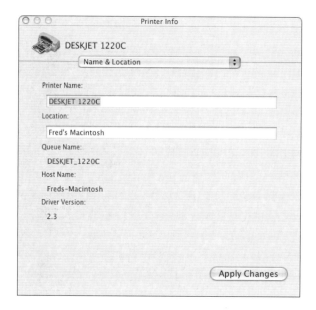

Printing Documents

Once you have added a printer using Printer Setup Utility as explained earlier
in this lesson, all Mac OS X applications can print to that device using a simple
process and a consistent interface.

Printing from Mac OS X Applications

Almost all Mac OS X applications that create or edit documents have Page Setup and Print commands in their File menus. If you've never printed from a particular application before, the first step is to configure Page Setup because each application maintains its own settings for this dialog.

Configuring the Page Setup Dialog

The Page Setup dialogs of Mac OS X applications allow you to change the appearance of pages to be printed. The choices for settings depend on the application you are printing from and the printer you are using to print.

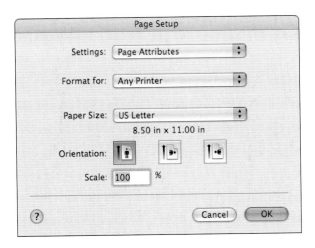

Because the printable area on a page varies for each type of printer, it is important to use the Page Setup dialog to specify the intended printer so that the application does not attempt to exceed the printable area. The configuration in Page Setup is used to determine the printable area.

The "Format for" pop-up menu is subtle in how it affects the page. Each printer has different page boundaries. Some can print closer to the top and bottom edges of the page; others can print closer to the left and right edges. Choose Any Printer from this pop-up to specify a lowest common denominator for the printable area, one that just about any printer can handle.

If you find that headers or footers are cut off when printed from your computer, but not from another computer, check the printer choice in Page Setup. (It is probably set to Any Printer.) Choosing the correct printer may fix the problem.

The default items in the Paper Size pop-up menu in Page Setup are country-specific. For example, if you selected United States as your country when you configured your computer using Setup Assistant, the Paper Size menu items include US Letter and US Legal.

Configuring the Print Dialog

In almost every Mac OS X application, if you choose File > Print, the Print dialog appears. Printers configured in Printer Setup Utility appear in the Printer pop-up menu in the Print dialog. You can configure and save options such as number of copies and pages, layout, output, paper feed, and error handling. Additional options depend on the printer driver being used and might be configurable in the Printer Setup Utility in the Show Info window.

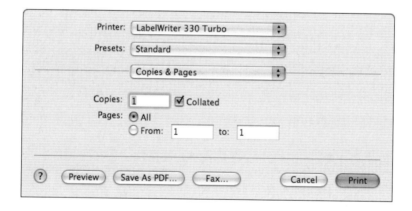

Printing from Classic Applications

The Classic environment uses some, but not all of the features of the Mac OS X printing architecture. You do not use Printer Setup Utility to configure printers for printing from Classic applications. Instead, you use the Chooser to select a printer. The Chooser is available from the Apple menu when you are running a Classic application.

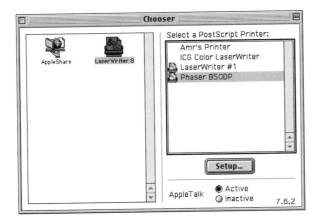

If you add an IP printer in Printer Setup Utility, you must choose LaserWriter 8 in the Classic's Chooser, then select the printer in the list at the right (see Knowledge Base article #106687, "Mac OS X: How to Select an LPR Printer in Classic"). For a USB printer, you must install a Mac OS 9 driver available from the manufacturer (see Knowledge Base article #106710, "Mac OS X: How to Print From a Classic Application"). Placing the PPD in /Library/Printers/PPDs/Contents/Resources/English.lproj allows Printer Setup Utility to find it auto-matically. You also could store it in some other directory. Then, when you add the printer, choose Other as a printer model and navigate to the PPD's location.

To print a document in a Classic application, choose File > Print (Cmd-P), configure the Print dialog that appears, then click Print.

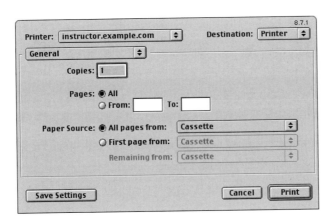

Mac OS 9 printer drivers are located in /System Folder/Extensions. You can install a Mac OS 9 PPD in Mac OS X. Most printer manufacturers include an installer to place the PPD into the correct location for Mac OS X. However, in some cases you might have to install the PPD under Classic, then manually move it to the Mac OS X location. In that case, you need to create a directory structure in /Library/Printers/PPDs/Contents/Resources/English.lproj and copy the PPD files from /System Folder/Extensions/Printer Descriptions to that new directory. Do not delete the copy in /System Folder/Extensions/ Printer Descriptions.

Printing Using Desktop Printers

If you create a desktop icon for a printer, you can quickly print documents by dragging and dropping document icons onto the printer icon in the Finder. You can also double-click the desktop printer icon to open the printer's queue window and monitor jobs while they print.

To create a desktop printer, either select the printer in the Printer Setup Utility and choose Printers > Create Desktop Printer (Shift-Cmd-D), or drag the printer's name from the Printer List to the Finder's desktop.

Printing from the Command Line

You can use either lp or lpr to print from the command line in Terminal (/Applications/Utilities). You can get printer status using lpstat and other information using lpinfo. You can use cancel to delete a print job. As an administrator, you can add, delete, and manage printers using the lpadmin command.

For more information about printing from the command line, see http://127.0.0.1:631/sam.html#4_3.

Using Other Print Options

Mac OS X has some unique options for outputting documents that don't involve printing, but they utilize the same interface because the process is virtually the same as printing.

Saving Documents as PDF Files

In Mac OS X, it is easy for you to save a document as a PDF file. All you need to do is choose File > Print (Cmd-P), then within the Print dialog, click Save As PDF. Enter a name and location for the PDF file, then click Save. You can open a PDF file with Preview (/Applications/Utilities) or any of Adobe's Acrobat applications on any platform, making PDF the perfect vehicle for sharing documents when retaining formatting is important.

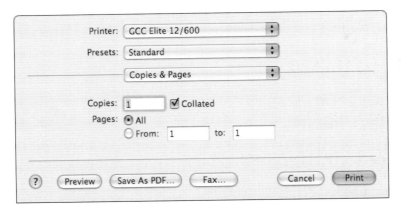

The ability to save any document as a PDF file in Mac OS X 10.3 is very useful. It can be extended almost infinitely through the PDF Workflow feature, which enables you to specify how you will prepare the PDF and what to do with it after creation. For example, you can open the PDF with Adobe Acrobat or optimize the PDF for onscreen viewing using a Unix tool.

By default, Mac OS X displays the Save As PDF button at the bottom of the
Print dialog. To replace this button with the PDF Workflow button, create a
new folder (Shift-Cmd-N) in either /Library or ~/Library, and name it PDF
Services.

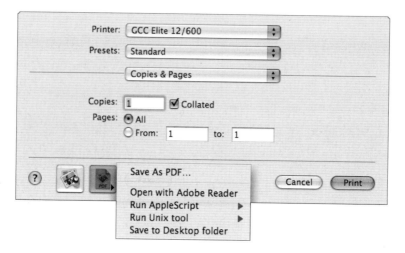

To add functionality to the PDF Workflow buttons, into either of these directories, place the following:

▶ A folder

▶ An application

▶ A Unix tool

▶ An AppleScript file

> **NOTE** ▶ You can also add items to /Network/Library/PDF Services.
> However, the local /Library/PDF Services or ~/Library/PDF Services/
> directory is required to activate the PDF Workflow feature.

Instead of putting original items in these directories, it's better to use aliases.
The PDF Workflow pop-up menu displays the exact names of the items in
these directories. By using aliases, you can leave the originals where they already
exist and then rename the aliases so they make sense when displayed in the
PDF Workflow pop-up menu.

The type of item determines what the item does when you choose it from the PDF Workflow pop-up menu. For example, if the item is a location (such as a folder), then the PDF is saved in that location. If the item is an application, the PDF is opened by that application. The real magic happens if you know how to create Unix tools or AppleScript scripts, since they can be used to specify complex workflow actions.

You can find more information about using PDF Workflows at http://developer. apple.com/ and in Knowledge Base article #151663, "Setting Up Workflows for Creating PDF Files."

Saving Documents in PostScript Format

The printing system in Mac OS X includes a PostScript interpreter that allows you to print a PostScript document to a non-PostScript printer. You can also convert a document to PostScript format without printing it. To do that, open the document, choose File > Print (Cmd-P), and from the Printer pop-up menu choose a PostScript printer. From the third pop-up menu, choose Output Options, select the Save as File checkbox, and then choose PostScript from the Format pop-up menu and click Save.

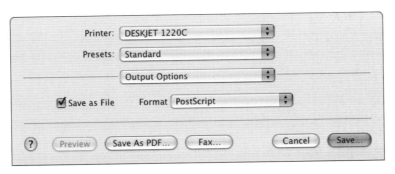

If you do not have a PostScript printer, you can create a virtual PostScript printer on your computer and choose it when you want to convert a file to PostScript. To create a virtual PostScript printer, open Printer Setup Utility, click Add, and choose IP Printing from the topmost pop-up menu. Choose Internet Printing Protocol from the Printer Type pop-up menu. Type *localhost*

in the printer's Address field and provide an easy-to-remember name in the Queue Name text box. From the Printer Model pop-up menu, choose a printer manufacturer's name, and then choose a PostScript printer in the Model list. Click Add. When you want to save a document as a PostScript file, in the Print dialog choose this printer from the Printer pop-up menu.

Once you have a PostScript file on your computer, you can print it on either a PostScript or a raster printer by dragging and dropping the file onto a desktop printer icon. You can also print a PostScript file from the command line. (You could open the PostScript file in Preview and print from there, but Preview would convert the file to PDF for printing, which might degrade the quality.)

Faxing Documents

With Mac OS X 10.3, you can "print" a document to a fax machine using your computer's internal modem. In any Mac OS X application that can print to a normal printer, choose File > Print to open the standard Print dialog. Click Fax, and a configuration sheet appears.

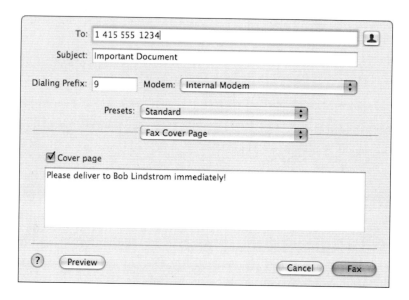

In the To field, enter the telephone number of the receiving fax machine. All other fields are optional. When you are ready to send your document, click Fax. Mac OS X transmits the document as a fax through the chosen modem, which must be connected to a working telephone line.

You can also share your faxing capability with other computers on the local network so they can fax through your computer, the same way you can share a printer.

When you enable Printer Sharing in the Services pane of Sharing preferences, users on other computers can add your fax modem to their Printer Lists. To add your fax modem to their Printer Lists in Printer Setup Utility, they choose View > Show Fax List, then select your fax modem in the list.

Note that when you are sharing your fax modem, computers on the network using your fax modem will spool jobs to your computer. This means that their print spool job will be stored on your system until it's faxed. The location for the spooled files is /var/spool/fax.

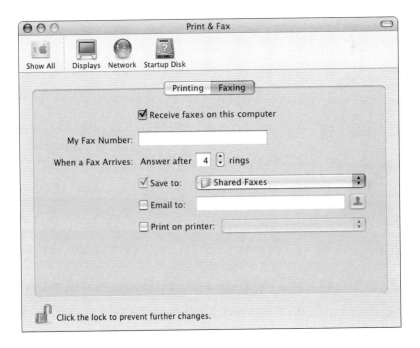

You can also set your system to receive faxes by selecting the appropriate check-box in the Faxing pane of Print & Fax preferences. If you don't want to leave your computer on all the time to receive an occasional fax, you can put it to sleep. But before doing so, in the Options pane of Energy Saver preferences, select the "Wake when modem detects a ring" checkbox.

Troubleshooting Printing

Here are some strategies for identifying and fixing problems with printing:

▶ Attempt to print to a different printer, if one is available, to see if the problem is with the printer or the application.

▶ Try deleting and then re-adding the printer in Printer Setup Utility.

▶ For USB printers, try adding them manually instead of relying on Mac OS X to add them automatically. If you are unable to locate the printer in Printer Setup Utility, use the troubleshooting techniques suggested in Lesson 9 to identify if you have a hardware or software issue.

▶ For network printers, use the network troubleshooting techniques in Lesson 6 to make sure that your network settings are correct and your network connection is functioning properly.

▶ If you've verified that you don't have a hardware problem, but you still can't see the printer listed in Printer Setup Utility, reinstall the printer's driver. Since the installation of printer drivers is optional while installing Mac OS X, it is possible that drivers were never installed. Check the manufacturer's Web site to get the latest version of the printer driver.

▶ If you're having problems with the format of the printed documents, make sure that you formatted the page for the correct printer in the Page Setup dialog.

▶ If a printer feature, such as duplex printing, isn't available or functioning, verify that the correct PPD is selected for the printer in Printer Setup Utility. You may need to configure the installable options in the printer's Show Info dialog in Printer Setup Utility.

▶ Read the log files related to printing. They are access_log, error_log, and page_log, all located in /var/log/cups. They serve as the best source of information for any problems you may have.

▶ Keep in mind that you might not have control over problems that occur with network printers and print servers. You should coordinate with the administrators of those computers and printers to resolve problems.

▶ Occasionally, you might have to call the printer vendor to resolve a problem.

What You've Learned

▶ Printer Setup Utility is the central utility for managing printers and printing. Through it, you can add and delete printers and manage print queues.

▶ You can share locally connected printers over the network by turning on Print Sharing in the Services pane of Sharing preferences or in Print & Fax preferences. Once you do that, other computers running Mac OS X 10.2 and higher will list your locally connected printers.

▶ Mac OS X printing is based upon Common Unix Printing System (CUPS).

References

The following Knowledge Base articles (located at http://kbase.info.apple.com) will provide you with further information regarding printing in Mac OS X.

External Devices

▶ 58648, "Mac OS X: Do Not Connect USB Printer to Apple Pro Keyboard"

▶ 106403, "Mac OS X: 'No Driver for This Platform' Message"

Printing

▶ 75216, "Mac OS X: USB Printer Drivers No Longer Available"

▶ 75413, "Mac OS X Server 10.2: How to Set Up Print Load Balancing Using CUPS"

▶ 106687, "Mac OS X: How to Select an LPR Printer in Classic"

- 106706, "Mac OS X: How to Print"

- 106710, "Mac OS X: How to Print From a Classic Application"

- 106714, "Troubleshooting Printing Issues in Mac OS X"

- 107060, "Mac OS X 10.2, 10.3: Sharing a Printer with Mac OS 9 Computers"

- 151663, "Setting Up Workflows for Creating PDF Files"

USB

- 31116, "USB Cable: Maximum Cable Length"

- 61237, "What to Do if a USB Device Isn't Working"

URLs

Visit the following Web sites for more information:

- CUPS: http://127.0.0.1:631 (Accessed on a computer running Mac OS X 10.2 or later)

- PDF Workflow: http://developer.apple.com/documentation/Printing/ Conceptual/PDF_Workflow/index.html

Review Quiz

Use the following questions to review what you have learned:

1. What utility is used to configure and control printing in Mac OS X?

2. What are the methods for connecting to a printer in Printer Setup Utility?

3. What printer information do you need to correctly select and print to a printer connected to the network via IP?

4. What quick fixes are particularly useful to consider when troubleshooting printing issues?

Answers

1. Printer Setup Utility.

2. AppleTalk, IP Printing, Open Directory, Rendezvous, USB, and Windows Printing.

3. Printer's IP address or URL and the printer type/model.

4. Verify printer is listed in Printer Setup Utility; verify correct printer is selected in Page Setup.

11

Time   This lesson takes approximately 1 hour to complete.

Goals   Identify the processes that run at system startup

Identify the location of important files and scripts used by the
startup sequence

Identify the different stages of the startup sequence and their
corresponding visual or auditory cues

Troubleshoot startup issues, including startup items and
login items

Startup Sequence

Most Macintosh users turn on their computers and wait for the Finder or login window to appear. That's all normal users need to know to begin working on a Macintosh computer. But power users and administrators benefit from understanding what goes on behind the scenes to run Mac OS X.

When the power is turned on, Mac OS X performs a series of tasks to prepare the system for operation. Visual and auditory cues help you follow the startup sequence. If something goes awry during startup, those cues can provide clues as to where the problem is and how to fix it. The following pages explain the Mac OS X startup sequence.

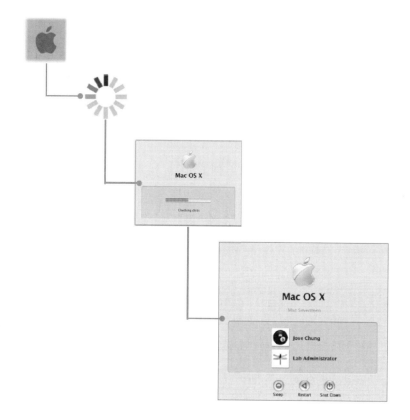

BootROM

BootROM is a hardware component that contains the startup (boot) programs, which are the first processes that run when the computer is turned on. These programs include the Power-On Self Test (POST) and Open Firmware.

POST

The Power-On Self Test checks basic hardware components for functionality. POST sets components such as the processor, random access memory (RAM), and crucial hardware interfaces to states expected by the system. In addition, POST verifies that the RAM is functioning to operating specifications.

If the system fails POST, the following error beeps occur:

▶ One beep—No RAM installed

▶ Two beeps—Incompatible RAM types

▶ Three beeps—No good memory banks

▶ Four beeps—No good boot images in the boot ROM

▶ Five beeps—Processor is not usable

Error beeps may vary, depending on the computer model. If no sound is present, some models will flash an LED to indicate a failure. Search the Knowledge Base for the specific hardware error messages.

If the system passes POST, you will hear the normal startup chime.

Open Firmware

Open Firmware initializes the rest of the hardware, builds the initial device tree (a hierarchical representation of devices associated with the computer), and selects the operating system to use.

Open Firmware also checks whether startup modifier keys have been pressed, including the C key for starting up via a disc in the optical drive, Cmd-S for single-user mode, and Cmd-V for verbose mode.

BootX

When the Open Firmware startup program in BootROM locates and selects the Mac OS X operating system, it transfers control to BootX (a process that Open Firmware starts from /System/Library/CoreServices on the startup disk). The primary task of BootX is to initialize the kernel environment and the drivers (such as the drivers for I/O buses) needed to boot the system.

When Open Firmware attempts to find BootX, one of the following icons will appear, indicating these results:

▶ Metallic Apple logo—Found BootX

▶ Circle with slash—Could not find BootX on the startup volume

▶ Flashing square with globe—Looking for BootX on a remote disk via the network

▶ Small metallic spinning globe—Found BootX on network
▶ Flashing question mark over a folder or floppy disk icon—Open Firmware did not find a startup disk (locally or on a network)

NOTE ▶ For more information, see Knowledge Base article #58042, "A Flashing Question Mark Appears When You Start Your Mac."

If Mac OS X components have been renamed or moved from the root level of the startup disk, a broken folder icon will appear. A black belt may appear around a folder icon if a Mac OS 9 restore has been installed incorrectly using the Restore discs that came with the computer. (See Knowledge Base article #106294, "Mac OS X: Reinstalling Mac OS 9 or Recovering from a Software Restore.")

When loading the kernel environment, BootX first attempts to load a previously cached set of device drivers. If this cache is missing or corrupt, BootX searches /System/Library/Extensions for drivers and other kernel extensions whose OSBundleRequired property is set to the appropriate value for the type of boot. (This is either a local or network boot, depending on the current selection in Startup Disk preferences.) You can recognize this stage by the metallic Apple logo and the spinning gear that appear on the screen.

Kernel

The kernel initializes the Input/Output Kit (I/O Kit), which controls input and output devices. The I/O Kit links the loaded drivers into the kernel based on the device tree previously created by Open Firmware.

The kernel then starts the mach_init process, the heart of the operating system. The mach_init process manages all CPU processes, including preemptive multi-tasking, memory usage and protection, and all interprocess communication protocols for the system, both local and remote.

mach_init and init

The mach_init process starts the BSD init process, which controls process IDs, basic file system security, and networking facilities of Mac OS X. During this stage of the startup sequence, the screen initially displays a blue screen and the Mac OS X progress window.

The init process performs four main tasks:

▶   It determines if the user is booting in single-user mode (Cmd-S) or from an optical disc. If the user is booting into single-user mode, the system initialization process displays an advisory message and hands control to the user.

▶   It runs the system-initialization shell scripts, which complete basic initialization tasks, and the SystemStarter program, which addresses more specialized initialization tasks specified in the /System/Library/StartupItems folder.

▶ It launches the loginwindow application, which displays the login window and manages the user login procedure.

▶ It configures and loads the user environment, including the Finder and the Dock.

Viewing the Init Process

1   Open Activity Monitor (/Applications/Utilities).

2   From the pop-up menu in the top-right corner, choose All Processes.

3   Locate and select the init process.

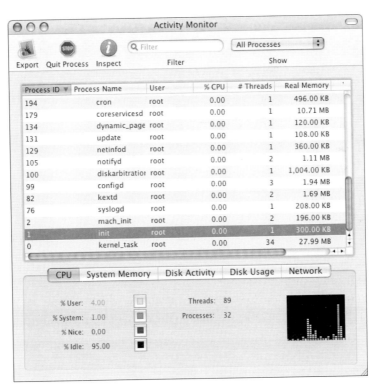

4 Click the Inspect button.

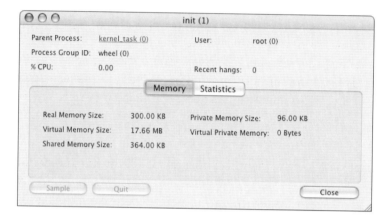

When you're inspecting a process, the name of the window will be the name of the process followed by the process ID in parentheses.

In this example, the process ID for init is 1. The parent process of init is kernel_task.

Startup Scripts and Startup Items

After the mach_init and BSD init processes execute successfully, the kernel runs the rc scripts located in /etc (an invisible folder) to perform basic system initialization tasks.

These tasks include a file-system consistency check (fsck), synchronizing memory within the file system (sync), and starting a process called SystemStarter, which launches the startup items.

NOTE ▶ By default, the fsck command does not run on journaled systems. To force this command to run on journaled systems, use fsck -f.

Startup items are processes that run during the last phase of the startup sequence to prepare a Mac OS X system for normal operation. Startup items consist of programs, including customizable shell scripts, that perform tasks such as clearing away temporary files and starting system daemons.

Startup items and any applications that run prior to the loginwindow application are referred to as system processes. These applications provide services to all users of the system and are usually children of the init process. (A child process is a process that is started by another process, which is called its parent.) Processes created after the launching of loginwindow are referred to as user processes. User processes are always associated with a particular user session and are usually children of the session's Window Manager process. You specify which user processes to launch in the Startup Items pane of Accounts preferences, discussed in Lesson 2.

System startup items are located in /System/Library/StartupItems, and consist of folders containing at least one program (typically a shell script) whose name matches the folder's name, and a configuration property list (plist) file that the shell script reads when the startup item loads.

> NOTE ▶ Administrator users should not add startup scripts to /System/Library/StartupItems. However, you can create and store custom startup items in /Library/StartupItems.

Appendix C lists the core startup items for Mac OS X.

Many startup scripts rely upon system configuration information stored in /etc/hostconfig. Some of the entries in hostconfig specify if certain services should be started with the computer. For example, when you turn on Personal Web Sharing in the Services pane of Sharing preferences, an entry is set in hostconfig:

WEBSERVER=-YES-

When the Apache startup item executes, it checks to see if the WEBSERVER value is set to YES, and, if so, starts the Apache Web server.

By the time the user logs into a Mac OS X system, a number of processes are already running. Most of these processes are daemons or system processes that run in the background. In addition to those created by the startup scripts, a handful of processes are created by the loginwindow application and the Window Manager daemon.

A daemon is a continuously running program that exists for the sole purpose of managing service requests that the computer system expects to receive. The daemon forwards the requests to the appropriate processes.

Appendix C lists the common system daemons and servers that are running after you log in to a Mac OS X computer.

Identifying the Startup Scripts

In this exercise, you will view the startup scripts as they start.

1   Restart your computer in single-user mode by pressing Cmd-S at startup.

> **NOTE** ► When operating in single-user mode, it's possible to make changes that are potentially disruptive because as the root user you have permission to access every file and folder. As such, always exercise extreme caution in single-user mode.

2   At the command-line prompt, type

fsck -y -f

3   At the command-line prompt, type

exit

4   Try to verify that the rc.script performs each of the followings steps by reading the messages that appear on the screen as each process starts:

> **NOTE** ► You might want to repeat steps 1–4 to have a chance to read all the messages that appear on the screen.

a   It starts the device-driver loader (kextd).

b   It starts the Apple Type Solution (ATS) server, enabling system-wide font management.

c   It starts the Window Server. (The user will see the blank blue screen.) When the Window Server is running, it manages the screen drawing functions.

d It runs the update background process, which periodically flushes the filesystem cache.

e It creates the swap file for the virtual-memory system and starts the dynamic pager for memory mapping.

f It starts the SystemStarter program to process local and system startup items. (The user will see the boot panel and the Mac OS X progress window.)

The loginwindow Process

Login occurs after system initialization with the appearance of the login window. The loginwindow process coordinates the login process and the individual user's session, calling on other system services as needed. Depending on the user's login preferences, the login window may prompt the user for a valid login name and password, or may use cached values to log in the user automatically. When the user's login name and password have been authenticated, loginwindow proceeds to load the user environment.

When the user logs in, loginwindow does the following:

▶ Loads the user's computing environment, including preferences, environment variables, device and file permissions, keychain access, and so on

▶   Launches the Dock, Finder, and SystemUIServer

▶   Launches the Setup Assistant if an installation is in progress

▶   Automatically launches applications specified in the Login Items pane of Accounts preferences

When all of these applications are launched and running, the login procedure is complete.

The loginwindow application uses Launch Services to launch all applications, including the Finder, Dock, SystemUIServer, and user-specified applications. Most applications in the user session run as child processes of the Window Manager process. They are not owned by loginwindow.

Once the user session is running, loginwindow monitors the session and user applications in the following ways:

▶   Manages logout, restart, and shutdown procedures

▶   Manages the Force Quit window, which includes monitoring the currently active applications, responding to user requests to force quit applications, and relaunching the Finder

▶   Displays alert dialogs when a notification is received from hidden applications (applications not visible in the user interface)

▶   Writes any standard-error (stderr) output to a log file (/var/tmp/console. log), which is then used as input by the Console application

NOTE ▶ If your computer is set to automatically log in, and you need to display the login window to log in as another user, hold down the Shift key when you see the progress bar for the login process until the login window appears.

User Environment Setup

Mac OS X requires user authentication prior to accessing the system. Although the loginwindow application manages the user authentication process, it does not itself authenticate the user. The loginwindow application passes the information specified in the login window to Directory Services for authentication.

When Directory Services authenticates the user, loginwindow initiates the user session and displays the status bar along with the text "Logging In."

NOTE ▶ If you select the "Automatically log in as" option in the Login Options pane of Accounts preferences, the loginwindow application does not prompt you for login information.

When a user logs in to the system, the loginwindow application sets up the user environment and records information about the login. It also configures the mouse, keyboard, and system sound using the user's preferences, and retrieves the user record from Directory Services.

Identifying Startup Processes

In this exercise, view the startup process as it happens, in both graphical and text startup.

1   If your computer is turned on, shut down your computer.

2   Start up your computer.

3   As the computer is booting up, follow along with the table to observe the major steps occurring during the startup process (from power on until the user environment has appeared).

Startup Sequence Stage	Cue
Power On	Black screen
POST	Flashing lights and beeps
Open Firmware	Startup chime
BootX	Metallic icon appears
Kernel Load	Gray screen with Apple logo and spinning gear
System Initialization	Blue screen followed by the Mac OS X progress window
Login	Login window appears
User Environment Setup	"Logging In" appears in login window, then Desktop and Dock appear

Troubleshooting the Startup Sequence

To troubleshoot issues during startup, try the following techniques.

Start Up Computer in Verbose Mode

Start up your Mac OS X computer in verbose mode (hold down Cmd-V at startup) to get more details on startup issues.

Start Up Computer in Safe Mode

Safe mode is the state Mac OS X is in after a Safe Boot (hold down Shift at startup)—a special way to start Mac OS X when troubleshooting. Starting up into Safe Mode simplifies the startup and operation of your computer in the following ways:

▶ It forces a directory check of the startup volume.

▶ It loads only required kernel extensions (some of the items in /System/Library/Extensions).

▶ It runs only startup items in /System/Library/StartupItems.

Starting up in Safe Mode is useful when you are trying to isolate the cause of a problem that may be caused by third-party kernel extension conflicts or startup items that cause the machine to act erratically.

Prevent Login Items from Launching

If you suspect that a login item (an application that launches automatically at login, as specified in the Startup Items pane of Accounts preferences) is preventing successful login, you can prevent startup items from launching as follows:

1   Start up the computer.

2   As soon as you see the blue background followed by the Mac OS X progress window, press and hold the Shift key.

By pressing Shift at this point, you prevent Mac OS X from logging in automatically, giving you the option of logging in as any user.

3 When the login window appears, release the Shift key, log in, then immediately press and hold the Shift key again.

4 Release the Shift key after the Finder's menu bar appears.

Examine Logs in Single-User Mode

Start up your Mac OS X computer in single-user mode (hold down Cmd-S at startup), and when the command-line prompt appears, examine the system log by typing

less /var/log/system.log

If the startup sequence is hanging, the system log shows where the process stops.

Remove Corrupted Preferences in Single-User Mode

Corrupted system, loginwindow, or directory services preferences can cause long delays and possibly stop the machine from completely starting up. Delete these preferences by starting your computer in single-user mode, moving them to a temporary location, and restarting. These preferences are located at

▶ /Library/Preferences/SystemConfiguration/preferences.plist

▶ /Library/Preferences/com.apple.loginwindow.plist

▶ /Library/Preferences/DirectoryService

▶ ~/Library/Preferences

Deleting Corrupted Preferences

In this exercise, you remove preference files that may be preventing or delaying startup. You'll also see that the system re-creates any removed preference files.

1 Reboot the machine, and after the startup chime, press Cmd-S to start in single-user mode.

2 Run a disk check by typing

fsck -y -f

> **NOTE** ▶ When operating in single-user mode, it's possible to make changes that are potentially disruptive because as the root user you have permission to access every file and folder. As such, always exercise extreme caution in single-user mode.

3   Mount the file system as read/write by typing

mount -uw /

4   Navigate to the login window and Directory Services preferences by typing

cd /Library/Preferences

5   Move the com.apple.loginwindow.plist to a backup file by typing

mv com.apple.loginwindow.plist com.apple.loginwindow.plist.backup

6   Move the DirectoryService directory to a backup directory by typing

mv DirectoryService DirectoryService.backup

7   Navigate to the SystemConfiguration preferences folder by typing

cd SystemConfiguration

8   Move the preferences.plist file to a backup file by typing

mv preferences.plist preferences.plist.backup

9   Restart the machine by typing

reboot

10   Log in as Apple Admin.

11   Navigate to /Library/Preferences in the Finder.

12   Verify that the com.apple.loginwindow.plist file and the DirectoryService directory were re-created.

13 Navigate to /Library/Preferences/SystemConfiguration.

Notice that preferences.plist has not been re-created. It will be re-created as preferences are set in System Preferences.

14 Open System Preferences.

15 Click Sharing.

Notice that Computer Name is blank.

16 In the Computer Name field, enter your name.

17 In the Finder, close and reopen the /Library/Preferences/SystemConfiguration folder.

The preferences.plist file has been re-created.

At this point, your computer is functional, and you could reconfigure all of the preferences back to their settings before this exercise. However, since you made a backup of the preferences.plist file, you can use that file to restore the preferences setting.

1 Reboot the machine, and after the startup chime, press Cmd-S to start in single-user mode.

2 Run a disk check by typing

fsck -y -f

3 Mount the file system as read/write by typing

mount -uw /

4   Navigate to the SystemConfiguration preferences folder by typing

cd /Library/Preferences/SystemConfiguration

5   Restore the preferences.plist file from the backup file by typing

mv preferences.plist.backup preferences.plist

6   Restart the machine by typing

reboot

Restore /mach_kernel, /etc, /var if Deleted

If you start up in Mac OS 9 (Macintosh models introduced after January 2003 don't boot in Mac OS 9) and delete the /mach_kernel, /etc, or /var folders, you must re-create these folders to start up the computer in Mac OS X. Refer to the following Knowledge Base articles for more information:

▶   107396, "Mac OS X: Cannot Print, Use Classic, Start File Sharing, Burn Discs, or Update Software if /tmp Missing"

▶   106908, "Mac OS X: Issues After Removing 'etc' and/or 'var' Directory Alias When Started Up from Mac OS 9"

If you deleted the /mach_kernel folder, restart the computer in Mac OS 9 and copy the mach_kernel folder from the root level of the Mac OS X Install Disc 1 to the root level of the Mac OS X startup volume.

If you deleted the /etc or /var folders, start up your computer in single-user mode, run fsck (use fsck -f to force fsck to run on journaled systems), mount the filesystem, and type the following to re-create the /etc and /var folders:

ln -s /private/etc etc

ln -s /private/var var

What You've Learned

In this chapter, you learned the basic description of the various stages of the Mac OS X startup sequence. The following table lists these stages. For each stage, the table lists the corresponding visual and auditory cues. Once you have identified the stage where startup is failing, you can isolate the cause and fix it.

Startup Sequence Stage	Cue
Power On	Black screen
BootROM-POST	Flashing lights and LEDs, and activity sound as POST mounts all devices, including hard disks and removable media
	One beep—No RAM installed
	Two beeps—Incompatible RAM types
	Three beeps—No good memory banks
	Four beeps—No good boot images in the boot ROM
	Five beeps—Processor is not usable
BootROM-Open Firmware	Startup chime
BootX	Metallic Apple logo—Found BootX
	Circle with slash—Could not find BootX on the startup volume
	Flashing square with globe—Looking for BootX on a remote disk via the network

Startup Sequence Stage	Cue
BootX	Small metallic spinning globe—Found BootX on network
	Flashing question mark over a folder or floppy disk icon—OpenFirmware did not find a bootable OS
	Broken folder icon—Missing Mac OS X components
	Folder icon with a black belt around it—Restored Mac OS 9 incorrectly on a drive with Mac OS X installed
Kernel	Gray screen with Apple logo and spinning gear
mach_init and init	Blue screen followed by the Mac OS X progress window
Startup scripts and startup items	Mac OS X progress window
loginwindow	Login window appears
User Environment Setup	The text "Logging In" appears in login window along with a progress bar upon successful login
	Desktop and Dock appear

References

The following Knowledge Base articles (located at http://kbase.info.apple.com) will provide you with further information regarding the startup sequence in Mac OS X.

- ▶ 106388, "Mac OS X: How to Start Up in Single-User or Verbose Mode"
- ▶ 106464, "Your Mac Won't Start Up in Mac OS X"
- ▶ 106805, "Mac OS X: 'Broken Folder' Icon, Prohibitory Sign, or Kernel Panic When Computer Starts"
- ▶ 106908, "Mac OS X: Issues After Removing 'etc' and/or 'var' Directory Alias When Started Up from Mac OS 9"
- ▶ 107392, "Mac OS X 10.2, 10.3: What Is Safe Boot, Safe Mode?"

Review Quiz

Use the following questions to review what you have learned:

1. What do one beep, two beeps, three beeps, four beeps, and five beeps at startup signify?

2. List the possible scenarios that may occur during the BootX sequence.

3. Describe what happens during the Kernel Load stage.

4. List five startup items in Mac OS X.

5. List the files and folder(s) required for a startup item to launch.

6. State three tasks that loginwindow performs after a user has logged in.

7. Identify the nine visual or auditory cues that are displayed during the Mac OS X boot process.

Answers

1. One beep: no RAM installed; two beeps: incompatible RAM types; three beeps: no good memory banks; four beeps: no good boot images in the boot ROM; five beeps: processor is not usable.

2. a) Kernel found

    b) System not found

    c) Network boot

    d) No startup disk found

3. Loads device drivers, initializes I/O Kit, loads and starts mach_init.

4. Accounting, Apache, AppServices, AppleShare, AppleTalk, AuthServer, BIND, ConfigServer, CoreGraphics, CrashReporter, Cron, DirectoryServices, Disks, IPServices, LDAP, LoginWindow, NFS, NIS, NetInfo, Network, NetworkExtensions, NetworkTime, Portmap, PrintingServices, RemoteDesktopAgent, SSH, Samba, SecurityServer, Sendmail, SystemLog, SystemTuning, mDNSResponder.

5. A folder containing at least one program (typically a shell script) whose name matches the folder's name and a configuration property list (plist) file that is read by the shell script when the StartupItem is loaded.

6. Loads the user's computing environment, launches the Dock, Finder, and SystemUIServer, and automatically launches applications specified in the Login Items pane of Accounts preferences.

7. Black screen, start-up chime, screen still black, gray screen or Apple logo, gray screen with Apple logo and spinning gear, blue screen followed by the Mac OS X progress window, login window, login window with spinning cursor, and "Logging In" text with progress bar.

12

Time

This lesson takes approximately 1 hour to complete.

Goals

Gather information about a computer problem and verify it

Use online tools such as Knowledge Base and Apple Help to research a problem and its possible solution

Use the Apple General Troubleshooting Flowchart to troubleshoot Mac OS X problems

Describe Apple and third-party resources for troubleshooting

Describe the difference between quick fixes and other types of fixes

Troubleshoot top Mac OS X issues

Perform a Knowledge Base search to identify known issues with a given system

Lesson 12
Troubleshooting

A user calls with the following complaint:

"I was working along just fine and suddenly I got this message about having to restart my computer. What's going on?"

You have 10 minutes or less on the phone.

How do you troubleshoot this issue?

In this chapter, you'll review basic troubleshooting techniques and follow the Apple General Troubleshooting Flowchart. As you examine each step in the flowchart, you will return to this sample scenario and see how to apply each step toward a solution.

Goals of Troubleshooting

There are two goals in technical troubleshooting: fix a problem properly and fix it quickly.

Goal 1: Fix a Problem Properly

Fixing a problem properly is the first of the two major troubleshooting goals. A correct and complete fix depends on many elements working together, including the following:

▶ Following systematic troubleshooting procedures

▶ Following proper procedures for take-apart and assembly

▶ Using up-to-date references and tools

▶ Not creating new problems

This results in a working system without a second or third service call.

Goal 2: Fix the Problem Quickly

The second major goal of the efficient troubleshooter is to fix the problem quickly. Users want their systems working again as quickly as possible. The more quickly you can troubleshoot and solve the problem, the more satisfied the client will be.

> **NOTE** ▶ Fixing a problem quickly does not mean taking shortcuts or doing sloppy work!

Keep in mind the following points when fixing a problem:

▶ You should never sacrifice quality for speed.

▶ Only complete the troubleshooting steps that are relevant and applicable to the problem.

Things to Do While Troubleshooting

Here are things that you should do throughout the troubleshooting process.

Keep Notes

What starts out as a simple troubleshooting job can sometimes unravel into a major task. Start taking notes from the very beginning of the troubleshooting process, even if it seems like a simple problem to fix.

Write down the following:

▶ Each piece of information you gather

▶ Each test that you perform (along with the results)

▶ Your proposed solution (to preserve a record of what you tried) each time you think you know what's wrong

Consult Resources

In addition to experience and skilled troubleshooting techniques, a good trouble-shooter possesses product knowledge. Consulting available resources is a vital part of obtaining knowledge about the product and about the specific problem you are troubleshooting.

Browsing through references such as Service Source or Knowledge Base can be particularly helpful when you find yourself without an idea of what to try next.

These resources can stimulate new thoughts and strategies toward finding the source of the problem.

Consider the Human Factor

When you have been working long and hard on a problem that has you stumped, try taking a break.

Frustration can impair your ability to think logically and rationally. You may be surprised how often a short break can allow you to think of solutions that you previously overlooked.

Don't fall prey to "confirmation bias." When you believe you have solved a problem, confirmation bias causes you to favor facts that confirm that solution, and to ignore or misinterpret factors that contradict that solution. The more intelligent an individual, the more skillful he or she can be at reinforcing a confirmation bias. Keep an open mind and don't be trapped by assumptions.

Another human factor to consider is whether the user should be present while you troubleshoot. Having the user present can be useful for gathering information about problem causes. However, having the user peer over your shoulder while you troubleshoot may also pressure you into making hasty and possibly bad decisions.

Additionally, users may later try to repeat some of the techniques on their own. Without adequate understanding of the techniques, users can cause irreparable damage. You can warn them not to try these techniques without a support person present. Unfortunately, people do not always pay attention to warnings.

Order of Elimination

While troubleshooting, you should generally check for problems in the following order:

1. User-related problems
2. Software-related problems
3. OS-related problems
4. Hardware-related problems

Statistically, most problems are user-, software-, or OS-related. Also, this order usually represents the least expensive to the most expensive repairs. If you approach your problem-solving in this order, you will be as efficient and cost-effective as possible.

User-Related Problems

You check for user-related problems in the course of gathering information, duplicating the problem, and trying quick fixes. You're looking for things like incorrectly set switches or preferences, incompatible equipment, and incorrect assumptions on the user's part.

Software-Related Problems

Incompatible, damaged, or outdated software, viruses, and other software problems can all cause symptoms that may look like hardware problems. Replacing hardware won't solve them, and it costs time and money. Always check for software problems before replacing any hardware.

Check for Viruses

A virus is a program that replicates itself and often modifies other programs. When a virus gets into system software, the computer may fail to boot, the system may crash, or the software may work incorrectly. Files downloaded from the Internet or exchanged between users are common sources of virus infection.

To check for a virus, ask users these questions:

▶ Did you recently receive software from another user or a common source and add the software to your system?

▶ Did you experience the problem before you obtained the software?

▶ Did you share the software with others? Are they having similar problems?

You can find up-to-date virus information on the Internet at a variety of locations. Third-party virus utilities such as Norton AntiVirus for Macintosh (NAV) and Virex can check systems and remove viruses.

> **NOTE** ▶ If you have a .Mac account, you can download Virex free from www.mac.com.

If you do detect a virus, make sure you find the original source file and eliminate it. Then remove and reinstall all affected system and application software and dispose of any corrupted data files.

Mac OS-Related Problems

You can identify Mac OS-related problems by their symptoms. Usually, they affect all applications, or they prevent the startup process from completing. We'll spend most of this chapter with a detailed look at how to troubleshoot Mac OS-related problems.

Hardware-Related Problems

When you are convinced that the problem is not caused by user error, a virus, or software, then hardware is left. Here are some tips:

▶ Remove external devices and internal cards (except for the video card if it is needed for the display) and test the CPU by itself.

▶ Remove third-party RAM.

▶ If the system can be tested with Apple Hardware Test, do so.

▶ Try to identify the functional area that the problem affects. For instance, a typical Macintosh computer could be viewed as having the following functional areas:

   ▶ Software

   ▶ Logic and control

   ▶ Memory

   ▶ Video

   ▶ I/O

   ▶ Power

▶ Inspect components, especially mechanical parts and fuses. You may be able to see the cause (a blown fuse or a visibly damaged chip), smell it (a burning smell is often a tip-off), or hear it (grinding noises are seldom a good sign).

▶ Work from largest to smallest components of the system.

▶ When testing, test only one thing at a time—it is ultimately more efficient.

If you isolate the problem to hardware, and you are an Apple-authorized service technician, follow the appropriate service procedures. Otherwise, contact an Apple-authorized service provider for repairs.

Using the Troubleshooting Flowchart

When you troubleshoot issues in Mac OS X, there is a basic process you can use to isolate and solve the issue. This process is described by the Apple General Troubleshooting Flowchart. It's an organized process, like a spiral, always circling toward the solution.

For example, let's say you have a malfunctioning Macintosh on your workbench. According to the flowchart, the first step is to gather information. Then, you make a decision: Has that step resolved the problem? If it doesn't, you then verify the problem, that is, you try to reproduce it and use a quick fix. (You can skip the on-site service decision, since you already have the computer in front of you.)

So, you think you may have identified the problem and skip to the repair or replace option. After completing the repair (often a quick fix is sufficient repair), you ask yourself if the problem is resolved. No? Go back to trying quick fixes. Often, you cycle through a number of quick fixes before resolving the problem or deciding that no more quick fixes apply, and you need to go on to running diagnostics.

In this way, the flowchart describes a series of tests and fixes you perform until you return the system to normal operation. You might want to keep the Apple General Troubleshooting Flowchart handy while you troubleshoot.

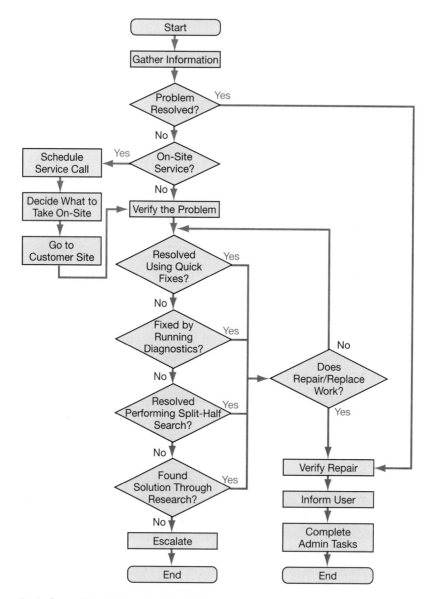

Apple General Troubleshooting Flowchart

Gathering Information

Your most powerful troubleshooting tool is your ability to ask smart, probing questions. Good questions can identify in detail the equipment used and uncover the steps to reproduce the problem. Gathering screen shots of the problem in action and collecting error messages can also help in reaching a solution.

One of the first things you should find out is: What exactly is the problem? Getting a clear picture of what is not working correctly is crucial to finding the solution. Try to get as specific a picture as possible about what problems are occurring, when they occur, and what error messages are displayed. Be familiar with the following Knowledge Base articles:

▶ 9804, "Mac OS System Error Codes: −299 to −5553"

▶ 9805, "Mac OS System Error Codes: 0 to −261"

▶ 9806, "Mac OS System Error Codes: 1 to 32767"

▶ 55743, "Common System Error Messages: What They Mean and What Might Help Resolve the Problem"

The following are tips you should follow when gathering information from users:

1   Start with open questions such as "What is the issue?" Open questions generally start with words like how, why, when, who, what, and where. They cannot be answered by "yes" or "no."

2   Let the user explain in his or her own words what was experienced. Do not interrupt the user. Interrupting someone generally prompts them to start over.

3   As you begin to understand the basics of the problem, start using closed questions that require more limited, specific answers. "What operating system are you using?" is an example of a closed question. Users might tell you the Mac OS versions they are using or tell you that they do not know. Closed questions often can be answered by "yes" or "no."

4   Verify your understanding of what you've been told. Restate what was said
and get the user's agreement that you understand the problem. An example
of restatement would be, "Okay, so what's happening is that when you do
X, Y happens. Is that correct?"

5   If the user agrees that you understand, continue to gather information. If
the user does not agree that you understand, clarify what you misstated and
reverify your understanding. Do not continue with the troubleshooting
until the user agrees that you understand the problem.

Here are some questions to ask a user before you continue to troubleshoot:

▶   What are the problems and symptoms?

▶   What were you doing when the problem occurred?

▶   What are the exact system hardware, Mac OS version, and exact versions
of software involved?

▶   Was any hardware or software recently added or removed?

▶   Are there environmental considerations (for example, is the system close
to a heater, window, other electrical devices)?

Sometimes, just looking at menus gives you important information. For example,
in Mac OS 9 and Classic, the quickest way to check if a control panel is enabled
is to see if it is listed in the Control Panels menu.

System Profiler

In situations where you don't have a user to question, use System Profiler to
gather information about the state and configuration of the system. System
Profiler gets its main information from the device tree that Open Firmware
builds at startup time. And, unlike many other applications or utilities, System
Profiler does not use a preference file (.plist), so its behavior cannot be corrupted by invalid or corrupted preferences.

Use System Profiler for situations where the OS or an application refuses to recognize hardware that is known to be connected to the system.

System Profiler provides detailed information about the system configuration, including the computer type and speed, the firmware version, the version of Mac OS, the amount of memory installed, and the types of network connections.

During the Gather Information step and throughout the troubleshooting process, remember that when you need to perform steps remotely, you can use tools such as the Apple Remote Desktop, Timbuktu (www.netopia.com), and secure shell.

If it's not appropriate for you to directly manipulate the other computer, you can have the user run System Profiler, save the generated report, and email it to you. If you have access to a Mac OS X computer, you can have the report saved in System Profiler's native file format, which you can easily view in System Profiler; otherwise, the user can export the report in a plain-text or rich-text format.

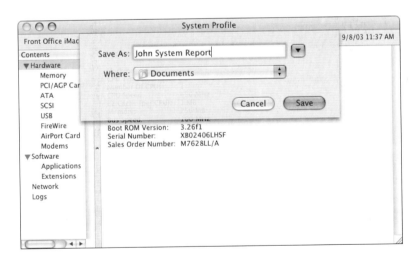

Apple Remote Desktop

Apple Remote Desktop is a real-time screen sharing and desktop management tool that allows system administrators to configure remote systems, distribute software, and provide online assistance from anywhere on the network or remotely across the Internet. With Apple Remote Desktop administration software, you can access your office computer from home as if you were sitting in your office.

In a classroom, Apple Remote Desktop enhances the learning experience by allowing the teacher to monitor and control the students' machines. In a corporate environment, it provides a solution for managing remote systems, reducing administration costs, and increasing productivity.

The client for Apple Remote Desktop is included with Mac OS X 10.3 and can be enabled from the Services pane of Sharing preferences. The Apple Remote Desktop administration software must be purchased separately.

Logs

You can use the Console utility (/Applications/Utilities) to view log files on a Mac OS X computer. To do so, open Console and click Logs in the toolbar to display a list of available logs in the Logs pane on the left. To view the contents of a log, select the log in the Logs pane. Console displays the contents of the log in the Contents pane.

For installer errors, look in the installer log (Mac OS X Log.txt) under the Library/Receipts entry in the Logs pane. This log lists information such as what files were copied, what partition was written to, and what errors were encountered. For Software Update errors, look in the Software Update log under the /Library/receipts entry. For application and system process errors, look in console.log.

To view messages about the system in Console (including error messages or messages that a task was carried out properly), choose File > Open System Log. Console displays the messages as Mac OS X adds them to the system.log file. (The system.log file is compressed periodically, and a new log is created.)

When using Console to track a message, the first thing you should do is note the date and time on the last entry or click Mark in the toolbar to add a time marker after the last entry. You can then examine actions that happen after that date and time. Whenever certain commands are carried out in Mac OS X, a series of messages should be listed in the Console. Typically, the first part of the message gives you the date and time stamp. The next part names the user of the process. After that the process and the process IDs are listed. After the colon, you can read the actual error or message. In this example, the only information is a repeat of the date, showing that the iCal helper will relaunch in an hour.

2003-05-28 14:48:48.906 iCal Helper[516] Launch of helper planned at : 05/28/03 15:48:48

Using Console is most helpful when no error occurs in the graphical user interface, and you cannot figure out why an application is no longer working. Console might show you an error message that would help focus your questions.

You can also use Console to view other log files, such as ftp.log, netinfo.log, and the Crash Reporter logs (listed under the CrashReporter entry). Most log files for Mac OS X are stored in either /var/log or /Library/Logs.

A common Console message is that a SIGHUP occurred. This software "interrupt and hang up" command tells a process to reread its configuration file and run with the new settings.

Verbose Mode

If you encounter a problem during the startup of Mac OS X, you may need to use verbose mode. If you press Cmd-V when you hear the chime during startup, Mac OS X boots in verbose mode, allowing you to see a command-line interface listing everything that happens during startup. If there is nothing wrong with the startup sequence, Mac OS X brings you to the Finder or login window.

If there is a problem during startup, Mac OS X usually stops at the problem and does not continue loading. When you start up in normal (graphical) mode (as opposed to verbose mode), the startup sequence runs displaying the Mac OS X progress window, so you may have no idea when during the startup process the computer stopped. Verbose mode gives you a way to find out.

Messages during startup are stored in the system.log file. Any "kmod destroy" messages that you see in the verbose mode are harmless. These are simply indications that Mac OS X is unloading kernel modifications that do not apply to your particular platform.

See Knowledge Base article #106388, "Mac OS X: How to Start Up in Single-User or Verbose Mode" for more information.

Problem Scenario—Gather Information

Going back to our original problem, posed at the beginning of this lesson, you try to get the exact wording of the alert message from the user. He explains that the message reads:

"You need to restart your computer. Hold down the Power button for several seconds or press the Restart button."

The message appears in several languages.

At the bottom of the screen, he sees

FF:FF:FF:FF:FF:FF

Here's a sample question and answer dialogue to show how you might approach the problem:

Question: What were you doing when the problem occurred?

Answer: I had just finished copying some files from my PowerBook to my desktop computer via target disk mode. When I restarted, I got an error message.

Question: What are the exact system hardware and Mac OS version involved?

Answer: PowerBook G4 (17-inch) and Mac OS X 10.3.

Question: Was any hardware or software recently added or removed?

Answer: No.

Question: Are there environmental considerations (for example, is the system close to a heater, window, other electrical devices)?

Answer: No.

So, now that you have gathered this information, you ask yourself if the problem is resolved. If not, can you eliminate any potential problem areas as the cause of the problem? In this example, you can eliminate user error and software-related problems for now. The next area to focus on is the OS, and your next step is to verify the problem.

Verifying the Problem

Verifying the problem—that is, reproducing the symptoms the user described— is extremely important in successful troubleshooting. It gives you a chance to objectively confirm the extent and nature of the problem. You also identify likely problem areas at this stage. In the long run, verifying the problem saves time.

For every symptom, there can be several explanations. Make sure you don't jump to a conclusion too fast. Trying to troubleshoot a nonexistent problem or a problem that has not been well defined is a significant waste of time.

Sometimes the problem can be solved by watching the user go through the process of re-creating the problem and observing that the user is operating the system incorrectly.

In other cases, watching a person re-create the problem yields additional information about the circumstances under which the problem occurs. (That is, the person may have forgotten to tell you some things about when and how the problem occurs.) Or, your observation of the problem may be quite different from the description you are given.

How you duplicate the problem depends on the problem the user describes. Basically, follow the steps the user followed to make the problem appear. It is best to follow the exact steps the user took to find exactly the same problem.

You must understand the Mac OS X theory of operation to learn something when you verify a problem. You must be able to compare the behavior you see with what you know should be happening. When there is a discrepancy, you must be able to make an educated guess as to what the problem is and where to start looking for the cause. Understanding the details of the Mac OS X startup sequence and the characteristics of a correctly functioning Mac OS X as described earlier in this book are essential to this process.

Problem Scenario—Verify the Problem

Let's get back to our problem scenario. During the Gather Information stage or when the user tries to reproduce the problem, you learn that the system stalls during startup. The system displays a metallic Apple logo and no spinning gear and then the error message appears.

> You need to restart your computer. Hold down the Power button for several seconds or press the Restart button.
>
> Veuillez redémarrer votre ordinateur. Maintenez la touche de démarrage enfoncée pendant plusieurs secondes ou bien appuyez sur le bouton de réinitialisation.
>
> Sie müssen Ihren Computer neu starten. Halten Sie dazu die Einschalttaste einige Sekunden gedrückt oder drücken Sie die Neustart-Taste.
>
> コンピュータを再起動する必要があります。パワーボタンを数秒間押し続けるか、リセットボタンを押してください。
>
> FF:FF:FF:FF:FF:FF

Clearly, something is going wrong during the startup sequence. A quick fix at this point might be a useful strategy as you try to isolate the malfunction.

Trying Quick Fixes

An effective troubleshooter quickly and systematically eliminates areas to explore and continually isolates likely solutions. Trying quick fixes is one of the most effective steps in this process.

A quick fix is a repair action that

▶   Can be performed quickly

▶ Involves little or no risk of harm to the system

▶ Has little or no cost

> **NOTE** ▶ A quick fix is not temporary or substandard.

A quick fix is not necessarily the most likely solution to the problem, but because it is easy to perform and takes little time or expense, it is worth trying.

For convenience, we divide the quick fixes applicable to troubleshooting the OS into three increasingly invasive strategies. We'll discuss each one next.

> **NOTE** ▶ Whether you try a quick fix or some other type of fix, try one at a time so that you know which fix corrected the problem.

Quick Fixes—Innocuous

For software related problems, you can try several quick fixes that do not significantly change the system (refer to Appendix A for more on quick fixes):

▶ Use System Profiler—For instance, you can use System Profiler to verify that the system detects a connected FireWire drive when the volume doesn't appear on the desktop.

▶ Start from a known-good operating system (such as the Mac OS X Install Disc 1), restart, or power off—If you press the Option key when you start up the system, the computer will display the Startup Manager screen, which lists drives and partitions with System folders. From this list, you can select a different System folder to boot from. Some of these quick fixes are further described in Knowledge Base article #107199, "Mac OS X: If Your Computer Stops Responding, 'Hangs,' or 'Freezes.'" The underlying goal is to start the system using a known-good OS, thereby narrowing the problem to the original OS (if the redirected startup succeeds) or eliminating the OS (if the startup still fails).

▶ Rebuild the desktop—Use this quick fix to troubleshoot Classic. For more information, see Knowledge Base article #10182, "Mac OS: Rebuilding Desktop File and Icon Recovery."

Quick Fixes—Less Innocuous

"Less innocuous" quick fixes are those that alter the user's system in some minor way.

For example:

▶   You can create a new administrator user to test whether faulty user settings or preferences were causing the original problem—although this will not resolve issues with system-wide preferences or the local NetInfo database. Or, when troubleshooting an application, such as iMovie, you can eliminate the possibility of a corrupt preferences file (plist file) by moving or renaming the application's preferences file. For details, see Knowledge Base article #25398, "Mac OS X: How to Troubleshoot a Software Issue."

▶   As mentioned in Lesson 4, you can force-quit an application that is not responding or is causing problems. If the application works fine after restarting, no further action is required. However, if the application continues to be problematic, you need to continue troubleshooting.

▶   You can try logging in as a different user. You may find that another user account works fine, allowing the user to complete any urgent tasks. You can then compare the working user account against the nonfunctional one to find out what difference may be causing the problem.

▶   For problems that involve network communications, you can try switching Ethernet ports if you're working with a Mac that has more than one port. Or you might try using an AirPort connection to the network, if one is available, instead of the Ethernet port.

▶   You may need to update the firmware on the computer. You can determine the current firmware version by running System Profiler (if the computer is functional enough), or by restarting into Open Firmware (restart while pressing Cmd-Option-O-F until the Open Firmware message appears). See Knowledge Base article #60351, "Determining BootROM or Firmware Version."

▶   Use the Repair Disk Permissions in Disk Utility. As mentioned in Lesson 2, erratic system behavior could be caused by incorrect permissions set on the boot volume.

Quick Fixes—Invasive

Invasive quick fixes, such as reinstalling the OS, are risky. They alter the computer or its software.

Before attempting invasive quick fixes, complete each of the following tasks, as appropriate:

► Make a backup of user data. You must do this before updating, reinstalling, or otherwise modifying the software on a system. This backup ensures that you can restore the system to its original state if you need to do so. If the system is unable to boot, and you have a FireWire-enabled system, you may be able to start up the system in target disk mode, which allows you to connect it to another system and copy critical data files.

► Make sure you are using only known-good software to modify the system. Avoid introducing new problems while trying to solve the original one.

► Look for the latest versions of software that you intend to update or reinstall. Be careful not to add new software components that can adversely affect applications and other software that the user has placed on the system.

If the problem occurs only with a single application, reinstalling the application may fix the problem. It is possible that key components for the application have been deleted or corrupted.

If the computer is having difficulties during the BootROM startup sequence, you may wish to reset parameter RAM (PRAM). Resetting PRAM will reset any Open Firmware variables that may have been incorrectly entered. Resetting PRAM also resets NVRAM.

> **NOTE** ► Mac OS X does not store as many parameters in PRAM as previous versions of Mac OS did. For more information, see Knowledge Base article #86194, "Mac OS X: What Is Stored in PRAM?"

To reset PRAM, press Cmd-Option-P-R at startup until you hear the startup chime twice. To reset NVRAM independently, start into Open Firmware and type

reset-nvram

See Knowledge Base article #42642, "'To Continue Booting, Type mac-boot and Press Return' Message."

These changes are invasive because changes to the system are required and could have later repercussions. For example, resetting NVRAM immediately after a kernel panic erases potentially useful log information.

Problem Scenario—Quick Fixes

Once again, we return to our scenario. You try the following quick fixes with the following results:

Quick Fix	Results
Restart the computer	If you didn't instruct the user to restart as part of gathering information or verifying the problem, instruct the user to do so now.
	In our example, the user reports that the computer displays a metallic Apple logo and no spinning gear, then the same error message.
	From this description, and from the knowledge gained completing Lesson 11, you know the computer got as far as BootX but not kernel load. Perhaps the system is not finding kernel extensions?
Start up with the install CD	The computer starts up fine. This means that you should concentrate your troubleshooting on the operating system installed on the computer.
Repair the system with Disk Utility	Instruct the user to run Disk Utility from the install CDs. The user reports that the startup disk is repaired without errors. On quitting the Installer and restarting, though, the computer again freezes and displays the same error message.

You're spending a significant amount of time troubleshooting this problem. At this point, it may be appropriate to consider more invasive quick fixes, such as reinstalling the operating system.

In this case, however, what would reinstalling the operating system involve?

If you can't perform an Easy Install when reinstalling, you'll have to perform an Erase and Install. Although erasing and installing the operating system might be a quick fix, the user might not want to go through all the steps it takes (reinstalling applications, reconfiguring preferences, and so on) to restore the system to its previous condition (but you can ask).

Before proceeding to the next step in the troubleshooting process, ask yourself if you have identified the fault. In this scenario, you haven't, nor can you eliminate the operating system as a possible source of the problem.

Running Diagnostics

If the system is still not functioning correctly after you've gone through the quick fixes, you should try running some diagnostics. Diagnostic tools are software packages that allow you to check the system performance. Refer to Appendix A for more on diagnostic tools.

If the computer can start up and run Network Utility, you can diagnose basic networking issues. If the computer shipped with a diagnostics CD, you can use it to verify that the hardware is operating correctly.

If you are trying to diagnose and repair disk problems with the boot drive, you'll need to boot from the Mac OS X Install Disc 1 and run Disk Utility from it. If you don't have access to an installation disc, you can boot into single-user mode and at the prompt use the fsck command to test and fix the disk:

 # /sbin/fsck -y

 # /sbin/mount -uw /

You can also use a virus scanner to check if the system has become infected. Although the number of Macintosh viruses is small, and the rate of infection is low compared to Windows systems, viruses are out there and can cause the loss of programs and data. In some instances, you may need to start up in Mac OS 9, if the computer allows it, and verify the directory structure with Disk First Aid. If Mac OS 9 and Mac OS X share the same volume, they share the same directory structure on the volume. (In Mac OS X, Disk Utility combines the functionality of Disk First Aid and Drive Setup.) To learn how to use Disk First Aid, search Mac Help.

Problem Scenario—Diagnostics

So, back to our problem. You already ran Disk Utility as part of quick fixes without fixing or finding the problem. Your next step is to try yet another technique for isolating and identifying a problem, this time by strategically removing hardware and software from the system.

Performing Split-Half Search

A split-half search is a technique for systematically isolating the source of a problem. You start by eliminating roughly half of the items you are checking. You then try to re-create the problem. You continue halving your search group until you isolate the source of the problem.

This part of the troubleshooting process can be the most difficult and the most time-consuming. Be sure to exhaust the tools and techniques in the earlier steps of the flowchart before performing a split-half search and, even then, make sure it wouldn't be faster just to reinstall.

Refer to Appendix A for more on split-half search techniques.

By holding down Cmd-S while you start up the computer, you start Mac OS X in single-user mode and eliminate all of the multiple-user processes as possible causes. You can then determine if the issue arises just when you are running in multiple-user mode or if it occurs in any operating system mode. Starting up in single-user mode and then using the exit command to return to the normal multiple-user mode can sometimes quickly fix a startup issue. Remember, single-user mode is only innocuous as long as no other commands are entered.

The /Library/StartupItems and /System/Library/StartupItems folders contain items that get started when the system boots. Holding down the Shift key at startup boots the system in Safe Boot mode, and the system uses only the startup items in the /System/Library/StartupItems that are installed by Apple as part of the base OS installation. The items in /Library/StartupItems are not executed. If the problem goes away, you can narrow your split-half search to find out which of the items in /Library/StartupItems could be causing the problem.

Similarly, if you press the Shift key right after you log in and hold it down until the Finder menu bar appears, you enter the Safe Login mode. The system will not open the login items that were activated in the Login pane of Accounts preferences. If the problem goes away while doing the Safe Login, you can narrow your split-half search to find out which login item is causing problems.

You can also systematically kill or forcibly quit processes using either Activity Monitor or the kill command in Terminal. Again, the strategy is to eliminate possible sources of the problem until you identify the specific process that is at fault.

Sometimes the problem is caused by a hardware device. By systematically unplugging peripherals from the system, you can track down the device that is causing problems.

In situations where you're trying to determine if the issue is with the computer system or with the network, you can run Network Utility.

As you try to eliminate potential causes, you might find it useful to compare the problem computer to another computer that is working correctly. By focusing on the differences between the two systems, you may cut down on the troubleshooting time.

Problem Scenario—Split-Half Search

Given what you know so far, is it worth doing a split-half search for our sample problem at this point? In our example, the answer is no. So, researching is the next step.

Researching

If you have completed the steps described so far and still can't determine the source of the problem, use additional resources to research the problem.

Check This Source:	For Information On:	Where
Read Me files	Last-minute compatibility and installation information	Installation disks and installation directories
Mac Help	Basic features, functions, and use	Help > Mac Help in the Finder
User manuals	Product-specific troubleshooting and installation information	Product installation disks and installation directories
Network Utility	Computer's network interfaces, access to specific hosts or IP addresses (Ping), network performance statistics, IP addresses and host names, user information, and active TCP ports	/Applications/Utilities
Console	Messages about the system and log files	/Applications/Utilities
Apple Support page	Top support questions, downloads, and updates (information organized by product)	www.info.apple.com

Check This Source:	For Information On:	Where
Knowledge Base	Technical articles, Read Me files, symptom/cure charts, specifications, late-breaking information, error codes	http://kbase.info.apple.com/
Service Source	Hot issues, product specification database, Apple Software Updates, troubleshooting symptom/cure charts	Available from Apple to Apple-authorized service providers and AppleCare Technician Training customers only
Email lists	Service that sends you information via email (from a mailing list so you can keep up with the discussion throughout the day)	http://lists.apple.com/
Discussion Lists	Discussion list where you post messages to forums, view messages by thread, and find solutions to issues that you are troubleshooting (can create bookmarks to postings that you want to return to later, customizing the Bookmarks page as your own personal support page)	http://discussions.info.apple.com/

One of the first research resources you should use is the Mac OS X built-in Help feature. You may find that the operating system is functioning correctly and the user is not following the correct steps to enable a particular feature to work.

The Knowledge Base (http://kbase.info.apple.com/) gives you detailed examples of issues and their resolutions. Knowledge Base makes use of an extensive set of keywords. These terms give you shortcuts to specific types of information. You can use keywords to assist you in making Knowledge Base searches. For example, using the keyword "kmosx" will list articles that cover Mac OS X issues.

In addition, Knowledge Base provides the Expert Search option, which lets you narrow down the search. For example, you can specify exact phrases to look for or limit the search to a certain product.

> **NOTE ▶** Knowledge Base categorizes documents into several types, which allows you to limit your search to these document types: Customer Installable Parts, Manuals, Mac OS System Updates, and SW Download.

If you've isolated the problem to a startup problem, you can search the Knowledge Base for Mac OS X startup. The results include, among other articles, #106464: "Your Mac Won't Start Up in Mac OS X."

Discussion forums are also available. Discussion forums give you the advantage of interacting with other users who are doing similar things with Mac OS X and, perhaps, running into similar issues.

Searching the Knowledge Base with Guided Search

The following steps will perform basic searches on the Knowledge Base.

1 Open Safari (/Applications).

2 Go to Knowledge Base at http://kbase.info.apple.com/.

You will be taken to the Guided Search page for Knowledge Base.

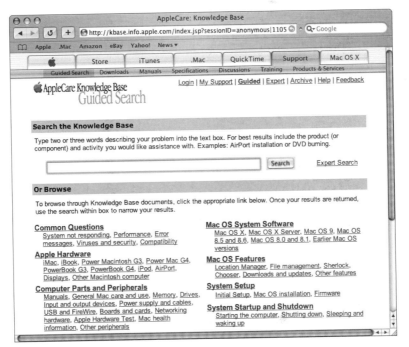

3 In the search field, type

    iPod update Mac OS X

    and press Return.

4 At the results page, you'll find links to Knowledge Base articles that will explain how to download the latest software for an iPod.

Search the Knowledge Base with Expert Search

The following steps will perform expert searches on the Knowledge Base:

1   Click Expert Search.

You will need an Apple ID to continue with this exercise. If you do not have one, you can create one if you'd like.

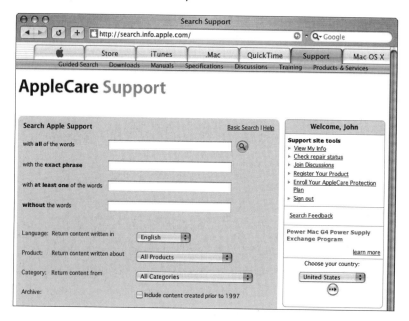

2   From the Category pop-up menu, choose Do-It-Yourself Repair.

3   From the Product pop-up menu, choose eMac.

4   Click the Search button.

5   Click eMac: Customer-Installable Parts from the search results to open the article.

6   Review this page and note that customer-installable parts instructions are available in a number of languages.

7 Click Expert to do a new search.

8 From the Product pop-up menu, choose iMac.

9 Enter *233* in the "all" search field.

10 Click the Search button.

11 Locate the article that lists the technical specifications for the iMac 233.

12 Do a new search for the specifications of the Macintosh you are using.

Problem Scenario—Research

In this case, the user can't use local resources to research the problem, so you try the Knowledge Base. What are you going to search for?

The Knowledge Base article leads you to continue your research by looking for clues in the panic log (/Library/Logs/panic.log).

You instruct the user to start up in target disk mode and look for the panic log. He can't find it. All he sees in the logs folder is AppleFileService (folder), DirectoryService (folder), and Software Update.log.

From the Knowledge Base article, you conclude that the log information is still in NVRAM. However, while looking around, the user notices a folder he doesn't recognize.

The folder has a nonsense name. Inside he sees another Library folder which, in turn, contains folders like these:

▶ CoreServices

▶ Extensions

▶ Filesystems

These are folders that typically reside in the System folder. It appears the System folder was accidentally renamed. Before proceeding in the troubleshooting process, once more ask yourself if you have you identified the fault and what your next step should be.

Escalating the Problem

If the troubleshooting process has not yet resolved the issue, you might have to contact Apple or a third party for help. AppleCare, the Apple service and support organization, provides a variety of online and phone-based support services, as well as support plans for different consumer segments. The service and support options for AppleCare are described at www.apple.com/support/.

Repairing/Replacing Components

Once you've located the trouble, you must fix it.

Before you replace software or hardware, it is appropriate to use the same precautions you would use when performing an invasive quick fix:

- ▶ Make a backup of user data.
- ▶ Make sure you are using only known-good software to modify the system.
- ▶ Look for the latest versions of software that you intend to update or reinstall.

Refer to the repair/replace text in Appendix A. This section groups repairs from easiest and involving the least consequences, to more difficult and/or time-consuming and involving greater consequences. Always consider repairs from the innocuous section first, then less innocuous, then invasive, unless you are certain what repair will solve the problem.

Notice that some of these repairs are also quick fixes. You will not necessarily try every quick fix while troubleshooting a particular problem. For example, it may be appropriate to run Disk First Aid during the Try Quick Fixes step while solving one problem, but with another problem it may not be appropriate until the Repair step.

You might need to reinstall the operating system and, if necessary, reconfigure it. This can be made less drastic if you do not select the erase option in the installer. Without selecting the erase option, the installer will fix files with incorrect checksums (corrupted files), user/group permissions, or locations (files that have been moved or deleted) by comparing the receipt for what is being installed with the receipt already on the hard disk. If you have upgraded Mac OS X since installing it, go to /Library/Receipts and delete the update packages for Mac OS X before reinstalling. After you reinstall Mac OS X, use Software Update to update the software again.

On computers that ship with Mac OS X preinstalled, you can use the erase and restore option to get the computer running again. Although this ensures that Mac OS X will be installed as it was when the computer was shipped, it does erase everything on the computer. If Mac OS X was not included on your computer when it shipped, you can start up from the Mac OS X Install Disc 1 and run the Installer. If you decide to erase the contents of the disk before installing Mac OS X, you will guarantee a fresh installation of Mac OS X, but you will also lose all the applications, configurations, and data files that were stored on the computer.

If you determine that the issue is not software related, you will need to investigate possible hardware issues. You should remove any additional hardware, such as peripherals or PCI cards, and see if the issue still persists. If you still cannot resolve the issue, you might need to have the Apple hardware repaired by an Apple-authorized service provider.

Problem Scenario—Repair/Replace

The repair for our sample problem is to correctly rename the System folder.

Before proceeding to the next step in the troubleshooting process, ask yourself if the problem is resolved? Yes, it is. So, your next step is to verify the repair.

Verifying the Repair

Make sure that the computer is functioning correctly before you return it to the user. Sometimes you may fix one problem only to find another. Or with hardware repairs, you may have swapped the right module but left a cable unplugged when reassembling the product. To ensure a positive user experience, make sure to thoroughly test every product you repair before telling the user it is fixed.

You need to make sure that

▶ The entire problem has been resolved

▶ No new problems have been introduced during the troubleshooting and repair

▶ All elements of the system work correctly together

To verify the repair, first try to re-create the problem as you did during the Verify Problem step. Once you are satisfied you cannot re-create the problem, you may want to run MacTest Pro, Apple Hardware Test, or Apple Service Diagnostic. Save any resulting logs to present to the user.

Here are some tips for verifying repairs:

▶ CPU systems—Use MacTest Pro and Apple Hardware Test to test the entire system, even if only one part of the system was repaired. If possible, run looping tests for several hours to catch any intermittent problems.

▶ Printers and other peripherals—If there is a diagnostic available for the specific product, use it!

Problem Scenario—Verify Repair
In our example, the steps to verify repair are as follows:

1   Restart the system. Do you get to the desktop?

2   Run some applications. Try printing.

3   Run System Profiler, refresh, and check logs.

4   Check the panic log.

Your next step is to inform the user and complete any administrative tasks.

Informing the User

The last steps in troubleshooting a problem are to explain to the user what you did and why, and to complete other administrative tasks.

The following are useful tips for informing the user:

▶ When verifying a repair with MacTest Pro, save the test log. You can show the log to the user as evidence that you have tested the system thoroughly and it passed the tests.

▶ Print other diagnostics reports and show the reports to the user.

▶ Explain any steps the user can take to avoid having problems reoccur. For example:

  ▶ If the user has shut the system off incorrectly, explain the hazards of not shutting down properly.

  ▶ If the user's system was corrupted by a virus, let the user know how to avoid such problems in the future.

  ▶ If the user has lost data, describe some ways to back up his or her information.

Taking time to teach users how to avoid future issues adds value and improves their computing experience.

Problem Scenario—Inform User

In our example, summarize the problem and its solution for the user:

▶ A kernel panic caused a startup failure.

▶ The kernel panic was caused by accidental renaming of the System folder.

▶ The solution was to locate the renamed System folder and correct the name.

After you summarize the problem and the solution, advise the user not to rename files or folders that Mac OS X needs for its operation, such as the System and Library folders. Explain to the user that it's possible to mistakenly rename system files when in target disk mode or when booted in to Mac OS 9.

What You've Learned

This chapter introduced you to Apple's systematic troubleshooting process. The troubleshooting steps outlined in this chapter are not hard-and-fast rules. They are a recommended, field-tested process. Your company may already have an established set of troubleshooting guidelines that you follow.

With whatever process you go through, you'll need to be flexible while completing it. Sometimes you'll have to go back and repeat earlier steps. For example, after you research the problem, you may find that you need to go back and try some different quick fixes. Still, following a systematic troubleshooting process helps save you time and money.

References

The following Knowledge Base articles (located at http://kbase.info.apple.com) will provide you with further information regarding troubleshooting Mac OS X:

- 9804, "Mac OS System Error Codes: –299 to –5553"
- 9805, "Mac OS System Error Codes: 0 to –261"
- 9806, "Mac OS System Error Codes: 1 to 32767"
- 10182, "Mac OS: Rebuilding Desktop File and Icon Recovery"
- 25398, "Mac OS X: How to Troubleshoot a Software Issue"
- 42642, "'To Continue Booting, Type mac-boot and Press Return' Message"
- 55743, "Common System Error Messages: What They Mean and What Might Help Resolve the Problem"
- 60351, "Determining BootROM or Firmware Version"
- 75178, "Knowledge Base: How to Use Keywords"
- 106227, "Mac OS X: What Is a Kernel Panic?"
- 106388, "Mac OS X: How to Start Up in Single-User or Verbose Mode"
- 106464, "Your Mac Won't Start Up in Mac OS X"
- 106991, "Mac OS X 10.2: Erroneous 'You Are Now Running on Reserve Battery Power' Alert"
- 107199, "Mac OS X: If Your Computer Stops Responding, 'Hangs', or 'Freezes'"

Review Quiz

Use the following questions to review what you have learned:

1. What are the 10 troubleshooting procedures suggested in this chapter?

2. What defines a quick fix?

3. Identify innocuous quick fixes that can be tried in Mac OS X.

4. Identify less innocuous quick fixes that can be tried in Mac OS X.

5. Identify invasive quick fixes that can be tried in Mac OS X.

6. Identify diagnostic tools that can be used in Mac OS X.

7. What is a split-half search?

8. What is Console used for?

9. If, after trying all previous troubleshooting steps, you still can't locate and fix the problem, what do you do?

10. Identify three Mac OS X repair or replacement techniques.

11. What are the three characteristics of a verified repair?

Answers

1. Gather information, verify the problem, try quick fixes, run diagnostics, perform split-half search, research, escalate, repair/replace, verify repair, inform user/complete administrative tasks.

2. A repair action that can be performed quickly, involves little or no risk of harm to the system, and has little or no cost.

3. Restart/shut down

    Run System Profiler

    Start in Safe Mode

    Start from Install Mac OS, Restoration, or MacTest Pro CD

    Suppress Auto-Login

    Suppress login items

    Use known-good disc (e.g., CD, DVD, Zip) (installation)

    Repair with Disk Utility

Start in single-user mode

Start in verbose mode

Start in another OS

Relaunch Finder

Disconnect all external devices

Turn off Screen Saver and Energy Saver (installation)

Verify with other users (network problem)

Connect to another device or volume (network)

Connect to PPP test server (modem)

4. Adjust user settings (Check Firewall setting; check Active Ports setting; check Startup)

Disk selection (startup)

Force quit

Log in as test user

Reset permissions

Move, rename, or delete preference file

Update printer driver (printing)

Update firmware

Change ports (for example, Ethernet and USB)

Use known-good peripherals (for example, monitor, disk drive, and printer)

5. Perform recommended (default) installation

Perform archive and install

Perform erase and install

Reinstall suspect application

Reset PRAM

Remove non-Apple RAM

6. Disk Utility

Network Utility

Apple Hardware Test

Tech Tool Deluxe (available with purchase of AppleCare Protection Plan)

Display Utilities (available to Apple-authorized service providers)

MacTest Pro (available to Apple-authorized service providers)

Apple Service Diagnostic (available to Apple-authorized service providers and AppleCare Technician Training customers only)

7. A split-half search is where half of the potential causes of a problem are removed or eliminated to help narrow down the potential cause of a problem.

8. Console is used to show you messages about the system and view log files.

9. Escalate the problem.

10. Run -fsck

Update driver

Repair with Disk Utility

Run AirPort Admin Utility

Run Setup Assistant

Use Directory Access

Run Unix commands

Use target disk mode

Adjust user controls

Reset PRAM

Perform recommended (default) installation

Perform Archive and Install

Erase and restore from Restore CDs

Perform Erase and Install

Repair with Apple Hardware Test

11. The entire problem has been resolved.

No new problems have been introduced during the troubleshooting and repair.

All elements of the system are compatible.

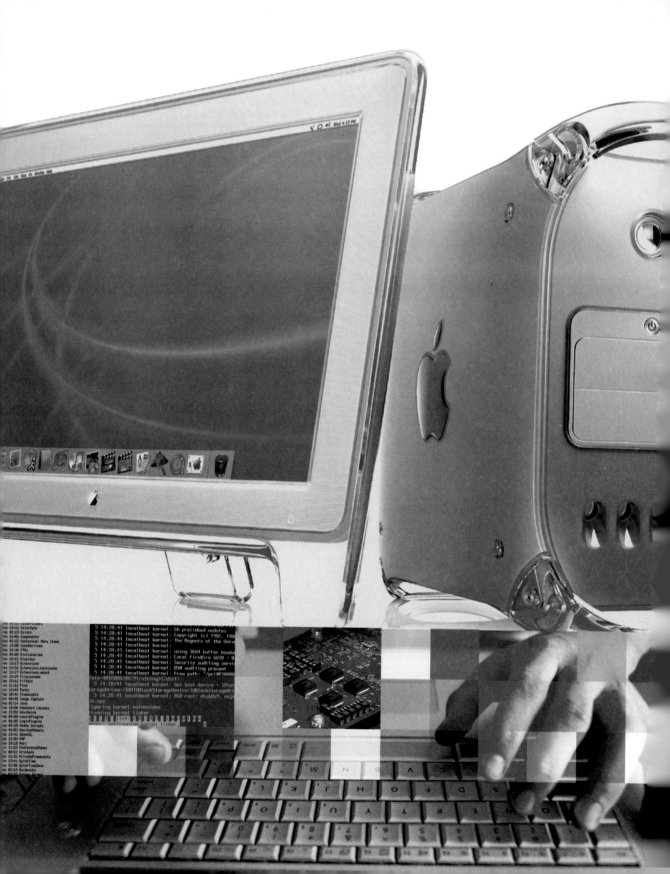

Apple General Troubleshooting Flowchart

This appendix serves as a quick reference to the Apple General Trouble-shooting Flowchart.

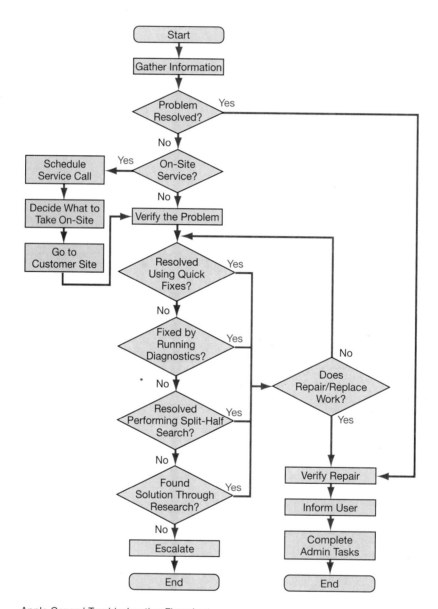

Apple General Troubleshooting Flowchart

Mac OS X Quick Fixes

We divide the quick fixes applicable to troubleshooting the OS into three increasingly invasive strategies, which we discuss in the following sections.

Innocuous (Consider These First)

The following fixes have little or no impact on the system:

- ▶ Restart/shut down
- ▶ Run System Profiler
- ▶ If the problem seems familiar, check Top Support Questions (available to authorized service technicians only)
- ▶ Perform a Safe Boot by holding Shift immediately on startup until the words "Safe Boot" appear below the progress bar
- ▶ Suppress automatic login during startup by holding Shift when the progress bar appears until the Login window appears
- ▶ Perform a Safe Login (suppress login items from launching) by holding Shift after logging in until the Finder menu appears
- ▶ Start up from Install Mac OS X Disc 1
- ▶ Repair the volume with Disk Utility
- ▶ Start up in single-user mode by holding Cmd-S during startup
- ▶ Start up in verbose mode by holding Cmd-V during startup
- ▶ Start up in Mac OS 9
- ▶ Relaunch Finder by choosing Apple > Force Quit
- ▶ Disconnect all external devices
- ▶ Turn off Screen Saver and Energy Saver during installation
- ▶ Verify with other users (to locate a network problem)
- ▶ Connect to another device or volume (network)
- ▶ Connect to PPP test server (modem)

Less Innocuous (Consider Next)

The following fixes have a moderate impact on the system:

▶   Adjust the user settings

▶   Check the settings in the Firewall pane of Sharing preferences

▶   In Network preferences, choose Show > Network Port Configurations

▶   Check the settings in Startup Disk preferences

▶   Choose Apple > Force Quit if an application is not responding

▶   Log in as a different user

▶   Reset permissions using the Info window (Cmd-I) or Terminal

▶   Move, rename, or delete the preference file

▶   Update the printer driver (for printing problems)

▶   Update the firmware

▶   Change ports (such as Ethernet, USB) in Network preferences

▶   Use known-good peripherals

Invasive Fixes (Consider Last)

The following fixes have a more drastic impact on the system:

▶   Perform a recommended (default) installation

▶   Perform Archive and Install of Mac OS X

▶   Perform Erase and Install of Mac OS X

▶   Reinstall the suspect application

▶   Reset PRAM by holding Cmd-Option-P-R at startup until you hear the startup chime twice

▶   Reset the PMU chip (consult your computer's documentation for location of PMU chip)

▶   Remove non-Apple memory from your computer

Mac OS X Diagnostic Tools

The following are common diagnostic tools used in Mac OS X:

- ▶ Disk Utility
- ▶ Network Utility
- ▶ Apple Hardware Test (included on disc with most current Macintosh computers)
- ▶ Tech Tool Deluxe (available with the purchase of an AppleCare Protection Plan)
- ▶ Display Utilities (available to Apple-authorized service providers)
- ▶ MacTest Pro (available to Apple-authorized service providers)
- ▶ Apple Service Diagnostic (available to Apple-authorized service providers and AppleCare Technician Training customers only)

Mac OS X Split-Half Search Techniques

The following are split-half search techniques:

- ▶ Start up in single-user mode by holding Cmd-S during startup
- ▶ Perform a Safe Boot by holding Shift during startup
- ▶ Suppress automatic login during startup by holding Shift when the progress bar appears until the Login window appears
- ▶ Perform a Safe Login (suppress login items from launching) by holding Shift after logging in until the Finder menu appears
- ▶ Systematically kill processes
- ▶ Disconnect peripherals
- ▶ Run Network Utility

Mac OS X Research Resources

The following are common resources to consult for troubleshooting Mac OS X issues:

- ▶ Read Me files
- ▶ Mac Help
- ▶ User documentation
- ▶ Network Utility
- ▶ Console
- ▶ Logs (viewable with Console)
- ▶ Activity Monitor
- ▶ Unix commands
- ▶ Apple Support Web page (www.apple.com/support)
- ▶ Knowledge Base (http://search.info.apple.com)
- ▶ Service Source (Apple-authorized service providers and AppleCare Technician Training customers only)
- ▶ man pages

Mac OS X Repair/Replace

When choosing to repair or replace items in a system, you can choose from three levels of troubleshooting strategy. The procedures should be used in the order they are discussed here.

First Choices

Try the following choices first when repairing or replacing items:

- ▶ Run -fsck in the command-line interface to fix disk problems
- ▶ Update drivers using Software Update preferences

- Repair permissions using Disk Utility
- Run AirPort Admin Utility
- Run Directory Access
- Run Unix commands
- Place the computer in target disk mode by holding down T during startup

Second Choices

Try the following choices after you've tried the appropriate first choices:

- Adjust the user controls
- Reset PRAM by holding Cmd-Option-P-R at startup until you hear the startup chime twice

Third Choices

Consider the following choices after you've tried the appropriate first and second choices:

- Perform a recommended (default) Mac OS X installation
- Perform Archive and Install from a Mac OS X Install Disc 1
- Erase and restore Mac OS X from the Restore discs
- Perform Erase and Install from a Mac OS X Install Disc 1
- Repair the computer with Apple Hardware Test (included on the disc with most current Macintosh computers)

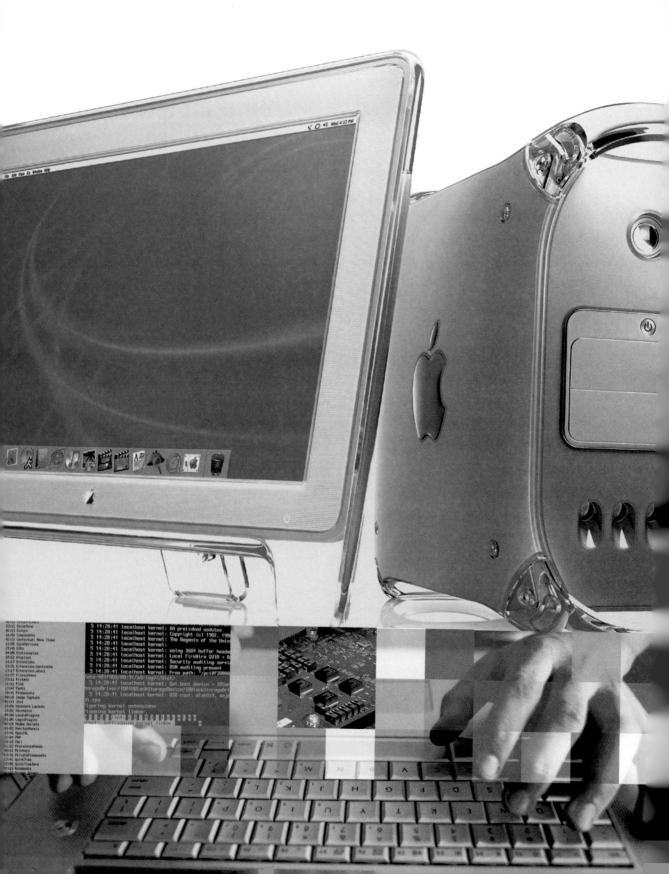

Appendix B
Networking Technologies

This appendix outlines useful information about some basic network technologies.

802.1X

This is the IEEE standard for network access control. It has these characteristics:

▶ Provides access control for both wired and wireless local area networks

▶ Is based on connection to a network rather than connection to a service

▶ Uses a central authentication server based on Extensible Authentication Protocol (EAP)

Apple Filing Protocol (AFP)

AFP uses a remote volume like a local volume and permits you to

▶ Mount a shared volume from a remote computer

▶ Navigate through the hierarchy for the remote file system

▶ Depending on your privileges, read/write/delete/execute

AFP saves documents and files directly to a remote volume like saving to a local volume. It can be used over AppleTalk or TCP/IP. It uses URL format to locate servers. For example:

▶ AppleTalk: aft/at/user:password@server/volume/path

▶ TCP: afp://user:password@server/volume/path

AFP uses AppleShare for shared volumes that are accessible using AFP over TCP/IP or AppleTalk.

Resources for AFP are located in /System/Library/Filesystems.

AFP can be enabled by turning on Personal File Sharing in the Services pane of Sharing preferences.

AirPort and AirPort Extreme

AirPort and AirPort Extreme are Apple's implementation of IEEE 802.11b and 802.11g wireless protocols, respectively, and use the same protocols as an Ethernet network.

Both use WEP (Wired Equivalent Privacy). AirPort has a range of 50 feet. AirPort Extreme has a range of 150 feet.

Both support TCP/IP, AppleTalk, and PPTP (for VPN connections).

Resources for AirPort and AirPort Extreme are located in /System/Library/ Extensions/AirPort Utilities. They include

- ▶ AirPort Setup Assistant (setup and configure AirPort)
- ▶ AirPort Admin Utility (configure and maintain AirPort network)

Both can be enabled in Network preferences and Internet Connect.

The default configuration shows a network port called AirPort when AirPort Card is installed.

Bootstrap Protocol (BOOTP)

This is the Internet protocol used for booting diskless workstations. Among its functions, BOOTP

- ▶ Discovers its own IP address
- ▶ Discovers the IP addresses of BOOTP servers on the network
- ▶ Locates a file to be loaded into memory to boot the computer
- ▶ Enables workstations to boot without a hard drive

The protocol is defined by RFC 951.

BOOTP can be configured in Network preferences.

Dynamic Host Configuration Protocol (DHCP)

DHCP provides a means to dynamically allocate IP addresses to computers on a local network.

To use DHCP, the system administrator assigns a range of IP addresses to DHCP and LAN clients. (Computers automatically lease the IP address for a period of time and renew leases upon expiration without user interaction.)

DHCP can be configured in Network preferences.

Resources for DHCP are found in /System/Library/PreferencesPanes.

File Transfer Protocol (FTP)

FTP is a broad-based protocol for downloading software from the Internet and is available for most operating systems.

FTP uses TCP for reliable delivery of information.

FTP employs login and password to authorize access to directories/files on a remote FTP server, but it transmits data in the clear, and is therefore insecure.

FTP can be enabled by turning on FTP Access in the Services pane of Sharing preferences.

After choosing Go > Connect to Server in the Finder to access an FTP server, users can see all files on the hard disk, even if they don't have permissions to change files/folders outside of shared directories.

HyperText Transfer Protocol (HTTP)

HTTP is a standard method of sending data over the Internet.

It uses TCP and is primarily used for retrieving Web pages.

Resources for HTTP are found in /System/Library/StartupItems/Apache.

The Apache HTTP server serves Web pages from your computer.

HTTP can be enabled by turning on Personal Web Sharing in Services pane of Sharing preferences.

Files and folders are shared from the Sites folder.

IP Addressing (IPv4 and IPv6)

Both IPv4 and IPv6 are Internet Protocol addressing standards supported by Mac OS X. They have common characteristics, as well as several differences that are described here.

IP Addressing

This provides a unique address to identify computers on the Internet.

It routes data when it moves from source to destination.

IP addresses are required because they are used as an identifier of the destination point.

IPv4 (Internet Protocol version 4)

IPv4 supports up to 4 billion public addresses.

It defines the use of unique 32-bit addresses.

IPv4 addresses are formatted as four 8-bit fields (4 octets). For example, 192.168.1.2.

Classes are determined by the first octet:

▶   Class A: Large networks 1–127

▶   Class B: Medium networks 128–191

▶   Class C: Small networks 192–223

▶   Class D: Multicast 224–239

▶   Class E: Experimental 240–255

The 127.0.0.1 address is used for loopback or localhost ID.

IPv6 (Internet Protocol version 6)

IPv6 is designed to increase the number of IP addresses, add features, and improve efficiencies of the IP protocol.

In 1995, Apple and Mentat announced IPv6 was integrated with Apple Open Transport in Mac OS.

It uses CIDR (Classless Interdomain Routing).

It provides increased flexibility in address numbers.

IPv6 allows networks to be flexible in size so IP addresses aren't wasted.

Here are some features of IPv6:

▶ Does not rely on class size to determine network numbers

▶ Translates between IPv4 and IPv6, seamlessly

▶ Uses 128-bit unique address

▶ Addresses written in hexadecimal

▶ Uses 16-bit fields separated by colons rather than 8-bit fields separated by decimals

▶ Includes MAC (Media Access Control) address of computer

▶ Addresses in URLs enclosed in brackets []

IPv6 is built in to drivers for various networking interfaces. You can see protocols by using Terminal.

Type

ifconfig -a

to show active network ports, addresses, and status.

Network Address Translation (NAT)

NAT is a method of segregating internal and external addresses and traffic.

NAT converts an internal address to a public address.

When set up, NAT has the following characteristics:

▶ One interface (port) is used for incoming and outgoing external traffic.

▶ One interface (port) is used for incoming and outgoing internal traffic.

▶ It can be a physical interface (Ethernet-to-Internet and AirPort-to-internal traffic).

▶ It can be a virtual interface (Ethernet card assigned two IP addresses—one external and one internal).

Devices providing NAT (sometimes called gateways) include cable/DSL (Digital Subscriber Line) modems/routers. NAT can be enabled in the Internet pane of Sharing preferences.

Point-to-Point Protocol (PPP)

PPP is a standard method for connecting a computer to the Internet, usually with a dial-up modem. It provides error-checking features.

PPP sends the computer's TCP/IP packets to a server, which puts packets onto the Internet.

PPP can be configured in Network preferences and Internet Connect.

Resources for PPP are found in /System/Library/ModemScripts.

Point-to-Point Protocol over Ethernet (PPPoE)

This is a specification for connecting users on an Ethernet network to the Internet via a gateway, such as cable/DSL modems and wireless devices.

It uses PPP and Ethernet.

PPPoE users share a common connection—they're supported by Ethernet in a LAN (multiuser) combined with PPP (serial connections).

PPPoE can be enabled in Network preferences.

Resources for PPPoE are found in /System/Library.

Rendezvous

Rendezvous is Apple's implementation of the Zeroconf (Zero configuration IP Networking) protocol.

It is designed to simplify setting up networks with different LAN standards (for example, AppleTalk and NETBIOS).

Rendezvous has three primary features:

▶ Computers can get dynamic IP address with or without DHCP server.

▶ Computers translate host names and IP addresses without DNS server.

▶ Computer users can find network services (printers/servers) without a directory server.

Uses in Mac OS X:

▶ Dynamically assigns an IP address to the computer (which would usually be done by a DCHP server).

▶ Network preferences set to attain an address using DHCP.

▶ Can talk to computer and devices via AirPort or Ethernet.

▶ iChat and Print Center dynamically discover other computers and devices, respectively, in your area without a server to provide information.

▶ Limited to finding computer and devices on same subnet.

It configures the host name in Sharing preferences.

Resources for Rendezvous are located in the plug-in to directory services:

/System/Library/Frameworks/DirectoryService.framework/Versions/
A/Resource/Plugins/Rendezvous.dplug

For more info, see www.apple.com/macosx/features/rendezvous/ and www.zeroconf.org.

Server Message Block (SMB)

SMB is the basic protocol for file sharing with Windows OS, connecting PC-compatible computers to a LAN.

It uses CIFS (Common Internet File System), a networking standard combining SMB connectivity with Internet file sharing.

Samba (www.samba.org) is an open source application developed to provide compatibility with CIFS and SMB client services.

In Finder, choose Go > Connect to Server to connect to SMB services (locate WORKGROUP in the list and double-click the host name).

SMB is enabled by turning on Windows Sharing in the Services pane of Sharing preferences.

Item	Description
Accounting	Handles process accounting, which logs every action a user or process takes in the /var/account/acct log
Apache	Runs the Apache HTTP server, httpd, if Web Sharing is enabled
AppleShare	Starts the AppleShare service if a network connection is present
AppleTalk	Runs the AppleTalk startup program in either router mode, multihoming (nonrouter) mode, or on a single port (as defined in /etc/hostconfig)
AppServices	Runs various support services for the graphical user interface and starts the core services daemon (coreservicesd)
AuthServer	Starts user authentication services
BIND	Starts up the local DNS server
Cleanup	Deletes temporary and log files
ConfigServer	Gets the computer configuration information
CrashReporter	Starts the crash reporting system (crashreporterd) and the kernel panic reporter (panicdump)
Cron	Runs the cron daemon
DirectoryServices	Starts the name-resolver daemon (lookupd) and manages directory information used when the Mac OS X Unix subsystem and graphical user interface exchange data
Disks	Starts the autodiskmount daemon, controls disk operations, and checks and mounts local disks
IPServices	Controls some services related to TCP/IP networking and starts TCP/IP services (inetd), host configuration services (BOOTP), and the NetBoot client management server

Item	Description
LDAP	Starts the LDAP service
Loginwindow	Signals that the system has the services it needs to start the loginwindow application (the init process launches the application while SystemStarter continues loading startup items in the background)
mDNSResponder	Starts up the multicast-DNS responder, which supports Rendezvous, Apple's implementation of zero-configuration networking
NetInfo	Starts the NetInfo servers (netinfod and nibindd)
Network	Configures the local network interfaces based on the data in /etc/iftab, sets the computer's host name, configures network routing (if specified), turns IP routing on or off (if specified), sets the machine's host ID in the kernel, and loads the Shared IP kernel extension to enable sharing of one IP address among all application environments (including Classic)
NetworkExtensions	Loads several network-related kernel extensions
NetworkTime	Interacts with the network time server and starts up network time service, which uses the Network Time Protocol (NTP)
NFS	Controls the use of and access to NFS, starts the NFS service that performs asynchronous block I/O (nfsiod), mounts remote file systems, starts the automounter, and, if the NetInfo database indicates that the computer should export a file system using NFS, starts the NFS server
NIS	Starts the network information services

Item	Description
Portmap	Determines the port number of a network service that a client needs to connect to and starts up the portmap daemon
PrintingServices	Starts the CUPS printing services daemon (cupsd)
Samba	Starts the Samba daemon (smbd), which provides network connectivity via the Server Message Block (SMB) protocol
SecurityServer	Starts the security server, which oversees system authorization, authentication, and keychain access
SendMail	Starts the outgoing mail services daemon (sendmail) and cleans up the outbound mail cue directory
SSH	Starts the sshd daemon if remote access is enabled, and generates the secure shell encryption keys as needed
SystemLog	Starts the system log daemon (syslogd)
SystemTuning	Optimizes the system's performance by turning on and off various services and sets up performance values for the system, based on such factors as available memory

The following table lists common system daemons and servers that are running after you log in to a Mac OS X computer.

Daemon or Server	Description
ATSServer	Enables the Apple Type Solution server for system-wide font management
autodiskmount	Mounts all devices automatically, including hard disks, and removable media
automount	Mounts NFS file systems automatically when they are first accessed and later unmounts them, when they are idle
	A mount point for a virtual file system first appears as a symbolic link on a local file system. Reading this symbolic link triggers automount to mount the associated remote file system
configd	Configures and maintains the network automatically
cron	Executes scheduled commands or scripts
dynamic_pager	Communicates with the kernel's default pager to create or delete the swap files (in /private/var/vm); these files are used as the storage for virtual memory
inetd	Listens for connections on certain ports (when a connection occurs, inetd decides what service the socket corresponds to and invokes the appropriate program to service the request)
init	Starts up processes during startup (init is the parent of most system-level processes)

Daemon or Server	Description
kextd	Loads the device-drivers During system startup, this daemon loads any remaining device drivers that were not loaded by BootX. After startup, kextd is responsible for dynamically loading and unloading device drivers
lookupd	Looks up requests to network information services such as NetInfo and DNS for name resolution
mach_init	Provides messaging between system-level processes, calls the Mach bootstrap port server, and starts the init process
mDNSResponder	Responds to network request for multicast DNS resolution
netinfod	Provides netinfo service (one netinfod process is created for each domain served)
nfsiod	Services asynchronous requests to an NFS server (most systems have multiple instances of this daemon running)
nibindd	Finds, creates, and destroys NetInfo servers (see netinfod)
pbs	Exchanges information between user processes via a pasteboard server and acts as the data transfer mechanism used in dragging operations
portmap	Converts RPC program numbers into Internet (DARPA protocol) port numbers (portmap must be running before RPC calls can be made)

Daemon or Server	Description
syslogd	Logs system error and status messages
update	Periodically flushes the filesystem cache to help prevent data loss in the event of a crash
Window Manager	Provides the graphical user interface, and is the parent process for most of the user applications, including Finder and Dock

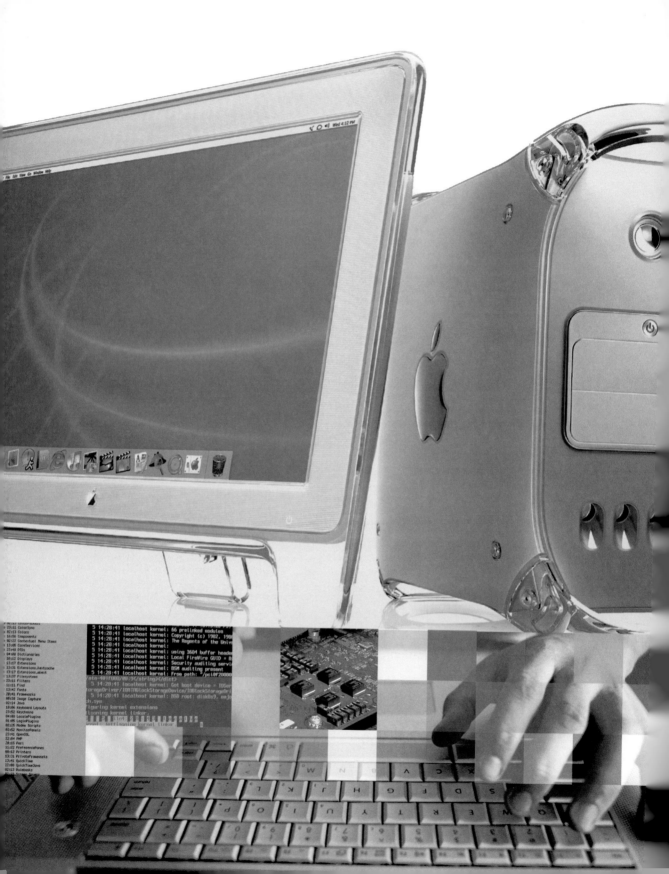

Glossary

802.1x Standard for access control on both wireless and wired local area networks. It provides a way to authenticate and authorize devices that attach to the network port.

Admin Type of user account that is created during the initial configuration of Mac OS X and can be created in Accounts preferences. When logged in as an administrator, user can add user accounts, change system settings, and install applications and resources to be accessed by any user on the computer.

A

AFP (Apple Filing Protocol) This protocol allows a computer on a network to access AppleShare file servers and view the items as though they were stored locally.

AirPort Apple's implementation of the wireless Ethernet standard, Ethernet 802.11.

alias A feature of the HFS/HFS Plus volume format that provides a lightweight reference, or pointer, to files or folders.

API (Application Programming Interface) APIs let application developers use functions of the computer and operating system without directly accessing the CPU.

Apple Events A messaging tool to transfer information, commands, and requests between applications, networks, and Mac OS X.

AppleTalk A set of networking protocols developed by Apple.

application environment Consists of the frameworks, libraries, and services (with associated APIs) necessary for the runtime execution of programs developed with those APIs. For example, applications developed with Carbon APIs run in the Carbon application environment.

Aqua Apple's graphical user interface for Mac OS X and Mac OS X Server, using color, transparency, and animation to enhance the appearance of the system and applications.

B

Binhex Encoding format that converts 8-bit files into 7-bit format. Binhex format preserves file attributes as well as Macintosh resource forks.

Bluetooth Short-range wireless technology for communication and synchronization between network devices.

BOOTP (Bootstrap Protocol) BOOTP is a method for acquiring an IP address with which a particular address is assigned to a particular host machine each time the machine starts up. It is used primarily for computers that start from a network server rather than their own hard disks.

BootROM Hardware that contains the first code to be activated at startup. Its two primary responsibilities are to initialize system hardware and select the operating system to boot.

BSD (Berkeley Software Distributions) BSD is a version of the Unix operating system developed at the University of California at Berkeley.

bundle A directory in the file system that stores executable code and the software resources related to that code. A bundle is also known as a package.

C

Carbon Application environment. Carbon is a set of programming interfaces derived from earlier Mac OS APIs that have been modified to work with Mac OS X, especially its kernel environment.

CGI (Common Gateway Interface) A script or program that adds dynamic functions to a Web site. A CGI sends information between a Web site and an application that provides a service for the site. For example, if a user fills out a form on the site, a CGI could send the message to an application that processes the data and sends a response back to the user.

CIFS (Common Internet File System) This proposed standard protocol allows applications to make requests for files and services on remote computers on the Internet.

Classic (Abbreviated term for Classic compatibility environment) Classic makes it possible for Mac OS 9.*x*, and all the applications capable of running in that version of the Mac OS, to run on a Mac OS X system.

Cocoa Application environment. Cocoa is based on two object-oriented frameworks that offer both Java and Objective-C APIs.

ColorSync Color management software used by the Quartz graphic system.

command-line interface Tool used to execute BSD commands; includes Terminal, single-user mode, console, and Telnet (SSH).

CUPS (Common Unix Printing System) Cross-platform printing solution for Unix environments based on the Internet Printing Protocol (IPP).

Darwin Core operating system in Mac OS X. Darwin is an open source operating system built on the Mach 3.0 kernel.

D

DAT files Virus definition files used by virus-protection software. They contain information about virus threats and their cures, and they must be kept up-to-date.

Desktop folder Storage for anything on the user's desktop.

DHCP (Dynamic Host Configuration Protocol) DHCP is a method for acquiring an IP address with which unique addresses are assigned to host machines from a range of addresses.

directory folder A directory is a named group of related files that are separated by the naming convention from other groups of files.

directory service A database service that keeps track of the resources that are available to the users of that database.

DNS (Domain name server) DNS servers are host machines that can translate domain names into IP addresses.

Dock Tool in the Mac OS X Finder that allows the user to open applications, documents, and other frequently used items.

driver Drivers are programs that enable a user to access and interact with hardware devices.

DSL (Digital Subscriber Line) DSL is a high-speed connection to an Internet service provider using the same wires as a regular telephone line.

E

Exposé Mac OS X 10.3 feature that automatically tiles open windows when F9 is pressed.

extension Software that extends the functionality of an operating system such as Mac OS 9 or earlier. See *kernel extension*.

F

FAT (File Allocation Table) FAT is a common volume format used by PC operating systems, including Windows.

favorites Aliases to frequently accessed folders, files, network volumes, or Web sites.

file extension Multicharacter suffix preceded by a period in a filename. File extensions are used to identify the correct application to execute the file.

file fork Method of storing data in a Mac OS file system with which each file has two portions: a data fork that contains the data and a resource fork that contains the information about the file itself.

file system The way in which files are named and where they are placed logically for storage and retrieval.

FileVault Feature that secures a user's home folder with AES-128 encryption.

Finder Carbon application that manages the user's desktop and mediates the user's access to any item in the file system.

firewall Hardware or software system designed to prevent unauthorized access to or from private networks.

FireWire Apple's implementation of the IEEE 1394 serial bus standard.

firmware Software contained in read-only memory, such as BootROMs or EPROMs.

framework A type of bundle that packages a dynamic shared library with the resources that the library requires, including header files and reference documentation.

FTP (File Transfer Protocol) This networking protocol is used to transfer files over a TCP/IP network, such as the Internet.

Get Info Dynamic window that shows permission settings, application settings, previews, and general information about an item; accessed using the Cmd-I keyboard sequence in the Finder.

G

GID (Group identification number) The GID is used in multiuser operating systems to uniquely identify groups of users.

HFS (Hierarchical File System) HFS and HFS Plus (also known as Mac OS Extended) are common volume formats for Macintosh operating systems. HFS Plus (Journaled) is a feature of the Mac OS Extended file system that tracks changes in an effort to prevent file systems from getting into an inconsistent state and also to aid in data recovery.

H

HTML (Hypertext Markup Language) The set of symbols or codes inserted in a file to be displayed on a World Wide Web browser page. The markup language tells the Web browser how to display a Web page's words and images.

HTTP (Hypertext Transfer Protocol) This networking protocol is used to transfer Web-based information.

IANA (Internet Assigned Numbers Authority) An organization responsible for allocating IP addresses, assigning protocol parameters, and managing domain names.

I

ICMP (Internet Control Message Protocol) A message control and error-reporting protocol used between host servers and gateways. For example, some Internet software applications use it to send a packet on a roundtrip between two hosts to determine roundtrip times and discover problems on the network.

IGMP (Internet Group Management Protocol) An Internet protocol used by hosts and routers to send packets to lists of hosts that want to participate, known as multicasting. QuickTime Streaming Server uses multicast addressing, as does Service Location Protocol (SLP).

IMAP (Internet Message Access Protocol) This networking protocol is used to access electronic mail from a mail server.

IPv6 (Internet Protocol version 6) This latest version of the protocol features improvements over IPv4, including 128-bit addresses rather than 32-bit addresses, and defines the rules for unicast, anycast, and multicast. These improvements were included to support future growth of the Internet.

ISO 9660 Standard CD-ROM file system that allows you to read the same CD-ROM disc whether you are on a PC, Mac, or other computer platform.

ISP (Internet service provider) An ISP is a company that provides a connection between client computers and the Internet.

J

Java An object-oriented programming language developed by Sun Microsystems.

K

KDC (Key Distribution Server) Maintains a list of user principals for a Kerberos authentication system.

Kerberos Authentication system based on a unique key, or ticket. Allows private information to be sent between two parties who have assigned tickets.

kernel Also known as a microkernel. The kernel is the underlying core of an operating system.

kernel extension (KEXT) A kernel extension is a type of loadable bundle that low-level system routines recognize and load into the kernel environment. KEXT bundles have a file extension of .kext.

kernel panic A type of error that occurs when the kernel receives an instruction in an unexpected format or that it fails to handle properly.

keychain Tool in Mac OS X that stores passwords and user identifications for applications, servers, or Web sites.

L

LAN (local area network) A LAN is a network of devices (computers, printers, and so forth) that are in the same general physical location.

LDAP (Lightweight Directory Access Protocol) This networking protocol is used to access online directory services that run over TCP.

link-local address An address assigned by an IP host in the absence of outside configuration information. It is part of the ZeroConf standard.

links In Unix, a method of referencing files. A hard link provides a file with more than one name and allows the name to be stored in different directories. A symbolic link is a lightweight reference to a file or folder using the path in the file system.

localhost Name given to a host machine if its IP address has no domain name associated to it.

location A set of network configurations composed of network ports and the protocols that run on those ports. The location is an organization tool used to manage network connectivity.

LPR (Line printer) LPR printers are network printers that use the Internet Protocol and are configured by identifying the IP address of either the printer itself or the printer queue it is connected to.

M

master password Feature of FileVault that allows the passwords of encrypted user accounts to be reset.

m-DNS (Multicast Domain Name Service) A means of translating host names to addresses without a dedicated domain name server. It is part of the ZeroConf standard.

MBONE (Multicast Backbone) A virtual network that supports IP multicasting. It uses the same physical media as the Internet, but it is designed to repackage multicast data packets so they appear to be unicast data packets.

MIME (Multipurpose Internet Mail Extension) An Internet standard for specifying what happens when a Web browser requests a file with certain characteristics. A file's suffix describes the type of file it is, and you determine how you want the server to respond when it receives files with certain suffixes. Each suffix and its associated response is called a MIME type mapping.

MX record (Mail Exchange record) An entry in a DNS table that specifies how mail is handled for a domain. When a mail server on the Internet has mail to deliver to a domain, it requests the MX record for the domain, and the record directs the mail to the computer specified in the MX record.

N

NetBIOS (Network basic input/output system) A program that allows applications on different computers to communicate within a local area network.

NetInfo A hierarchical database system used for directory services.

network port Network interface unit. In Mac OS X, a network port is a device that serves as a common interface for various other devices within a local area network, or as an interface to allow networked computers to connect to a network.

NFS (Unix Network File System) NFS allows a user to access files on a remote computer as though the files were part of the user's own file system.

normal user A user account type that can use a basic set of applications and tools and is limited to making configuration changes that affect only the user's account. A normal user cannot make changes to any settings that are system-wide. Also, a normal user cannot use Directory Setup and NetInfo Manager to change configurations.

NSL Provides a protocol-independent way for applications to discover network services. See *SLP*.

NTFS (Windows NT File System) The NTFS volume format is used by Microsoft Windows NT.

O

Open Firmware Cross-platform standard for controlling hardware. Open Firmware is used by all PCI-based computers running the Mac OS.

OpenGL Industry standard application programming interface for 2D and 3D graphic systems.

open source Software that is developed, tested, and improved through public collaboration and distributed with the intent that it be shared with others.

ORBS (Open Relay Behavior-modification System) A database, accessible via DNS lookups, that tracks known spammers (senders of junk mail). The database contains SMTP servers that are known to allow third-party relay; senders of junk mail use these servers to forward their junk mail.

package See *bundle*.

P

pane Any region of changeable content within a dialog or window.

path Route through a file system to a particular item.

partition Isolated section of a hard disk.

PC Card Also known as PCMCIA, a PC Card is a standard that contains the physical, electrical, and software specifications for an integrated circuit card usually used in laptop systems.

PCI (Peripheral Component Interconnect) Bus standard that provides a channel or path between the components in a computer.

PDF (Portable Document Format) PDF is a standard graphics format used for rendering and printing. It was developed by Adobe Systems, Inc.

permission In a multiuser operating system, provides a measure of security needed to keep one user from modifying or viewing another user's items on the computer. The three permissions are read, write, and execute. Also known as privilege.

PID (Process identification number) The PID is used in multiuser operating systems to uniquely identify running processes.

plug-in A software module that extends the functionality of an application or framework.

POP (Post Office Protocol) This networking protocol is used to access electronic mail from a mail server.

POSIX (Portable Operating System Interface) POSIX is a set of standard operating system interfaces based on the Unix operating system.

PostScript This programming language, developed by Adobe Systems, describes the appearance of a printed page.

PPP (Point-to-Point Protocol) This networking protocol is used to connect two peer machines using a common solution, such as a modem.

PPPoE (Point-to-Point Protocol over Ethernet) This networking protocol is used to connect two peer machines using a broadband solution, such as a DSL modem.

preemptive multitasking Method of running multiple processes simultaneously where the operating system can interrupt, or preempt, a currently running task to run another task.

process A task. A process is a running program or set of threads.

protected memory Memory scheme in which an operating system allocates a unique memory address space in RAM for each application or process running on the computer and prevents applications from accessing memory outside of their allocated space.

protocol Networking language. A protocol is a special set of rules that relates to intercommunication between systems.

Q **Quartz** 2D graphics application programming interface based on PDF.

QuickTime Multimedia development, storage, and playback standard developed by Apple.

R **RAID (Redundant Array of Independent Disks)** Software or hardware system that uses two or more disk drives at the same time to improve fault tolerance and performance.

Rendezvous A protocol developed by Apple for automatic discovery of computers, devices, and services on IP networks.

receipt A bundle that acts as a record of what was installed by the Mac OS X Installer. The receipts are stored in the Library folder.

resource fork See *file fork*.

root (user) Short name for System Administrator. Root has read and write permissions to all areas of the file system.

root (file system) Beginning of a file path. The root of the file system is designated by a forward slash (/).

router Gateway between two networks. A router determines the next network point to which networking information should be forwarded toward its destination.

RTP (Real-Time Transport Protocol) This networking protocol is used to transmit, or stream, QuickTime data.

RTSP (Real-Time Streaming Protocol) This networking protocol is used for two-way communication with a unicast streaming server.

SCSI (Small Computer System Interface) SCSI is a fast communications bus that allows for multiple devices to be connected to a computer.

S

SDP (Session Description Protocol) Used with QuickTime Streaming Server, an SDP file contains information about the format, timing, and authorship of the live streaming broadcast.

search domain Provides the TCP/IP configuration with a domain name or list of domain names to use in the event one is not specified in a IP search or request.

Secure Empty Trash Feature that overwrites deleted files in the Trash when emptied, making the files nearly impossible to recover.

share point Server volume that can be mounted by a network user.

sheet Modal dialog attached to a specific document window.

single-user mode Mode in which Mac OS X is started without the multi-user components or graphical user interface. Single-user mode is entered by holding down Cmd-S at startup.

SLP (Services Location Protocol) This networking protocol is used to discover and advertise TCP/IP-based services, such as personal file sharing, personal Web sharing, or USB printer sharing. Some of these discovered services are viewed in the Finder by choosing Go > Connect to Server.

SMB (Server Message Block) This networking protocol allows a computer on a network to access Windows and Samba file servers and view the items as though they were stored locally.

SMTP (Simple Mail Transfer Protocol) This networking protocol is used to send electronic mail using a mail server.

SSH Program to log in to another computer over a TCP/IP network and execute commands on the remote computer. SSH provides authentication and secure communications over unsecure channels.

SSL (Secure Sockets Layer) An Internet protocol that allows you to send encrypted, authenticated information across the Internet.

subnet mask Used to determine what part of an IP address identifies a network and what part identifies an individual host machine.

superuser Another name for root. See *root (user)*.

System Administrator Long name for root. See *root (user)*.

System Preferences Application used to configure the system settings and preferences for Mac OS X.

T

TCP/IP (Transport Control Protocol/Internet Protocol) TCP/IP is the primary networking protocol used to communicate over the Internet.

Telnet Program to log in to another computer over a TCP/IP network, execute commands on the remote computer, and move files from one computer to another. Telnet provides authentication but not encryption of information.

thread Information needed to serve a particular service request or set of instructions.

ticket In a Kerberos authentication system, an embedded unique key that allows private information to be passed between parties.

TTL (Time-to-Live) The specified length of time that DNS information is stored in a cache. When a domain name-IP address pair has been cached longer than the TTL value, the entry is deleted from the name server's cache (but not from the primary DNS server).

UDF (Universal Disk Format) Standard CD-ROM and DVD file system designed to ensure consistency in optical media.

U

UDP (User Datagram Protocol) A communications method that uses the Internet Protocol (IP) to send a data unit (called a datagram) from one computer to another in a network. Network applications that have very small data units to exchange might use UDP rather than TCP.

UFS (Unix File System) This volume format is used primarily by Unix and Unix-based operating systems.

UID (User identification number) The UID is used in multiuser operating systems to uniquely identify a user.

Unix Pronounced YEW-nihks. Nonproprietary operating system used on computers.

URL (Uniform Resource Locator) The URL is an address of a file, or resource, accessible on the Internet.

USB (Universal Serial Bus) USB is a serial interface between a computer and add-on devices.

verbose mode All of the startup information (drivers loading, services starting) is listed as Mac OS X starts up. Verbose mode is entered by holding down Cmd-V at startup.

V

virtual memory Scheme for managing the protected memory space and allocating the amount of memory needed by applications.

VPN (Virtual Private Network) Private data network that uses public telecommunications infrastructure but maintains privacy with tunneling protocols.

W

WebDAV (World Wide Web Distributed Authoring and Versioning) WebDAV is an extension of HTTP that allows the viewing of a Web server file system as though is was a local file system.

WEP (Wired Equivalent Privacy) Security protocol for wireless networks designed to offer the same level of security as wired networks.

WINS (Windows Internet Naming Service) A name resolution service used by Windows computers to match client names with IP addresses. A WINS server can be located on the local network or externally on the Internet.

X

X11 The X Window System. Common windowing environment for Unix.

XML (Extensible Markup Language) The universal format for documents and data accessed on the Web.

Z

ZeroConf An Internet standard for Zero Configuration IP Networking.

Index

Symbols and Numbers

- (minus sign), 20–21
% (percent), 181
* (asterisk) wildcard, 195
. (dot), 99, 100, 115
.. (dot-dot), 99
/ (forward slash), 98, 189
: (colon), 180
? (question mark), 195, 406–407
[ ] (square brackets) wildcard, 195
\ (backslash), 188
| (pipe character), 205
~ (tilde), 98–99, 180
> (greater than), 183
802.1x, 245–246, 474, 491

A

absolute paths, 98–99
access levels, 81–82, 94. *See also*
    permissions
accounts, user. *See* user accounts
ACDT (Apple Certified Desktop
    Technician), 5
ACHDS (Apple Certified Help Desk
    Specialist), 4
ACPT (Apple Certified Portable
    Technician), 5
ACSA (Apple Certified System
    Administrator), 5
ACTC (Apple Certified Technical
    Coordinator), 4
Active Directory authentication, 291–292
Activity Monitor utility, 168–170
Address Book picture, 42
administrator users
    defined, 491
    deleting Admin account, 55
    Directory Access changes, 271–273
    forgotten passwords, 63
    group permissions, 83

local vs. network user accounts, 39–40
login options, 46–47
overview of, 38–39
system passwords, 75–76
Advanced Technology Attachment (ATA),
    335, 356, 366
AES (128-bit Advanced Encryption
    Standard), 129
AFP (Apple Filing Protocol)
    characteristics of, 474
    connecting to, 279–280
    defined, 491
    file sharing, 303–311
    managing with directory services,
        287–288
AirPort
    characteristics of, 475
    configuring AppleTalk, 239
    configuring IP addresses, 228–229
    configuring ports, 227
    defined, 491
AirPort Extreme, 475
alerts, 278
alias, 491
AOL Dialup, 237
API (Application Programming
    Interface), 491
Apple Admin account, 40–41
Apple Certified Desktop Technician
    (ACDT), 5
Apple Certified Help Desk Specialist
    (ACHDS), 4
Apple Certified Portable Technician
    (ACPT), 5
Apple Certified System Administrator
    (ACSA), 5
Apple Certified Technical Coordinator
    (ACTC), 4
Apple Events, 491
Apple Filing Protocol. *See* AFP (Apple
    Filing Protocol)

Apple General Troubleshooting
    Flowchart, 434–435, 466–471
Apple Remote Desktop, 437
Apple Software Restore (ASR), 33,
    126–127
Apple Support Page, 450
Apple>About This Mac, 26–27
AppleCare, 456
Applet Launcher, 162–165
AppleTalk
    configuring over Ethernet, 239–240
    defined, 216, 491
    enabling for AFP file sharing, 306
    enabling printer, 372
    service discovery protocols, 269, 297
    troubleshooting with, 248, 285
applets, Java, 162–163
application environments
    BSD/X11, 165–166
    Classic. *See* Classic
    defined, 491
    Java, 162–165
    Native, 144–146
    references, 175–176
    review quiz, 176–177
    troubleshooting, 145–146
    types of, 144
application management
    fast user switching, 58–59
    force quitting, 172–174
    installing additional applications,
        20–21
    monitoring system activity, 168–171
    references, 175–176
    with System Profiler, 166–168
Application Programming Interface
    (API), 491
apropos command, 185, 187
Aqua, 492
Archive and Install, 18
Archive.zip file, 132

archives, file and folder, 132
ASR (Apple Software Restore), 33,
   126–127
asterisk (*) wildcard, 195
ATA (Advanced Technology Attachment),
   335, 356, 366
attributes, file, 196–200
authentication
   with Active Directory, 291–292
   in Directory Access, 271–273
   with directory services, 287–288
   with Kerberos, 292–295
   with LDAP, 288–290
   overview of, 286–287
   startup and, 414–415
   troubleshooting, 296
Automatic location, 221

B
backslash (\), 188
backups
   file system, 137
   installation and, 15, 31–32
   quick fixes requiring, 445
   reference guide for, 139
Berkeley Software Distribution. *See* BSD
   (Berkeley Software Distribution)
/bin directory, 190
Binhex, 492
Bluetooth, 343–352, 366, 492
boot problems, 138
BOOTP (Bootstrap Protocol), 229,
   475, 492
BootROM, 404–405, 422, 445
BootX, 405–407, 422–423
browsers, 163–164
BSD (Berkeley Software Distribution)
   customizing installation of, 20–21
   defined, 492
   Network Utility requiring, 248
   using, 165–166
bundles, 114, 492
burning CDs/DVDs, 133, 137
burning disk images, 128–131, 136
buses
   ATA and Serial ATA, 335
   Bluetooth, 343–352
   defined, 333
   FireWire 400/800, 337–342
   PC card, 335
   PCI and PCI-X, 335
   SCSI, 336

USB 1.1/2.0, 336–337
viewing peripherals with System
   Profiler, 353–357

C
Carbon, 145, 492
Cardbus. *See* PC cards
case sensitivity, 24, 111, 132
cat command, 193
cd command, 191
CDs
   backing up data, 137
   burning, 135–137
   erasing volumes, 124
   installation, 10
   transferring files, 133
certification, Apple, 4–5
CGI (Common Gateway Interface), 492
chmod command, 196, 198
Chooser, 390
chown command, 196, 198
CIFS (Common Internet File System), 492
classes, device, 357–360
Classic, 146–162
   choosing partition method, 13–15
   configuring Mac OS X to run, 156–157
   control panels, 149–151
   defined, 493
   force quitting in, 173
   Mac OS 9.2, 149
   menu, 161
   misassigning permissions, 82
   Multiple Users control panel, 37
   partitioning hard drives, 125
   preparing for installation, 15–16
   printing documents from, 390–392
   process, 146–147
   references, 175
   review quiz, 176–177
   starting, 147
   Startup Disk restrictions, 39
   troubleshooting, 162, 443
   upgrading from, 13
   USB support of, 336–337
Classic, preferences
   Advanced, 153–154, 159
   configuring Mac OS X for, 156–157
   Memory/Versions, 155–156
   Start/Stop, 151–152
   troubleshooting, 158–160
Cmd-S, 182
Cmd-Z, 180
Cocoa, 144, 493

colon (:), 180
ColorSync, 493
command prompt, 180–182
command-line interface, 179–207
   accessing, 181–182
   advanced commands, 204–205
   defined, 493
   dial-up connections, 236
   disks and volumes, 203–204
   edit keys, 187–188
   entering commands, 182–183
   file system representations, 188–201
   in graphical environment, 204
   issues with, 180, 205–206
   monitoring system usage, 203
   online help, 184–187
   overview of, 180–181
   printing documents from, 392–393
   processes, 202–203
   references, 206–207
   review quiz, 207
Common Gateway Interface (CGI), 492
Common Internet File System (CIFS), 492
Common Unix Printing System (CUPS),
   370, 493
compressed files, 129, 132–133
concatenation, 193
Connect to Server
   mounting AFP volume, 279–280
   mounting FTP volume, 283–284
   mounting NFS volume, 284
   mounting SMB volume, 280–282
   mounting WebDAV volume, 282
   overview of, 278–279
   troubleshooting, 285
   verifying AFP file sharing, 306–309
   verifying FTP access, 316–317
   verifying SMB file sharing, 313–314
connectivity, 218–220, 327
>console, 181
Console, 29–31, 438–439, 450
control panels, Classic, 149–151
Core OS layer, 9
Core Services, 9
cp command, 192, 205
CpMac command, 201
CUPS (Common Unix Printing System),
   370, 493
cursor keys, 188

D
daemons, startup, 411–412, 487–489
Darwin, 8, 493

DAT files, 493
data forks, 112–113
desktop
    folder, 493
    printers, 392
    rebuilding in Classic, 154, 443
destination volume, 16–17, 18
Developer Frameworks, 10
device classes, 333, 357–360
device drivers, 360–363
df command, 204
DHCP (Dynamic Host Configuration
    Protocol)
    assigning IP addresses, 233–234
    characteristics of, 476
    configuring IP addresses, 229
    defined, 493
diagnostic tools, 447–448
dial-up connections, 235–236, 259
dig command, 252–253
digital cameras, 358–359
digital subscriber line (DSL),
    237–238, 494
directories, 190–193, 493. *See also*
    FileVault
Directory Access, 270–275
directory services, 287–288, 493
discussion lists, 451–452
disk drives, 31, 122–125
Disk First Aid, 448
disk images, 128–131, 136. *See also* .dmg
    (disk image files)
disk management, from command-line,
    203–204
disk space, 11, 66
Disk Utility
    burning discs, 133, 136–137
    command line utilities vs., 203–204
    diagnostic tools of, 447
    disk images and, 128–131, 136
    ejecting storage devices, 360
    Erase pane, 124
    First Aid pane, 122–124
    Information pane, 118–121
    overview of, 117–118
    Partition pane, 15, 125
    quick fixes, 446
    RAID, 126
    reference guide, 139
    troubleshooting permissions, 82, 92–93
diskutil command, 203–204
ditto command, 201
.dmg (disk image files), 54–57, 93, 128

DNS (domain name server), 234–235,
    252–253, 493
Dock, 172–174, 493
documents
    fast user switching conflicts, 59
    permissions, 84–85
    printing. *See* printing documents
    troubleshooting opening of, 145–146
domain name server (DNS), 234–235,
    252–253, 493
dot (.), 99, 100, 115
dot-dot (..), 99
drivers, 398, 494
drives, 125, 339–342
DSL (digital subscriber line),
    237–238, 494
du command, 204
DVDs
    burning, 135–137
    erasing volumes, 124
    transferring files, 133
Dynamic Host Configuration Protocol.
    See DHCP (Dynamic Host
    Configuration Protocol)
dynamic IP addresses, 233–234
dynamic service discovery protocols,
    269, 271

E

Easy Install, 20–21, 447
edit keys, 187–188
Edit>Undo command, 180
email lists, 451
encryption, 129. *See also* FileVault
Energy Saver, 31
Erase and Install, 18–19, 447
Erase pane, Disk Utility, 124
error codes, 285
Essential System Software, 20–21
/etc directory, 190, 421
Ethernet configuration
    AppleTalk, 239–240
    IP addresses, 228–229
    overview of, 242–243
    ports, 227
    PPPoE, 237–238
Execute permission, 82
Expert Search, Knowledge Base, 452,
    454–455
Exposé, 494
Extensible Markup Language (XML), 504
Extensions Manager, 151, 160

F

fast user switching, 47, 57–62, 80
FAT (File Allocation Table), 9, 494
favorites, 494
faxing documents, 396–398
File Allocation Table (FAT), 9, 494
File Exchange, Bluetooth, 349–352
file extensions
    for compressed files, 132
    defined, 494
    for disk images, 128–129
    hiding, 115–116
    from Internet, 115
file forks, 112–113, 494
file locations
    absolute and relative paths, 98–99
    fonts, 104–110
    hidden folder views, 99–100
    search paths, 104
    special folders, 100–104
file permissions
    access levels, 81
    accessing home folders, 91–92
    changing, 85–88
    groups, 83
    interacting with document
        permissions, 84–85
    overview of, 80–83
    references, 94
    review quiz, 95
    testing, 89–90, 92
    troubleshooting, 91–92
file sharing, 301–331
    AFP, 303–311
    FTP, 314–317
    services, 302–303
    SMB, 312–314
    troubleshooting, 317–318
file system representations, 188–201
    changing file attributes, 196–200
    executing commands as System
        Administrator, 196
    file-related commands, 193–195
    frequently used commands, 191–193
    hidden files, 190
    locating files, 190–191
    logging in remotely, 200
    Mac OS X–specific commands, 201
    overview of, 188–190
    shell filename wildcards, 195
file systems
    access levels, 81
    archiving, 132

backing up, 137
burning discs with Finder, 135
CDs or DVDs transferring, 133
defined, 494
disk images, 128–131, 136
Disk Utility. *See* Disk Utility
expanding compressed files, 132–133
ignoring volume ownership, 133–134
references, 139–140
review quiz, 140
troubleshooting, 138
volume formats for, 110–117
file transfers, 242
FileVault, 65–77
defined, 494
home folder encryption, 68–70
master password, resetting, 72–73
master password, setting, 64, 67–68
overview of, 65–67
password, resetting, 71–77
security settings, 43
Final Cut Pro, 175
find command, 195
Finder
burning discs, 133, 135
connecting to servers, 277
defined, 494
directories/files not seen in, 190
exchanging files with shared volumes, 268–269
mounting remote volumes, 265–268
using service discovery, 264
viewing hidden folders, 99–100
Finger, 249
firewalls, 328–329, 494
FireWire, 337–342, 366, 494
firmware
defined, 494
Knowledge Base articles for, 33
password protection, 94
quick fixes, 444
troubleshooting installation, 31
updates, 12
First Aid pane, Disk Utility
overview of, 122–124
repairing disk permissions, 82, 92
troubleshooting file system with, 138
folder locations
Library, 103–104
Shared, 103
Simple Finder, 44
System, 103
top-level and home, 101–102

Trash, 102–103
viewing hidden, 99–100
folder management, 127–137
archiving, 132
backing up, 137
burning disk images, 128–131, 136
expanding compressed files, 132
ignoring volume ownership, 133–134
transferring files onto CDs or DVDs, 133, 135
folder permissions, 80–90
access levels, 81–82
accessing home folders, 91–92
changing, 85–88
groups, 83
interacting with document permissions, 84–85
overview of, 80–83
references, 94
review quiz, 95
testing, 89–90
troubleshooting, 91–92
fonts
language, 20–21
overview of, 104–110
reference guide, 139
force quitting, 170–174, 444
forked files, 19, 112–113
forward slash (/), 98, 189
frameworks, 167–168, 495
FTP (File Transfer Protocol)
characteristics of, 476
configuring proxies, 242
connecting to, 283–284
defined, 495
file sharing, 314–317

G

Get Info, 80, 93, 115–116, 495
GetFileInfo command, 201
GID (Group identification number), 495
GimpPrint drivers, 371
graphics
disk images, 128–131, 136
login picture, 42
Mac OS X technologies, 8
using command-line with, 204
using PDFs for, 9
greater than (>), 183
grep command, 204–205
Group identification number (GID), 495
groups, permissions, 83

Guided Search, Knowledge Base, 453
.gzip format, 132–133

H

hard drives
connecting FireWire, 339–342
partitioning, 125
hardware
peripherals. *See* peripherals
problems, 432–433
repairing/replacing, 456–458
standards, 9
updating for installation, 12–13
hdiutil command, 203–204
Help feature, 184–187, 450, 452
HFS (Hierarchical File System), 495. *See also* Mac OS Extended (HFS Plus) format; Mac OS Standard (HFS) format
hidden files, 190–191
hidden folders, 99–100
Hierarchical File System (HFS), 495. *See also* Mac OS Extended (HFS Plus) format; Mac OS Standard (HFS) format
home directories, encrypting. *See* FileVault
home folders
accessing, 91–92
creating, 41–42
defined, 39
deleting user accounts, 54–55
encrypting with FileVault, 68–70
reviewing deleted user's files, 56–57
subfolders appearing in, 101–102
home page, 324–326
HTML (Hypertext Markup Language), 324–325, 495
HTTP (HyperText Transfer Protocol), 282, 476–477, 495
hubs, 247
human input devices, 358

I

I/O Kit (Input/Output kit), 407
IANA (Internet Assigned Numbers Authority), 495
iChat, 42
ICMP (Internet Control Message Protocol), 495
icons, 25–26, 128–129
id command, 203
iDisk, 137

IEEE (Institute of Electrical and Electronics Engineers), 9, 245–246, 337
IGMP (Internet Group Management Protocol), 495–496
iMac, 18
images. *See* graphics
IMAP (Internet Message Access Protocol), 496
.img extension, 128
iMovie, reference guide, 175
Information pane, Disk Utility, 118–121
Init process, 408–410, 423
input, 183, 205
Input/Output kit (I/O Kit), 407
installation. *See* Mac OS X, installation
Institute of Electrical and Electronics Engineers (IEEE), 9, 245–246, 337
Internet
  enabling disk images, 128
  file extensions and, 115
  networking references, 259
Internet Assigned Numbers Authority (IANA), 495
Internet Connect
  defining, 211
  for ports, 218
  for VPN server, 244
Internet Control Message Protocol (ICMP), 495
Internet Explorer, 163
Internet Group Management Protocol (IGMP), 495–496
Internet Message Access Protocol (IMAP), 496
Internet Protocol Version 4. *See* IPv4 (Internet Protocol Version 4)
Internet Protocol Version 6. *See* IPv6 (Internet Protocol Version 6)
Internet Service Provider (ISP), 496
Internet sharing, 318–331
  connections, 327
  enabling, 321–322
  firewalls, 328–329
  home page files, 324–326
  main Web sites, 319–320
  overview of, 318–319
  references, 330
  review quiz, 331
  services, 302–303
  user Web sites, 320–321
  verifying, 322–324

IP addresses
  characteristics of, 477–478
  configuring in TCP/IP pane, 228–230
  dynamic, 233–234
  looking up, 252–254
  network routing with, 213–215
  static, 230–233
  troubleshooting, 259
IP printers, 372, 391
iPhoto, 175
IPv4 (Internet Protocol Version 4)
  characteristics of, 477
  comparing IPv6 with, 229–230
  configuring, 228–229
IPv6 (Internet Protocol Version 6)
  characteristics of, 478
  configuring, 229–230
  defined, 496
ISO 9660, 9, 496
ISP (Internet Service Provider), 496
iSync, 175–176
iTunes, 175

J
Java, 162–165, 176, 496
journaling, file system, 111, 140

K
KDC (Key Distribution Server), 293, 496
Kerberos, 292–295, 496
kernel
  cues, 423
  defined, 496
  panic, 496
  startup sequence, 407
KEXTs (kernel extensions), 361–363, 496
key combinations, in Classic, 153–154
Key Distribution Server (KDC), 293, 496
keyboard shortcuts, 98–99, 187–188
keychains, 77–79, 287, 496
keywords, Knowledge Base, 452
kill command, 202–203
killall command, 203
Knowledge Base articles
  accessing network services, 285, 296–297
  application environments, 150, 175–176
  command-line interface, 206–207
  file sharing, 330–331
  file systems, 111, 133
  installation, 12, 14, 18–19, 32–34

networking configuration and troubleshooting, 222, 258–259
  overview of, 3–4
  peripherals, 366
  printing, 370, 399–400
  startup sequence, 407, 421, 424
  troubleshooting, 440, 443, 446, 451–455, 460
  users and permissions, 63, 82, 93–94

L
L2TP (Layer Two Tunneling Protocol), 243–245
language, fonts and translations, 20–21
LANs (large area networks), 213, 497
last command, 203
Layer Two Tunneling Protocol (L2TP), 243–245
layers, 10
LDAP (Lightweight Directory Access Protocol), 288–290, 497
Library folder, 103–104
Limitations pane, Account preferences, 40, 43–44, 50–53
Line printer (LPR), 497
link-local addresses, 234, 497
links, 497
local accounts, 39–40. *See also* user accounts
localhost, 497
locate command, 193–194
location, network connectivity
  configuring, 215–216
  creating and choosing, 221–222
  defined, 497
  with static IP addresses, 230–233
  troubleshooting, 259
log files
  checking console, 29–31
  gathering information with, 437
  troubleshooting installation, 31
  troubleshooting network issues, 285
  troubleshooting printing, 399
  troubleshooting startup sequence, 418
  viewing from command line, 203
login. *See also* authentication
  FTP passwords for, 284
  items opening automatically at, 45
  keychain password, 78
  picture, 42
  quick fixes for, 444
  remotely from command line, 200
  setting login options, 46–53

SMB passwords for, 282
troubleshooting passwords, 79
troubleshooting with split-half
searches, 449
loginwindow process, 413–415, 423
Lookup, 253–254
LPR (Line printer), 497
ls command, 183, 191

M

MAC (Media Access Control) addresses,
216, 249–250
.Mac Backup feature, 137
Mac Help, 450, 452
Mac OS 9. *See* Classic
Mac OS Extended (HFS Plus) format
characteristics of, 19, 110–111
defined, 14–15
file extensions, 115
file forks, 112–113
for installation, 16
manipulating files from command
line, 201
reference, 34, 140
Mac OS Standard (HFS) format,
111–113, 115
Mac OS X
configuring to run Classic applications,
156–157
defined, 7
upgrading, 13
Mac OS X, installation
console logs, 29–31
logs, 437
overview of, 10
partition method, 13–15
performing, 16–21
preparing, 15–16
references, 33–34
review quiz, 34–35
Setup Assistant, 22–25
Software Update, 28–29
system information, 26–27
System Preferences, 25–26
troubleshooting, 31–32
understanding, 8–10
updating hardware and software, 12–13
verifying requirements, 11–12
mach_init process, 408–410, 423
mach_kernel, 421
macosx directory, 55–57
Mail, 176, 287–288. *See also* authentication

Mail Exchange record (MX record), 498
man command, 184–187
man pages, 205
master passwords
defined, 497
encrypting home folder, 64
resetting, 71–73
setting, 66–68
MBONE (Multicast Backbone), 497
m-DNS (Multicast Domain Name
Service), 497
Media Access Control (MAC) addresses,
216, 249–250
memory, 31–32, 155–156, 158–159
MIME (Multipurpose Internet Mail
Extension), 497–498
minus sign (-), 20–21
mkdir command, 193
modems, 227–229, 259
more command, 193
MS-DOS file system, 111
Multicast Backbone (MBONE), 497
Multicast Domain Name Service
(m-DNS), 497
Multiple Users control panel, 37
Multipurpose Internet Mail Extension
(MIME), 497–498
mv command, 192, 205
MvMac command, 201
MX record (Mail Exchange record), 498

N

naming conventions, 24, 41–42, 83
NAT (Network Address Translation), 478
Native application environments,
144–145
NetBIOS (Network basic input/output
system), 498
NetInfo, 24, 273–274, 498
Netstat, 248
network accounts, 39–40, 46
Network Address Translation (NAT), 478
Network File System (NFS), 284, 498
network interface cards (NICs), 216
network ports. *See* ports
Network preferences, 210, 216–220, 247
See also ports
network services
authentication. *See* authentication
connecting to servers. *See* Connect to
Server
references, 297–298

review quiz, 298–299
service discovery. *See* service discovery
Network Setup Assistant, 210, 221
Network Status pane, 216–220, 233–234
Network Utility
diagnostic tools of, 447
overview of, 248–255
reference, 259
researching problems in, 450
networking configuration, 209–261
802.1x, 245–246
applications, 210–211
location, 215–216, 221–222
monitoring connectivity, 218–220
ports. *See* ports
protocol, 216
quick fixes, 444
references, 258–259
review quiz, 260
routing, 212–215
status, 216–218
VPNs, 243–245
networking configuration,
troubleshooting, 246–258
file sharing, 317–318
Lookup, 252–254
Network Utility overview, 248–250
overview of, 246–247
Ping, 251–252
printers, 398
scanning ports, 256–258
TraceRoute, 254–255
networking technologies, 473–481
802.1x, 474
AFP, 474
AirPort and AirPort Extreme, 475
BOOTP, 475
DHCP, 476
FTP, 476
HTTP, 476–477
IP addressing (IPv4 and IPv6),
477–478
NAT, 478
PPP, 479
PPPoE, 480
Rendezvous, 480–481
SMB, 481
NFS (Unix Network File System),
284, 498
NICs (network interface cards), 216
No Access permissions, 81–82

normal users. *See* users, normal
  changing passwords, 73–74
  creating two accounts, 47–49
  defined, 498
  group permissions, 83
  limitations of, 80
  local vs. network user accounts, 39–40
  overview of, 38–39
notes, troubleshooting process, 428
NSL, 498
nslookup command, 252–253
NTFS (Windows NT file system), 498
NVRAM, 34, 445–446

O

octets, 213–214
online help, 184–187
open command, 201, 204
Open Directory, 264, 271, 372
Open Firmware
  Boot X and, 405–407
  defined, 498
  overview of, 405
  setting password protection, 63, 207
Open Relay Behavior-modification
  System (ORBS), 499
open source, 499
OpenGL, 498
opening documents, 145–146
ORBS (Open Relay
  Behavior-modification System), 499
output, 183, 205
ownership, 82, 103, 133–134, 198–200

P

packages, 20–21. *See also* bundles
Page Setup dialog, 389–390
pane, defined, 499
Paper Size pop-up menu, 390
Parallel ATA, 335
parameter RAM (PRAM), 34
Partition pane, Disk Utility, 125
partitions
  choosing method, 13–15
  defined, 499
  erasing contents of, 124–125
  getting information about, 119–121
  hard drive, 125
  installation destination, 16
Password pane, Account preferences, 41
passwords
  creating, 47–49, 63–64
  encrypted. *See* FileVault

forgotten, 63
FTP login, 284
Open Firmware, 63, 207
security, 64–65
SMB login, 282
storing in keychains, 77–78, 287
troubleshooting, 79
paste command, 204
paths
  absolute and relative, 98–99
  defined, 499
  Traceroute, 254–255
pbcopy command, 201, 204
pbpaste command, 204
PC cards, 335, 499
PCI (Peripheral Component
  Interconnect) cards, 335, 499
PCMCIA (Personal Computer Memory
  Card International Association),
  335, 499
PDFs (Portable Document Formats)
  with CUPS, 370
  defined, 499
  Mac OS X using, 9
  saving documents as, 393–395
percent (%), 181
Peripheral Component Interconnect
  (PCI) cards, 335, 499
peripherals, 333–367
  buses. *See* buses
  configuring Universal Access, 363–364
  device classes, 357–360
  device drivers, 360–363
  references, 366
  review quiz, 366–367
  troubleshooting, 364–365
  viewing with System Profiler, 353–357
permissions
  AFP file sharing, 310–311
  defined, 499
  references, 94
  review quiz, 95
  setting file and folder, 80–90
  troubleshooting, 91–92
Personal Computer Memory Card
  International Association (PCMCIA),
  335, 499
Personal Web Sharing. *See* Internet
  sharing
pictures, 42, 49
PIDs (process identification numbers)
  from command line, 202–203, 205
  defined, 499
  determining, 169

ping command, 186–187, 251–252
pipe character (|), 205
plug-ins, 499
Point-to-Point Protocol. *See* PPP
  (Point-to-Point Protocol)
Point-to-Point Protocol over Ethernet.
  See PPPoE (Point-to-Point Protocol
  over Ethernet)
Point-to-Point Tunneling Protocol
  (PPTP), 243–245
POP (Post Office Protocol), 499
Port Scan, 256–258
Portable Operating System Interface
  (POSIX), 500
ports
  activating and prioritizing, 223–224
  AppleTalk, 239–240
  checking status of, 217–218
  configuring, 226–227
  defined, 498
  DNS servers and, 234–235
  Ethernet, 242–243
  firewall, 328–329
  location of, 221–222
  overview of, 216
  PPP, 235–237
  PPPoE, 237–238
  prioritization, 224–226
  proxies, 241–242
  scanning, 256–258
  sharing Internet connections, 327
  TCP/IP, 228–230
  using dynamic IP addresses, 233–234
  using static IP addresses, 230–233
POSIX (Portable Operating System
  Interface), 500
POST (Power-On Self Test), 404–405
Post Office Protocol (POP), 499
PostScript format
  adding networked printer, 382–384
  defined, 500
  saving documents in, 395–396
  troubleshooting printers, 398
PostScript Printer Description (PPD)
  files, 372–373
Power-On Self Test (POST), 404–405
PPD (PostScript Printer Description)
  files, 372–373
PPP (Point-to-Point Protocol)
  characteristics of, 479
  connecting with Internet Connect, 211
  defined, 500
  overview of, 235–237
  troubleshooting, 259

PPPoE (Point-to-Point Protocol over Ethernet)
  characteristics of, 480
  connecting with Internet Connect, 211
  defined, 500
  overview of, 237–238
PPTP (Point-to-Point Tunneling Protocol), 243–245
PRAM (parameter RAM), 34, 445
preferences. *See also* System Preferences
  port prioritization, 224–226
  Print & Fax, 378, 398
  quick fixes, 444
  security, 64–65
  Sharing preferences, 302–303
  Start/Stop, 151–152
  troubleshooting file, 146
  troubleshooting startup sequence, 418–419
  Universal Access, 363–365
  user account. *See* user accounts
Print & Fax preferences, 378, 398
Print dialog, configuring, 390
Printer Drivers package, 20–21
Printer Setup Utility, 265, 371–388
printing, 369–401. *See also* USB printers
  adding networked PostScript printer, 382–384
  adding printers, 371–375
  with CUPS, 370
  faxing documents, 397
  to local printer, 375–376
  managing print queues, 386–388
  to network printer, 384
  references, 399–400
  review quiz, 400
  setting printer info, 388
  to shared USB printer, 379–381
  sharing printers, 377–379
  sharing printers with Windows, 385–386
printing documents
  from Classic, 390–392
  from command-line, 392–393
  configuring Page Setup dialog, 389–390
  configuring Print dialog, 390
  with desktop printers, 392
  faxing, 396–398
  overview of, 388–393
  saving as PDFs, 393–395
  saving in PostScript format, 395–396
  troubleshooting, 398–399
privacy policy, Apple, 23

process identification numbers. *See* PIDs (process identification numbers)
processes
  Classic, 146–147
  defined, 168–169, 500
  displaying PID from command line, 205
  force quitting with Activity Monitor, 170–171
  identifying startup, 415–416
  managing from command-line, 202–203
  monitoring with Activity Monitor, 169–170
  network routing, 214–215
  startup sequence, 482–489
protected memory, 500
protocols, 216, 500
proxies, 241–242
ps command, 202, 205
Public folder, 91
pwd command, 192

Q
Quartz, 500
question mark (?), 195, 406–407
queues, print, 386–388
quick fixes, 442–447
QuickTime, 500

R
RAID (Redundant Array of Independent Disks), 126–127, 500
RAM (Random Access Memory), 11, 34
Read & Write permissions, 81
Read Me files, 450
Read Only permissions, 81–82, 91
Real-Time Streaming Protocol (RTSP), 501
Real-Time Transport Protocol (RTP), 501
Rebuild Desktop button, 154
Redundant Array of Independent Disks (RAID), 126–127, 500
registration, 22–23
relative paths, 98–99
Remote Apple Events, 302–303
Remote Login, 200, 302–303
Rendezvous
  characteristics of, 480–481
  connecting printer, 372
  defined, 500
  Directory access configuration, 273

service discovery protocol, 269, 297
  troubleshooting, 285, 318
Repair Disk Permission, 444
research, 450–455
Reset Password window, 76–77
resource conflicts. *See* fast user switching
resource forks, 112–113, 501
resources, troubleshooting process, 428
Restart button, 47
restarting computer, 446
restore. *See* ASR (Apple Software Restore)
rm command, 192
rmdir command, 193
root (file system), 501
root (user), 501. *See also* System Administrator
root directory, 189, 190
routing, network, 212–215, 254–255, 501
RTP (Real-Time Transport Protocol), 501
RTSP (Real-Time Streaming Protocol), 501

S
Safari, 163
Safe Login mode, 449
Safe Mode, 416–417
/sbin directory, 190
scanners, 358–359
Screen Saver, 31
SCSI (Small Computer System Interface), 336, 357, 501
SDP (Session Description Protocol), 501
search domain, 501
search paths, 104
searches, split-half, 448–449
Secure Empty Trash, 103, 501
secure shell (ssh), 182, 203, 502
Secure Sockets Layer (SSL), 502
security, 62–95
  encryption. *See* FileVault
  file and folder permissions, 80–90
  home folder access, 91–92
  with keychains, 77–79, 287
  login options, 46–47
  options, 64–65
  passwords, 63–64
  review quiz, 95
  troubleshooting, 79–80, 92–93
  user accounts, 43
Serial ATA, 335
Server Message Block. *See* SMB (Server Message Block)

servers, 487–489. *See also* Connect to
  Server
service discovery, 264–277
  authenticating, 271–273
  configuring, 270–271
  connecting to volumes from Finder,
    265–268
  disabling, 275–277
  dynamic protocols, 269
  exchanging files with shared volumes,
    268–269
  Knowledge Base articles, 297–298
  making changes to protocols, 271
  methods of, 269–270
  overview of, 264–265
  references, 297–298
  review quiz, 298–299
  viewing configuration options,
    273–275
Service Location Protocol (SLP), 269, 502
Service Source, 451
services, Internet and file sharing,
  302–303
Session Description Protocol (SDP), 501
SetFile command, 201
Setup Assistant, 22–25, 38
share point, 501
sharing files. *See* file sharing
Sharing preferences, 302–303
sharing printers. *See* printing
sharing volumes. *See* volumes, shared
Sharing, over Internet. *See* Internet
  sharing
sheet, 501
shell, 170
SIGHUP, 439
Simple Finder, 44, 82
single-user mode
  accessing command line from, 182
  defined, 502
  performing split-half searches, 448–449
  troubleshooting startup sequence, 418
.sit format, 132–133
sleep, 47, 154
SLP (Service Location Protocol), 269, 502
Small Computer System Interface (SCSI),
  336, 357, 501
SMB (Server Message Block)
  characteristics of, 481
  connecting to, 280–282
  defined, 502
  Directory access configuration,
    274–275
  file sharing, 312–314, 330

service discovery protocol, 269, 297
  troubleshooting, 285, 318
.smi extension, 128
software
  Apple Software Restore, 33
  extensions, 153, 160, 494
  installing essential system, 20–21
  problems related to, 431
  quick fixes for, 442–447
  repairing/replacing, 456–458
  updating for installation, 12–13
Software Update, 28–29, 201, 437
special folders, 100–104
split-half searches, 448–449
spooled files, 397
square brackets ([ ]) wildcard, 195
ssh (secure shell), 182, 203, 502
SSL (Secure Sockets Layer), 502
standards, 9
Start/Stop pane, Classic, 151–152
Startup Disk, 39
startup items
  cue, 423
  overview of, 410–413
  preventing from launching, 417–418
  Startup Items pane in Accounts
    preferences, 40–41, 45
startup scripts, 410–413, 423
startup sequence, 403–425
  BootROM, 404–405
  BootX, 405–407
  Classic, 147, 151–152, 154
  kernel, 407
  loginwindow process, 413–414
  mach_init and init, 408–410
  overview of, 422–423
  processes, 415–416, 482–489
  references, 424
  review quiz, 424
  scripts and items, 410–413
  troubleshooting, 416–421, 452
  user environment setup, 414–415
  in verbose mode, 439–440
static directories, 269
static IP addresses, 229–233
storage devices, 359–360
storage, getting information about,
  118–121
subnet masks, 214, 502
sudo command, 196
SuperDrive, 133
superuser, 502. *See also* System
  Administrator
switches, 180, 247

symmetric multiprocessing, 169
System Administrator
  defined, 502
  executing commands as, 196
  group permissions and, 83
  overview of, 39
System folder, 103–104
System Preferences
  configuring, 25–26, 38
  defined, 502
  managing user accounts with, 40
System Profiler
  finding applications, 166–167
  finding firmware version, 12
  finding frameworks, 167–168
  gathering information, 27, 436–437
  installation requirements, 11–12
  MAC address identification, 250
  quick fixes, 443
  upgrading with, 16
  viewing extensions, 362–363
  viewing peripherals, 353–357
  viewing volume information, 111–112
system.log file, 437, 440
system_profiler command, 201

T

tab completion, 187–188
.tar format, 132–133
target disk mode (TDM), 337–339
TCP/IP (Transmission Control
  Protocol/Internet Protocol)
  defined, 216, 502
  Mac OS X using, 9
  network configuration, 228–230
  network routing, 212–215
TDM (target disk mode), 337–339
Telnet, 182, 502
Terminal
  accessing command line from, 182
  command reference guide, 207
  edit keys, 187–188
  viewing man pages, 186–187
thread, 503
tickets, 292–295, 503
tilde (~), 98–99, 180
Time-to-Live (TTL), 503
top command, 202
top-level folders, 101
Traceroute command, 254–255
training series, Apple, 5
Transmission Control Protocol/Internet
  Protocol. *See* TCP/IP (Transmission
  Control Protocol/Internet Protocol)

Trash, 94, 102–103
troubleshooting
    applications, 145–146
    authentication, 296
    Classic, 158–160, 162
    connecting to servers, 285
    file sharing, 317–318
    file systems, 138
    installation, 31–32
    network configuration. *See* networking
        configuration, troubleshooting
    peripherals, 364–365
    permissions, 82, 92–93
    printing, 398–399
    software, 176
    startup sequence, 416–421
    user accounts, 79–80
troubleshooting process, 427–463
    Apple General Troubleshooting
        Flowchart, 434–435, 466–471
    escalating problem, 456
    gathering information, 435–441
    goals, 428
    informing user, 459
    order of elimination, 430–433
    quick fixes, 442–447
    references, 460
    repairing/replacing components,
        456–458
    researching, 450–455
    review quiz, 461–463
    running diagnostics, 447–448
    split-half searches, 448–449
    things to do, 429–430
    verifying problem, 441–442
    verifying repair, 457–458
TruBlueEnvironment, 147–148
TTL (Time-to-Live), 503

U

UDF (Universal Disk Format), 503
UDP (User Datagram Protocol), 503
UFS (Unix File System)
    characteristics of, 111
    defined, 503
    Mac OS X format, 9
    references, 34
    selecting for installation, 19
UID (user identification number), 39, 503
undo feature, shells, 205

Uniform Resource Locators (URLs),
    98, 503
Universal Access, 363–364
Universal Disk Format (UDF), 503
Universal Serial Bus. *See* USB (Universal
    Serial Bus)
Unix, 8–9, 503
Unix Network File System (NFS), 284, 498
updates, 12–13, 18, 31
upgrades, 13, 16
URLs (Uniform Resource Locators),
    98, 503
USB (Universal Serial Bus)
    1.1 and 2.0, 336–337
    defined, 503
    installation requirements, 11–12
    Mac OS X support of, 9
    references, 366
    viewing with System Profiler,
        354–356
USB printers
    overview of, 373–375
    printing from Classic, 391
    printing to, 375–376
    references, 400
    sharing, 379–381
    troubleshooting, 398
user accounts. *See also* administrator
    users; normal users
    creating, 40–45
    creating local, 24
    deleting, 54–57
    local vs. network, 39–40
    login options, 46–54
    managing with directory services,
        287–288
    references, 94
    security. *See* security
    switching between users, 57–62
    types of, 38–39
User Datagram Protocol (UDP), 503
User Environment Setup, 414–415, 423
user identification number (UID),
    39, 503
users
    gathering information from, 435–436
    problems related to, 431
    researching manuals, 450
    summarizing problem and solution to,
        459–460
/usr/bin directory, 190, 201

V

verbose mode, 416, 439–440, 503
Verify Disk command, 123
Virex, 431
virtual memory, 503
Virtual Private Networks. *See* VPNs
    (Virtual Private Networks)
viruses, 431–432, 447–448
volumes
    ejecting storage, 360
    formats, 110–117
    managing from command-line, 203–204
    using Finder to connect to, 265–268
volumes, shared
    connecting to, 278
    disabling AFP file sharing, 309–310
    exchanging files with, 268–269
    using Finder to connect to, 265–268
    verifying AFP file sharing, 306–309
VPNs (Virtual Private Networks)
    configuring, 243–245
    connecting with Internet Connect, 211
    defined, 504

W

WANs (wide area networks), 213
WebDAV (World Wide Web Distributed
    Authoring and Versioning), 282, 504
WEP (Wired Equivalent Privacy), 504
which command, 193
Whois, 249
wide area networks (WANs), 213
wildcards, 195
Windows
    NT file system, 498
    printing and, 372, 385–386
Windows Internet Naming Service
    (WINS), 504
Wired Equivalent Privacy (WEP), 504
World Wide Web Distributed Authoring
    and Versioning (WebDAV), 282, 504
Write Only permissions, 81–82

X

X11, 166, 176, 504
XML (Extensible Markup Language), 504

Z

ZeroConf, 504
.zip extension, 132

Take the Mac OS X Help Desk Essentials Exam for a reduced price!

Code: PPC400

Use this promotion code for $50 off the regular price of the **Mac OS X Help Desk Essentials Exam**. See below for registration details.

www.2test.com/888-APL-EXAM (888-275-3926)

This promotion code may be used only for the **Mac OS X Help Desk Essentials Exam**, delivered at an Authorized Prometric Testing Center™. This promotion code is good while the Mac OS X Help Desk Essentials Exam is available.

To redeem this coupon:

- To register by phone, call the phone number listed above. Tell the phone representative that you want to use the **promotion code PPC400**.

- To register online, go to **www.2test.com**, select **Information Technology Certifications** from the pop-up window, and follow the onscreen directions. Enter the **promotion code PPC400** in the appropriate field to take advantage of this promotion.

NOTE: This promotion code may not be redeemed for cash, credit, or refund; and may be used only for the stated exam.